"Sid Shroyer's *When Once Destroyed* is a marvelous hybrid, a poignant investigation of the life of his silent but influential father and a forensic account of the destruction of a small town in Indiana by the forces of 'progress.' Composed as a long letter to Shroyer's infant grandson, Vern, this book conveys the admirable rural rectitude of Shroyer's own father, also Vern. At the same time, Shroyer undertakes extensive research in libraries and archives to uncover the reasons for building the dam that flooded his small town and upended the lifeways of its inhabitants."

–**STEPHEN FREDMAN**, professor emeritus of English, University of Notre Dame, and author of many books on poetry and poetics

PRAISE FOR *WHEN ONCE DESTROYED*

"This is hands down one of my most compelling reads of the year. Even with all the historical facts, statements, and details, this book never strays from feeling like the letter it is. The amount of research that went into this book is evident, and it's proof of Sid Shroyer's dedication to making sure this story is told through the voices of the community. As a journalist and a Hoosier, I'll be recommending this book to friends: It's a brilliant example of the craft of storytelling. It's also a painful reminder of all the stories that exist around us yet go untold or become forgotten."

–**BÁRBARA ANGUIANO**, producer,
National Public Radio's *1A* podcast

"Part advisory letter to a beloved grandson, part meticulously researched reportage, and all heart, *When Once Destroyed* captures the tragedy of one community's destruction at the hands of the powerful and shows how this can happen anywhere.

In fast-moving chapters, Sid Shroyer has crafted a detective story with shocks and surprises around every corner. He skillfully pieces together newspaper stories, personal letters, government reports, archival papers, survey maps, secret plans, oral histories, outright lies, a murder, broken promises, small-town politics, and congressional acts in order to corroborate a complex story of American power and its victims.

Shroyer captures in his distinctive and winning voice the fine grain of life in Somerset, Indiana—the church clothes and farm meals, passed-along stories and silences, roars of a packed basketball gymnasium, and the soft voices of casual racism and resistance—so that we mourn what was lost when the Army Corps of Engineers dammed the Mississinewa River and destroyed a way of life forever. And yet this book discovers what we lost and invites us to reflect on our own communities' stories of location and dislocation, loss and growth, and the stories we, too, must preserve for the next generation."

—**APRIL LIDINSKY**, professor of women's and gender studies, Indiana University South Bend

"Having grown up in a small rural community and spent years as a sociologist studying small towns, I was impressed with the depth of detail and insight in these pages. Sid Shroyer has captured a profoundly moving piece of American history."

—**ROBERT WUTHNOW**, professor emeritus of sociology, Princeton University, and author of *The Left Behind: Decline and Rage in Small-Town America*

"Sid Shroyer's family story, written as letters to his grandson, centers on the dramatic loss of his family's homestead. Their town of Somerset, Indiana, was submerged as the result of a 1960s flood control project, a project he sees as an example of the link between progress and profitability.

Shroyer uses personal memories, research, and interviews to recover as much as he can of his family story. This includes moving testimonies of others who lost their homes. Somerset was rebuilt on higher ground, but as the title implies, when once destroyed, the past is lost."

—**GABRIELLE ROBINSON**, professor emeritus of English, Indiana University South Bend, and author of *Better Homes of South Bend: An American Story of Courage* and *Api's Berlin Diaries: My Quest to Understand My Grandfather's Nazi Past*

WHEN ONCE DESTROYED

A Historical Memoir
of the Life and
Death of a Small Town

WISE INK

SID SHROYER

Disclaimer: This is a creative nonfiction memoir. As such, it is based on my memories as to events and how they occurred. I recognize that the people described in this book may have memories of the events described that are different from my own. Extensive editorial precautions have been taken to ensure diligence to factual accuracy.

ISBN 13: 978-1-63-489815-7
Library of Congress Catalog Number: 2025918022
Printed in the United States of America
First Printing: 2026

30 29 28 27 26 5 4 3 2 1

Cover design by Emily Mahon
Interior design by Dan Pitts
Cover photo by Judy Shroyer
Author photo by Hanna Kjeldbjerg
Edited by Imani Josey and Sara Robb (ScriptAcuity)
Proofread by Caitlin Fultz and Abbie Phelps
Index by Ina Gravitz
Production editing by Lindsay Bohls

WISE INK

Wise Ink Media
PO Box 580195
Minneapolis, MN 55458-0195
wiseink.com

Wise Ink is a creative publishing agency for game-changers. Wise Ink authors uplift, inspire, and inform, and their titles support building a better and more equitable world. For more information, visit wiseink.com.

FOREWORD

I've known Sid Shroyer since before he married my baby sister, enough years ago that they now have the grandson to whom this book is addressed. I have followed Sid's career as a radio essayist with a unique voice and as an English teacher in a rural Indiana high school. None of that is in this book—but in one way or another, practically everything is in this book.

Every story we've ever heard or told is about particular people in a particular time and place. But a good story, one worth retelling and remembering, bleeds into other times and places. It may have taken place elsewhere, but it finds us where we live. So it is with this book, *When Once Destroyed*.

First, about Sid's grandson: His name is Vern. Sid's father was named Vern too. Sid awakens on the morning after his grandson's birth and decides to write to him about his great-grandfather. Thus begins this book, in which Sid tells a true story spanning many decades, linking one Vern to the other.

The main character in this book is not the younger Vern. It is not Sid. It is not even the elder Vern. It is his voice echoing through Sid.

In that voice, Sid tells his grandson an extraordinary story. It is a story of the deliberate obliteration of his father's hometown, Somerset, Indiana. It is now underwater—in the literal sense that a lake covers it. The families who had lived there since before the American Civil War and their descendants moved elsewhere.

The plan to drown the town was hatched in governmental bodies in Indianapolis and Washington, DC, and on the drafting tables of the US Army Corps of Engineers. The aim was flood control across the north central Indiana plain. During the mid-1950s, awareness of the plan to drown the town dawned gradually on the people who lived there. An army report that had been advertised as "interim" turned out to be a final report.

"We're going to have to move." It took years for this thought to seep into family conversations. Some older people died from stress. Because the government had undertaken such projects before, it knew the percentages. It knew how many older people wouldn't make it through.

Sid's message to young Vern is: "This is where you come from. It doesn't exist anymore. But it's important. I know about it. And I'm going to tell you . . ." in that unmistakable voice of Sid's father that has been in his head forever.

There can be no authentic Indiana story that does not include basketball. The state high school tournament is known as "Hoosier Hysteria." I've seen people who have fainted from the tension carried out of arenas horizontally on the shoulders of friends. If you are sixteen or seventeen and have made a play that won a meaningful game, that moment will endure in the memories of those who were there, or heard about it, as long as you live.

In the final game of the 1932 sectional (local rung of the state tournament), Vern hits the winning free throw. As the crowd erupts, Vern, the hero, turns to his brother Maurice and says, "Let's get out of here."

He could have gone out to dinner on that free throw for a long time. But he never mentioned it. Ever. Sid had to hear about it years later from one of his uncles.

"Let's get out of here." It is one of the fundamental tropes in Sid's rendering of Vern.

There are a few others. Same voice. Same tone. Same reverence for the basic. Some uttered by Vern. Some just passed along through him.

"Watch number six." Authority. Respect. (Also about basketball.)

"Get down on the floor." A woman's memory of a voice that came to her in a tornado, drawing her into the life-saving arms of her mother, who failed to survive the storm.

"John Brown was right." Celebrating forebears whose move to Kansas before the Civil War helped secure it as a free state.

"It's our flag, too." Vern's voice steeling the teenage Sid in the face of Vietnam era rage.

This was the stuff of the life of a father and son. This voice. Extended seamlessly down the ages to the great-grandson.

Young Vern, you're four and a half years old at the time your granddad's book is being published. You have something extraordinary waiting for you.

–**PETER FIRESTEIN**, author of *Crisis of Character: Building Corporate Reputation in the Age of Skepticism*

CONTENTS

For Linda

My sister, Linda Riggs, taught me to read when I was four. She taught third grade for forty-two years in the community where we were raised. Linda died between the time I finished When Once Destroyed *and when it was published. She was an important source of information for the events I describe, and she was an even more important source of encouragement.*

We talked more regularly because of this work.

She liked what I shared, she liked the idea, and she was anxious to hold it in her hands. I'm very sorry that can't happen. In her absence, I more clearly sense her presence. I can't believe she's gone.

INTRODUCTION

On the morning after the day my grandson was born, I woke up with the notion that I ought to tell him about my dad. This book is a 3:00 a.m. letter to my grandson, Vern, about my father, Vern. Bringing my dad and my grandson together in the same room is a gift. To me. From me. A letter to my grandson about my dad provides me with purpose, focus, foundation, and voice. The voice I assumed in the form of a letter to my grandson is in precisely the proper vernacular for the telling of this story. So, too, is the perspective.

When new Vern was born, I saw myself suddenly in the middle of a thread of five generations that stretched from my grandfather to a baby boy, my son's son. It's a line of sons. In my mind's eye, I could see Pop. I had a picture of the new Vern.

I knew when I started writing this letter to my grandson that I would have to find out more about what happened to Somerset. If I were to tell him the story of my dad, I'd have to tell him about the decimation of his boyhood home and the community where he grew up.

In my journey to do that, I was surprised by how much of what I discovered was information that nobody knew. I learned that the path in the guidance of my imagination was wrong. What I had followed a hundred other times in the last sixty years was not even close to where I had needed to go.

But then, six months after he was born, six months after I began writing to a new Vern, I looked at a map and said to a man who wanted to help, "That's it, Dave."

Found it.

Like Dave Compton, all the people I interviewed for this work gave me an openness that exceeded my expectations. "I want to tell my grandson about my dad" was all I had to say.

"I have something to share" was the response.

In telling Vern about Dad, I had to explain that Dad's boyhood home and the nearby town where he went to school were destroyed in the development of a man-made lake. I soon realized that I'd discovered a story that transcended my family's experience. There's something here for an audience beyond Vern.

"I might be writing a book," I shyly acknowledged to my friends and family. I'd discovered the secrets behind a mystery connected to my earliest memories.

"I'd like to read that," people replied.

I dove into the work. My initial research and interviews had led me to the Indiana State Library in Indianapolis, where the story unfolded before me in the files of a former congressman and a Marion, Indiana, jeweler who initiated the flood that killed Somerset. I remember that flood as well as I remember when my grandmother died and when her grave had to be moved because of it.

"I'm writing a book," I began saying aloud to more than just close family and friends.

But as the book grew, its initial purpose remained. It is a "Dear Vern" letter to my grandson. That's how it began. That's what gave me the appropriate manner and the freedom to go where it led. That's also where it ends: "Sincerely."

One of the stories in my path that I found most compelling is in the episode of the moving of the graves that stood in the way of the US Army Corps of Engineers. Sixty years later, people who were in the area (but were not actual witnesses) describe the event precisely the way it was depicted by local, army, and government officials and in area newspapers.

"Respectfully," they said then.

"Respectfully," the neighbors say now.

"Everyone agrees," they may as well echo in unison.

But that's not true. My brother, Stan Shroyer, for instance, was a witness. That's not what he saw. And if asked, "To what end, the difference?" I would say that more than half a century later, his testimony still matters. So do the testimonies of others like him that found me in the process.

My research into the story of the Upper Wabash Valley Flood Control Project was as much a passion as it was daunting, but it also revealed familiar themes. It showed how status can affect access to social policy decisions and avenues of communication as well as the casual destruction of the culture of the "other" for the sake of a dominant ideology. It wove a tale of "progress" that meant profitability. The story illustrated how the meaning of "value" has changed since my father's time and place from the moral to the monetary. Finally, this experience highlighted the alienating effect of community destruction on succeeding generations. Robin Wall Kimmerer's wonderful adage from *Braiding Sweetgrass* about "leadership rooted in power and authority," not "in service and wisdom," was startlingly clear.

This little story about a little place became a big story about a big place. Though it grew beyond its original intent, I maintain its original purpose. I am speaking to my grandson about my dad. I invite you to listen in on what I had to tell him. It could mean something to you too.

But a bold peasantry, their country's pride
When once destroyed, can never be supplied.
–OLIVER GOLDSMITH, "The Deserted Village," 1770

Vern

1. THE BEGINNING

Dear Vern,

My dad, like you named Vern, died when I was thirty-three. I had then only recently come to the realization that we could be friends. The winter before, I had gone to visit him in the hospital in Marion, Indiana. He had cut off part of a finger trying to fix a jam in his snowblower while he was clearing the driveway. I think that was the machine he had converted from a self-propelled garden tractor into a walk-behind rototiller that then evolved into the snowblower, but I could be wrong. He was always converting stuff and inventing things.

Vern's great-grandfather was an inventor. There's a story about him in the *Indianapolis Star*, April 4, 1953. Richard Harrison "Had" Arrick was the grandfather of Dad's mom, Eva. Her maiden name was Arrick. When I was a kid, we attended the Arrick reunion.

In a column called "Taking a Look Around at Indiana Rural Life,"[1] author David I. Day said that Had, a Miami County man, was an "inventor of tools and machines for the farms." He was a man who "could take almost nothing and from it make almost anything," according to a Chicago woman named Mrs. Emma Wills, whom Day said heard about Had from her father. Had invented a mechanical horse-drawn corn planter. It was "the first of its kind," Day reported.

Had ran a sawmill and a blacksmith shop as well and farmed until he lost a hand in a corn shredder in 1893. It was a long, long time ago, but be careful, Vern, about the impulse to stick your hand in moving mechanicals. By my count, you're next in line for that sort of thing.

Had was my father's great-grandfather, and Vern is your great-grandfather. Your great-uncle, Stan, is my big brother. Stan remembers that when we were kids, Vern submitted a product he created for work to what General Motors called a "Rewards Program." He'd spent a lot of time on it. He had an idea, and he brought it to life. They accepted it and were going to put it into use to make the plant more efficient.

"It was complicated," Stan told me, "but I can't tell you what it did."

I've got a picture. It looks hydraulic. And it's on wheels, so it could move around the factory floor from one job to another. That's what Vern did at the Fisher Body plant in Marion. He was a maintenance welder who moved around the factory from one job to another. Sometimes he was busy and sometimes he was not. On those occasions when he was not, he read. Vern loved to read. The machine he created looks to me like something that could lift things that were too heavy for one person to move. It's got a sliding mechanism like a trombone, so it's adjustable to fit the whatever-it-is that it would be trying to move. I know what it looks like because, as Stan told me, Vern took pictures of it.

Stan then sent me the photo. "The 'Rewards Program' reward wasn't enough," Stan said. "That's why there is a picture." Vern eventually took his invention back along with the picture so the company couldn't steal his idea. Then he took the hydraulic mover machine apart. Maybe the pieces ended up in the snowblower that took his finger twenty years later.

"'Nope. Wasn't enough money.' That's what Dad said," Stan said. "He used the pictures to make sure nobody ever copied it."

With the stuff he worked on, it was hard to keep track of what became what over the years, even when I lived at home. So, later, it would not be a surprise to come home to discover that the lawn mower had become a device that chopped wood. It was a surprise to see damage. For example, after the snowblower accident, even though Vern was lying in a hospital bed, it didn't seem like he needed to be lying in a hospital bed. He'd cut off a finger, that's all. Vern wasn't one for fuss. He reminds me of your dad that way. Suck-it-up-and-move-on kind of guy.

So, I announced, "Kinda late in life to be pulling this kind of shit, isn't it?" This was not the way I had ever talked to my father before. He laughed.

Our eyes met as if to say, "We can relax now. We like each other."

Ten months later, he was dead.

It still makes me sad that I never saw him as a grandparent for my children. But I did recognize pieces of him in them. I realized that no one had to tell your dad or your aunt Lily about the nature of life and responsibility. I didn't know it at the time, but they just knew. I grew up wanting to do right by my dad, and he didn't have to spend a lot of time telling me what that was. I could tell by watching him. And as your dad grew up and became the person he is, I was reminded of my dad's character: his common sense, his integrity, his work ethic, and the humanity in his sense of humor. They would have liked each other, too.

Somerset

2. ORIGINS

Dear Vern,

There's a lot about your great-grandfather that I didn't know before I started writing this letter to you. There was even more that I didn't know about Somerset, the town in southern Wabash County, Indiana, where he grew up. Eventually, it was flooded by the Mississinewa Reservoir in the Upper Wabash Valley Flood Control Project, but more on that later.

The town began as a single-cabin settlement. From a 1998 reproduction of an 1875 Wabash County atlas, I learned that when Somerset was first "laid out" in 1844 and "known as a half-way point on the road between Peru and Marion," it was only a log cabin tavern, kept by a "Frenchman named Krutzan."[2] The environment around Somerset had been conducive to the Indigenous lifestyle, and the atlas says the Miamis were "hospitable."

French missionaries and fur traders had been the Miamis' first contact with Europeans. The atlas says that the "missionaries who visited their villages along the southern shore of Lake Michigan in 1672 had spoken of the Miamis at that time as being one of the most powerful nations of the west."[3] It says, "They claimed and occupied the land from the lake . . . on the north to the Ohio River on the south." That's the whole length of Indiana, Vern.

The Indigenous presence was gradually extinguished amid conflicts for power and control with the French, the English, and finally, the Americans. At the end of a series of forty-four treaties imposed by the United

States between 1795 and 1840, all the land held by and for the Miamis in Indiana was officially gone. In 1845, the year after Somerset became a town, the army forced six hundred natives from their homes in surrounding Waltz Township and marched them to "their new home" in Kansas. A few Miamis remained, adapting as best they could to the new American ways, but for settlement, the land was clear of them.

Fifty years before Somerset would be decimated by a second forced removal of residents by the US Army for the Mississinewa Reservoir, it was destroyed by fire. FLAMES WIPE OUT SOMERSET was the front-page headline on the November 3, 1914, *Wabash Daily Times Star* story. "It started in the Ed Cochran general store, apparently, and spread to other buildings."[4] The township hall, a barbershop, the post office, the Odd Fellows Hall, a drugstore, and three barns were destroyed. Without even a volunteer fire department, I guess it mostly burned itself out. It's hard for me to visualize the 1914 drugstore. Did the shampoo then have its own aisle?

Local historian Ron Woodward's March 2009 Wabash County Genealogical Society newsletter says that after the fire, the town had returned "pretty well" by 1920.[5] On the same spot, not up the hill. That would come later.

Along with some bits about Dad's basketball prowess, as I searched for "Somerset, Indiana" and "Vern Shroyer" in newspaper archives online, I found some pretty revealing stories.

In 1934, a Somerset man shot himself in the chest when a woman married to somebody else refused to "accompany him out of town," according to the April 18 *Indianapolis News*.[6] She told police she loved him, but not that much, I guess. He survived. Her husband filed for divorce.

That year, too, on June 2, Woodward says, my great-aunt Vernie's second husband, John Knee, opened the Riverside Resort along the Mississinewa River two miles west of town, with "entertainment by 4-piece military band, the Hill-Billies, Billy Frank and Rus Knee."[7]

Two years later, the *Indianapolis Star*[8] reported a story about a man named John Huddleston who lived a mile north of town and connected an electric fence to his windmill for power. Also that year, a group of thirty-four people from the little town of Hackleman in Grant County traveled twenty-one miles by bus from their Center Grove Church to

Somerset to attend church services on a Sunday evening.[9] That's the kind of information that popped up when I searched for Somerset, Indiana, and my dad in newspaper archives online. Small-town stuff.

Another article from 1936 showed more promise, though, and it made me wonder about Vern. It shared that Somerset had a party in October of 1936. Dad was twenty. I wondered if he may have been there.

The party happened during a three-day weekend on the Mississinewa River shore in Somerset, in honor of a new park's dedication. According to an advance article in the *Indianapolis News*,[10] it was "the first link in the proposed chain of small historic parks to be established along the banks of the Mississinewa River between Peru and Marion."

The chain of parks was an idea from the Indiana State Parks Commission from back in 1930, which was then taken more locally by a group headed by the leader of northern Wabash County's Manchester College. That was an organization called the Mississinewa Park Association. Otho Winger, the North Manchester school president, grew up in the area and, by virtue of his research and writing, had become renowned for his understanding of local history. He wrote about Frances Slocum, a.k.a. Maconaquah. He wrote books called *The Lost Sister among the Miamis*, *The Last of the Miamis*, *Little Turtle*, *Kenapocomoco*, *The Potawatomi Indians*, and *The Frances Slocum Trail.*

That last one, *The Frances Slocum Trail*, describes following the trail that was originally an Indigenous people's route from what is now roughly Marion to Peru, through parts of what are now three Indiana counties: Grant, Wabash, and Miami. The proposed chain of parks was to follow that road with Somerset in its middle.

Winger's *The Frances Slocum Trail* came out first as a pamphlet in 1933, so it, too, was in the middle of things, like a guidebook to the important places along the way. It marked where the parks should go, like the grave of Maconaquah, marked FRANCES SLOCUM, on the west, and the Indigenous people versus newcomer colonialists on Mississinewa Battleground on the east. In the middle was Somerset, originally a Miami settlement area and, as Winger described it, a place "with plentiful supplies of wildlife and fresh water from the numerous groundwater springs in the area."[11]

Somerset was on a low cliff overlooking the Mississinewa River. It was high enough to mimic how the original Indigenous settlers stayed dry.

Nature never flooded Somerset; we will see that it took men to do that. Likewise, in the spirit of control, Somerset is one of the places where the descendants of European men annihilated the five hundred Indigenous nations of what Europeans called *America*.

The perspective Americans have in telling human history has changed since the days of Otho Winger, Vern. The definition of *our* has changed since those days. We've learned that to learn from the past, history must include the perspective of people whose stories have been traditionally denied. That inclusion hasn't always been the case. For some, even as they read my letter to you, that inclusion will be a bone of contention.

Back to the party I mentioned. The occasion, then, in October of 1936, when the cooling temperatures and the colorful leaves on the canopy of Somerset trees most certainly made for an idyllic scene, happened to celebrate a new park. I hope Vern was there. He might have skipped it, though, thinking that someone there might have recognized him. That would be the Vern I knew. It was a celebration for the new park, and it was a celebration for the parks that were to be. Winger had a lot to do with it. A lot of people have ideas. Winger wrote those down, and he put them into action.

Somerset had a vibe, a presence, that artists shared. In South Bend, there's a James Whitcomb Riley High School, named for an Indiana poet who wrote "Amongst the Hills of Somerset" and "When Frost Is on the Punkin," and "Little Orphant Annie" among others: "An' the Gobble-uns 'at gits you / Ef you / Don't / Watch / Out!"[12] I remember that I had to learn that when I was in grade school. That's Riley.

According to Wabash County historian Ron Woodward, Riley worked as a sign painter around Somerset when he was young. He was well known and popular in his day—the "Hoosier Poet," he was called—but today, critics and scholars are inclined to diminish his patronizing attempt at colloquialism and rather traditional verse in the shadow of more original nineteenth-century work like that of Walt Whitman and Emily Dickinson.

In any case, whether it was "good" and whether it was intended for Indiana or, as some say, for a hilly town in Pennsylvania, that "Somerset" poem made the people in Somerset, Indiana, proud, and a look around that weekend would have made it understandable if someone wanted to glorify its beauty.

"Let's get out of here," I imagine Vern saying, though. As I would learn in writing this to you, even on the day of his greatest glory, that was his response. It's hard for me to visualize him enjoying all the public displays of affection at the three-day park dedication festival.

Maybe, I'd like to think, he could have enjoyed a little part of it. With a group of guys, or a girl, or his brother, Burnell, or his little sister, Lenore, or his mom, I like to think of him walking around, having a look and a good time that weekend. There was a baseball game in the new park. He could have played in that. If I had to guess, though, I'd say he spent the weekend at home, two miles away. That was his favorite place to be. No fancy touches.

Another artist who glorified Somerset was a painter by the name of Homer Davisson. His studio was open for visitors that weekend. He lived there in a house in the middle of town along the river, where the cool breeze blew through the shade in the hot months of summer. He lived there like it was a resort, away from his other home in Fort Wayne and his frequent trips for painting landscapes to New England.

Kay (Shroyer) Peas told me she remembers seeing Davisson painting. "In the spring, summer, fall, he would have a class. They would be on the street."

"He lived right across the street from us," Kay's sister, Janet, told me. "I remember riding my tricycle in front of our house and he would have an easel out and he'd be painting and I would say, 'Hello, Mr. Davisson,' and he wouldn't reply and I would pedal by on my bike."

Kay and Janet are the daughters of my grandfather Pop's cousin Bob. I remember Bob a little. He was only a year older than Vern, an almost brother.

According to Somerset native Tom Snyder, "Homer Davisson was a loner. We were always told as kids, 'Don't go around him; don't go and talk to him; ride your bike the other way.'" Looking at Davisson's work, and from what Janet and Tom said, I'd guess that, like my dad, he preferred scenery and keeping people at a distance.

Somerset wasn't the kind of place where people spent a lot of time telling themselves, or one another, or outsiders, how great things were. I think Vern's silence was connected to that. James Whitcomb Riley, Homer Davisson, and Otho Winger were all outsiders to Vern, and he wouldn't care how great they were, supposedly, or how they sang Somerset's praises. When the celebration started, I imagine Vern would have said he had a better place to be.

The Mississinewa Park Association provided some money to spruce up the park before the dedication that October weekend in 1936. There were a thousand MPA members, from Wabash, Miami, Huntington, and Grant Counties, and as far as they were concerned, they were just getting started on an ambitious plan for parks along the Frances Slocum Trail, all the forty-mile way from Marion to Peru.

The land for the park in Somerset came from Dr. Charles Taylor, who was a physician from Bluffton, about an hour east in Huntington County, where he started a clinic in 1897 that, according to its website, is today one of the biggest doctor groups in northeast Indiana. Dr. Taylor and Winger both spoke at the dedication on a cool October Friday afternoon with a fifty-voice chorus providing atmosphere. Folks browsed farm, food, and craft exhibits that were being judged for awards that evening. For the real fun, event planners had "pulling contests" and that baseball game. What a day for Somerset!

Organizers worked around some Saturday rain for a "baby show" and a livestock exhibit and a Halloween parade. Some folks must have ducked into the opened Davisson art studio who wouldn't have gone in otherwise. For Somerset, staying dry would get harder.

Flood

3. THE IDEA

Dear Vern,

Two and a half years after the park dedication weekend, a jeweler from Marion by the name of Ralph Roessler had an idea that occurred to him while visiting Lake Shafer near Monticello, Indiana. I suppose he wanted to spruce things up around him, too. His was an idea, though, that would destroy Somerset.

Lake Shafer is really a reservoir, one of two created when the Indiana Hydro-Electric Company dammed the Tippecanoe River near Monticello, Indiana, between 1923 and 1925. It includes the Indiana Beach amusement park and areas for cottages, boats, and swimming.

When Roessler was there in 1939, he must have thought that it would be nice to have something like this back at his home in Marion. He committed his vision to a diary. I found his words at the Indiana State Library in Indianapolis about a year after you were born.

> May 21, 1939.
>
> Dinner at Fishermans' Paradise, Monticello, Indiana, and a trip around the reservoir suggesting the possibilities of a similar development on the Mississinewa River. Possible now because of the construction of a sewage disposal plant at Marion to remove pollution from the river. Visualizing the

> construction of a dam at or near Conners Mill and the building of a state park to take in historical burial grounds, Mississinewa Indian battle grounds, the old mill reconstructed with water wheel turning. Visualizing backing up the water in a lake four to six miles long, confined largely in the stream bed, but spreading at various points to a wider lake effect. Visualizing a development of marginal lands for resort purposes and the development of a state park both in construction and maintenance.[13]

Ralph Roessler's idea for the turning of what he called "marginal lands" into a reservoir "for resort purposes" began with him there at Lake Shafer. It concluded thirty years later with him on more than one flag-draped dedication reviewing stand.

To deliver his idea, though, it had to be for flood control. For flood control it became.

While there's no mention of "flood control" in Roessler's initial idea, it's true that flood control had been in the news around that time. The *Journal and Courier* newspaper of nearby Lafayette carried an April 26, 1939, page 1 story noting that an Ohio congressman said the House of Representatives was considering both $75 million and $110 million separately for flood control in upcoming budgets.[14] Three years earlier, the US Flood Control Act of 1936 had included levee and flood wall money for Peru, Wabash, and Logansport on the upper Wabash River.

Roessler's idea quickly shifted in focus away from recreation to flood control, clearly, because there was federal money available for flood control that wasn't available for recreation. Roessler's idea morphed into the Upper Wabash Valley Flood Control Project, promoted by a state agency that Roessler helped create called the Indiana Flood Control and Water Resources Commission and by the US Army Corps of Engineers. The corps controlled the money. Lawmakers and policymakers followed its lead.

The project would be designed to prevent flooding in areas downstream from Marion, especially the Miami County city of Peru, which had a terrible flood in 1913. There were similar Army Corps of Engineers projects in many places around the country. As it turned out, this one wouldn't be designed to help Roessler's hometown, and, in fact, some people in Marion eventually thought it would hurt them. He stuck with it, though, and Roessler became "the Father of the Mississinewa Reservoir."

The town of Somerset would be washed over, drowned, by one of three new reservoirs created in the Upper Wabash Valley Flood Control Project, the one that is now referred to as Mississinewa Lake. The people of Somerset lost their community for "the greater good." Vern was part of that community, and that's why I want to include that story in my letter about him to you. Who he was, and who we are, is tied up in that.

Somerset

4. FOUND IT

Dear Vern,

While Somerset was in the process of being destroyed, some homes and businesses and a church were moved up the hill to a spot about half a mile away along State Road 13. For a while, that settlement was called New Somerset. Then, maybe because it was confusing for the post office, they reverted the name back to Somerset, which is a nagging, if minor, bone of contention for the old-timers who know for a fact that what came to be called Somerset isn't Somerset.

Old and new town resident Larry Stouffer said of the flood, "It hurt a lot of people, older people. It put a lot of stress on people." But, he added, "there's a lot of people who moved up here to the new town who are better off."

"Greg went through it," Larry said, nodding to Greg Bowman, who sat to my left at a Somerset Lions Club meeting. "His folks lived right in Somerset, right on the riverbank, right at the bridge in old Somerset."

"My father wasn't very happy about it, I can tell you that," said Greg. And there were others. "Merrill Lindsey was a nice lady, but she was one who could never accept that. Poor soul," Greg said, his voice tapering into one talking to oneself.

An invitation to a Somerset Lions Club meeting from a "new" Somerset resident led me to Greg and Larry. I had found a Wabash County Historical Society page on Facebook that connected me to Lucinda Holderman. She lived at Somerset. Lucinda invited me to the Lions Club meeting. There, for the first of many times, I discovered that telling people that I'm writing my grandson a letter about my dad made them receptive to the idea of sharing information with me.

On the phone the Monday morning before the evening meeting, Lucinda said, "I've already told them you're coming. We're having roasted chicken and potatoes from Rusty's Chicken in Roann. I ordered you a meal."

She introduced me when I came into the community building, just after the group finished a prayer circle, at five minutes after 6:00 p.m., and gave me the lay of the land. I moved awkwardly to a table and set up some pictures I'd brought. They were family group shots and pictures of the old farm.

On the wall there, I spotted Dad's photo, top-row center, in a framed class of 1935 senior picture. Proud and distinguished in their finest clothes, ten boys and two girls, the Somerset High School class of 1935 was one class on the wall among many.

In about half an hour, a man named Dave Compton was telling me, "I've got a lot of information, and you're welcome to look at any of it you want. I've got about two thousand pictures and maps and all that."

I proudly shared a picture of you.

Dave would connect me to Janet Schenkel and Kay Peas, the daughters of Vern's second cousin, Bob, and his wife, Mary Shroyer. They grew up in the center of Somerset at the time when the Upper Wabash Flood Control Project happened. Bob's and Mary's signatures are on a petition opposing the dam at Peoria on the Mississinewa River that backed up the water that flooded Somerset. I found them on the petition pages along with a lot of other familiar names that pop up in the research your grandma Judy and I would do in the Indiana State Library.

Janet would later tell me, "The forties and fifties, Somerset sort of froze at that point. In the sixties, it was flooded, so it sort of stayed in the thirties, forties, fifties."

I continued to reach out to people who might help me tell you about Dad. His only living sibling was Wayne Shroyer, whom I hadn't seen for twenty-five years. "Somerset always had a lot going on," Uncle Wayne told me from his home in Ocala, Florida, when I reached him on the phone.

"On Friday night, before there was such a thing as drive-in theaters, Somerset and Red Bridge, Converse, a lot of the communities around, they had their own, like a drive-in. You would park in the street, and they would show movies. Friday night was Somerset, and Saturday night, I think, was Converse.

"They were free," Wayne said. "They would have popcorn and stuff like that. You bought popcorn and took it back to the car and sat there and watched movies. They had a great big screen, twenty by twenty foot. It was a big canvas. They tied it between boards. They had a frame, and they put that canvas between the frame. And it was on rollers, and they had it sitting where they could roll it out, right onto the street. I went to Converse, Red Bridge, and Somerset for movies. They had big speakers on the side of the frame. You could hear good.

"We had a hardware store, and it was a big hardware store. They'd roll the screen out beside the hardware. They'd take the speakers off, and they'd put them in the hardware, where they stored them. It was called Somerset Hardware. They did a lot of business. Every farmer from around went there.

"Somerset had two garages that did work on cars, tractors, and everything else. If you had something broke, you could take it there.

"They had two grocery stores, and they were across the street from each other. They had a little restaurant there. They cooked hamburgers and stuff like that. Aunt Vernie was involved in that." Aunt Vernie was my grandpa Shroyer's sister, my great-aunt, and, as I learned, Tom Snyder's grandmother. Tom became my most important source for information about Somerset. Small world.

Small town. "The houses," said Kay. "You could walk anywhere, and you could play, and a mother would come out and say, 'Kay, it's time for your supper. Your mother will be looking for you.'"

"Everybody looked out for everybody else," said Janet. "It was that kind of a place. You didn't worry about locking doors. It was just one big family. We would go out and play up and down the street, and then everybody would go home at night."

"There wasn't a bit of it I hadn't had my bicycle on," Tom Snyder said. "Even the cemetery."

Helen and Aden Adkins lived in Somerset in its final years, after they were married in the mid-1950s. Dave Compton also connected me to Helen.

"We always went down to the local [to shop]," Helen said, "because you always found somebody you knowed. We'd go there and gossip with the guys. And there was a little restaurant across the road there downtown. We'd go into it a lot. At one time, they had a barbershop. Vic Fierstos had a garage, with gas, and so did Floyd Bowman, and then King's store there, I think, had gas. There were two or three gas stations there. And years before that, there was a locker plant there. A grocery store. That was about the time I come to town, I think. Tom Snyder's mother had a little restaurant there at one time. I'd go in there and eat." That's the Aunt Vernie place dad's brother Wayne told me about.

"Between the two churches in town and the school, life just circled around church and school and family and kids," said Janet. In that memory, she paused. "We can't go back to share the things that we liked when we were growing up. We can't take our kids there."

Kay said, "There's something about saying, 'This is the tree I climbed.' We used to go across the river to the woods every spring and pick violets. You had three or four different kinds of violets that grew there wild, so we would always make it a practice of going over and picking violets."

"There are some things that trigger a memory that you had forgotten about," said Janet. "We miss not being able to have the space that triggers a memory."

"My kids," Helen Adkins said, "were in kindergarten and seventh grade when we had to move, so they don't remember much about Somerset, except what they've been told. My youngest boy, he goes fishing on the reservoir, and he says to people, 'This is where we used to live,' and he wasn't even born then. We lived on the farm when he was born."

"It colors your thinking and your reaction to other people and other events," said Kay.

"Not only was it home, it was also a generational home that you couldn't replace with anything. Most of the houses were not real fancy. They were very plain and very simple. People made do with what they had."

"The move? They talked a lot about it. There was just a lot of anger," said Janet.

"People had gone to meetings and done everything they could for the most part to try to keep the flooding out, even though they understood the reasoning for it," said Kay.

Since then? "I don't think people buried it. I don't think that was it at all. Everybody moves on. It's not healthy to sit in that spot."

The way people talked about Somerset—Kay and Janet, Dave, Greg and Larry, Lucinda, Tom, Helen, and Uncle Wayne—very quickly, I got a sense of what was lost from the place where Vern grew up. In the detail, I felt like the people telling me about it wanted me to keep the community alive.

None of it surprised me.

I have always been attracted to "Somerset," the idea of it, the mystery. I had been curious about what happened to Somerset for a long time, Vern, when I started writing to you. I'd poked around down there from time to time over the years, around No Trespassing signs, down a hill on a path that used to be a road that disappears into the water. I'd looked for the place where a kid learns not to touch an electric fence and not to stick his finger into a lawn mower. I'd looked for cousins, aunts and uncles, Grandma and Grandpa. I'd looked for my mom and dad, laughing. If I could find that place, somehow, it had occurred to me long before you were born that the people I remember would be there, too.

Where I had been looking, though, was wrong. Your presence pointed me in the right direction.

After we met at the Lions Club meeting on August 16, 2021, in Somerset, I traveled on September 3 to Dave Compton's home to look at the two thousand documents he'd said I "might be interested in."

Dave Compton was a longtime business owner and resident of Somerset who was directly involved with the town residents' resettlement in the mid- to late 1960s. At the time we met, he lived with his wife at the United Methodist retirement home complex called Heritage Pointe in Warren, Indiana. That's in Huntington County. It's big and attractive, the nicest retirement place I'd ever seen. It was like a small college campus, with a range of living and care options, a swimming pool, a chapel, and a nine-hole golf course. As part of that, Dave and his wife had their own house. It's not far from the Salamonie Lake reservoir, and I drove by what's now called Roush Lake, the Huntington reservoir, on the way there from my home in South Bend. Along with the Mississinewa, the Salamonie and Roush reservoirs make up the Upper Wabash Valley Flood Control Project that the US Army Corps of Engineers designed to prevent downriver flooding in small cities like Wabash, Peru, and Logansport.

At his home, Dave Compton helped me find the exact location of where Vern's family had lived when Vern was growing up.

Dave and I spent at least half an hour at his table trying to figure out exactly where your great-grandfather's boyhood home was located. He had some pretty detailed area maps, and I had my memory, the memory of a sixty-eight-year-old man reaching backward sixty years, and a couple of pictures. I'd showed him the snow-dappled barn, farmyard, and house, and a picture of me and some of my cousins in the front yard that gave us a glimpse down the hill at the gravel road out front that headed west and then south, as I remembered.

The life I was searching for, so that you could better know your name, was mostly unknown to me. I didn't even know where exactly he lived. Vern could have easily pointed to a map and said, "Here," to me a thousand different times. We never got within two hundred miles of that conversation.

"I think it's down here," I said to Dave while his attention was elsewhere. Again, I said, "I think it's around here," pointing on a map to an area that is south of the river and north of the Frances Slocum Trail, tucked into a squiggly curve as the Mississinewa River heads briefly more north, then west.

"I remember driving up 513 to where it ends, from Converse, and continuing north past the Slocum Trail intersection. Since the flood," I continued, "I've parked the car there and walked down the hill on the path where the gravel road used to be, several times. The woods are pretty thick and the path dissolves before I ever recognize anything, and I turn around. I think I'm going to come to the road that my grandparents lived on, dead-ending into the path I'm on, if I can only go a little farther." That seems like the memory of a dream when I tell it to you now.

Sometimes when we went to their house, we drove down 13 and then through Somerset on the way there, and sometimes we avoided the town altogether by coming in on 513. I think, now, that Dad didn't want anyone to see him. We'd drive down the hill after going past the Slocum Trail, and at the hill bottom, we turned right at a gravel pit, and there on the north side of that road was the farm where they lived. Grandma and Grandpa's. Where Vern grew up. Right there. The place where I stuck this finger in the lawn mower and touched the electric fence. That was my memory.

Dave and I continued to gaze at one map in particular. We pointed and looked, but the names and the label on the land sections that seemed right, in Areas 29 and 32—"John Ziegler," "E. & R. Rogers," "H. & R. Schaaf," and "H. 1 B"—didn't mean anything to me or to Dave. As we looked, I thought it must be a problem with the map. We looked at other maps and other pictures and other newspaper clippings and talked some more.

In a few minutes, the map with the names on plots of land areas within the numbered square-mile sections came past my eyes again. I widened my view, and suddenly, three map miles away from where I had been sure my grandparents lived, and on the river's north side, not to the south, I saw in the southwest corner of Area 21, "C. & E. Shroyer." Charles and Eva Shroyer. Grandpa and Grandma.

The path in the guidance of my imagination that I had followed a hundred times in the last sixty years was not even close to where I needed to go. "That's it, Dave."

Found it.

Flood

5. THE INDIANA STATE LIBRARY

Dear Vern,

At the Indiana State Library at the capitol complex in Indianapolis, I discovered a lot of documents about the Upper Wabash Valley Flood Control Project in the Somerset area congressman's files. Republican John Beamer represented Indiana's Fifth Congressional District from 1951 to 1959. Just as important were the documents preserved by the man who would later be called "the Father of the Mississinewa Reservoir," Ralph Roessler. I got the impression that Ralph Roessler was saving things that might help him write a book about the Upper Wabash Valley Flood Control Project someday. He didn't write a book, maybe because the story didn't end the way he had hoped and maybe because there were story parts that he did not want to tell. Maybe he got busy with other things. He was running his retail business at the same time. His records are significant, and his record summaries were like a map for me to follow.

Marion jeweler Ralph Roessler led the Marion, Indiana, Kiwanis Club Public Affairs Committee on the day he visited Lake Shafer, near Lafayette, at the invitation of a friend in May 1939. He shared his idea with the club president and a few other club members the next day, suggesting that what he began to call the Conners Mill Mississinewa River Project would be a "feasible project" for the club.

According to the May 31, 1939, *Whetstone*, the Marion Kiwanis Club newsletter,

> The Public Affairs Committee, headed by Ralph Roessler had a very special meeting last week at which objective for Kiwanis was discussed. The idea as presented to the committee is the biggest thing which has been brought before the Objective Committee in the history of Kiwanis in Marion. It will make you proud that you belong to a club which can even conceive such a splendid objective, though it dies aborning.[15]

That same day, the Marion Kiwanis Club endorsed the idea and put Roessler in charge of publicizing it. Roessler's original idea was for damming the Mississinewa River at Conner's Mill in Grant County, near the village of Jalapa, creating a lake that would extend east and south into the area of Marion's Matter Park. According to the diary he saved, that day he also heard from an agency called the Federal Water Conservation Department "with support." Members at a Mississinewa River Association (MRA) meeting in Wabash would be "enthusiastic" the next day, he noted. Area newspapers, Roessler said, were "instructed" to make mention of that and "what this idea is all about." In the MRA meeting, Roessler said, "John Knee of Somerset" suggested that the dam be farther west, "below Somerset."[16]

Farmer and small businessman John Knee was Aunt Vernie's second husband. As things turned out, putting the dam "below Somerset," so the water would back up behind it, was what happened. That destroyed John and Vernie's own property and doomed the town. John Knee didn't cause that, of course, but his is the first "below Somerset" mention I found.

Quickly, Roessler says in his diary, he learned that federal money could be available for the project. He wrote their new congressman, Forest Harness of Kokomo, telling him in a June 3, 1939, letter that the Marion area should get some of that money. Miami County had benefited from federal aid already, he wrote him. *Now*, he thought, *it's Grant County's turn.* As it turned out, Miami County's Peru benefited the most from the Upper Wabash Valley Flood Control Project.

Roessler mentioned in the letter to Harness that he'd already described the project to Indiana governor Clifford Townsend of nearby Blackford County. Townsend, a Democrat who was best known for his work on 1937 flood relief along the Ohio River, had attended college in Grant County. And Roessler told the Republican Harness that getting behind the project would be good for him politically. The Marion jeweler also noted that a Water Conservation Department member Ralph did not identify had told him that "our river could well come under the heading of flood control and as such become a part of the army program of Mississippi Valley control by damming the head waters of tributaries to the Ohio." It's clear, Vern, that the army had already done flood control work elsewhere in the country. It did not take long for Roessler to learn about the connection to the money.

Ralph continued to tell Congressman Harness that "by damming at Conners Mill or below, a lake five or six miles long can be created. I find this to be one of the most popular projects ever proposed, and everyone is enthusiastic about it. If you want to set yourself up in a big way in Marion, get on the job to help us get this in the flood control program. Leave it to me to publicize your efforts."[17]

Roessler wanted the project for the purposes of recreation and development, like what he saw at Lake Shafer. But he knew within a matter of days that to get the money for that, the project had to be under the army's umbrella of "flood control." Critics all along would make the case that the Upper Wabash Valley Flood Control Project was subterfuge for recreation disguised as flood control. Supporters said that argument was spurious.

Roessler wasted little time. On June 6, 1939, he called the office of Congressman Harness and spoke with an assistant. According to Roessler's diary, he "explained carefully to secretary that we do not want flood control that means merely damming up the river and controlling the water flow. *Our primary objective is the creation of a lake or reservoir by backing up the river*" (my emphasis).[18]

That same day, in a letter, Harness informed Roessler that the following day, June 7, 1939, Harness would be introducing a bill in Congress to authorize a study into the project. That was a mere fifteen days after Roessler brought the idea to the Kiwanis Club in Marion, five days after the club approved it.

Then, that day, June 6, 1939, Roessler met with the president and other Marion Kiwanis Club members.

Roessler's diary:

> Suggestion made that I call Harness and inform him he should investigate very carefully his procedure so that we will get a lake and not simply a series of dams to control the water flow. Called Washington, Rep. Harness out of city. Talked to secretary. Bill already in hands of committee and in hopper. Explained carefully to secretary that we do not want flood control that means merely damming up the river and controlling the water flow. Our primary objective is the creation of a lake or reservoir by backing up the river.[19]

The next day, according to the Roessler diary, he met with Congressman Harness in the regular Kiwanian meeting place, the Spencer Hotel in downtown Marion, and "stressed the importance of the lake. Harness says he will rewrite the bill with that in mind."

With that in mind, the phrase "and the securing of incidental benefits" was included. Here it is:

> *IN THE HOUSE OF REPRESENTATIVES A BILL June 7, 1939
>
> To authorize a preliminary examination and survey of the Mississinewa River and its tributaries in the State of Indiana, from Matters Park to Conners Mill in Grant County, for flood control, for run-off

> and water-flow retardation, and for soil-erosion prevention. Be it enacted by the Senate and House of Representatives of the United States of America in Congress assembled,
>
> That the Secretary of War be, and he is hereby, authorized and directed to cause a preliminary examination and survey to be made of the Mississinewa River and its tributaries in the State of Indiana, from Matters Park to Conners Mill in Grant County, with a view to the control of floods, and the securing of incidental benefits, and the Secretary of Agriculture be, and he is hereby, authorized and directed to cause a preliminary examination and survey to be made for run-off and water-flow retardation, and soil-erosion prevention on the watershed of said waterway, in accordance with the provisions of the Flood Control Act approved June 22, 1936, the costs thereof to be paid from appropriations heretofore or hereafter made for such purposes.[20]

The June 7, 1939, *Whetstone* reported that "the Conners Mill-Mississinewa River project as outlined to the Club by Ralph Roessler caught on like a forest fire in dry weather. The Board of Directors adopted the idea as a major project and committees are being appointed to work out the details."[21]

The Harness study-the-Kiwanis-Club-plan bill passed the House of Representatives on July 6, 1939. It passed the US Senate on August 2, 1939, and it was signed and became law August 11, 1939, "as authorized by section 6 of the Flood Control Act."

In an August 12, 1960, column, Paul Hillsamer, editor of the *Marion News Herald*, which was reprinted at the request of Indiana senator Vance Hartke as part of the *Congressional Record*, said the years of US Army Corps of Engineers study that followed shifted the project west.

The "details" would change when the army engineering cavalry rode in, but Roessler's idea, Hillsamer said, was the start of the project that would later wash away Somerset, the place where Vern grew up.

Vern turned twenty-three that summer.

Vern

6. CIVIL DISOBEDIENCE

Dear Vern,

Your great-grandfather never answered the phone. Our phone was on a kitchen cabinet shelf by the doorway to the living room, and he could be sitting at the kitchen table or in a living room chair when it rang, but he wouldn't budge. The whole genius key to the old phone system was that you had to pick up the receiver for it to quit making a repetitive, loud, annoying noise, and that completed the connection. It makes us flinch, it's a jolt, the unexpected sudden ringing that interrupts whatever state of mind we are in, like the alarm clock in the morning taking us from reverie to immediacy against our will and against our better nature. "Make it stop," pick it up. It's a system that worked. Except for Vern. He did not comply.

I didn't want to answer it, either. I was trying to make sense of Bob Dylan's "Subterranean Homesick Blues" down the hall in my room when it rang, and it was a strain for me when it beckoned, but I could fight it and not budge from my state of being, either, and I could count how many times the phone would ring, thinking, *Well, he's bound to answer it if it rings again*, up to twenty times, and yet Vern was not gonna answer it.

The rings would stop. There was no answering machine or voicemail recording, only the caller who'd been defeated by Vern's iron will. One minute—or five minutes or fifteen minutes—later, the process would start again, and hungover from the first time, I would run down the hallway, defeated, to make it stop.

"Tell your dad that your uncle Johnny got a new car," Mom would say when I answered. That, or something else insignificant that she could have told him when she got home. I'd be pissed that I fell for Mom's telephone tyranny, and my only retribution would be not to tell Dad that Johnny had gotten a new car.

I'd call home from college on Sunday evenings. Mom would blather about the ladies at church or the children of relatives I hadn't seen, and I'd eventually ask, "Is Dad home?"

And Mom would say, "Yes."

And I'd say, "Can I talk to him?"

And Mom would say, "Yes."

And I'd say, "Can you call him to the phone?"

And Mom would say, "Yes."

And I'd say, "Now?"

And I was prepared to wait for no matter how long it took, but, in fact, it didn't take that long for him to come to the phone, and I'd say, "Hi, Dad."

And he'd say, "Hello."

And I'd say, "Okay, bye. Put Mom back on the phone."

I sensed our shared sense of humor and that he liked the little game I had played. It seemed like the more meaningful conversation. I didn't give a shit about Johnny's Cadillac.

Vern didn't like to talk on the phone. In fact, he didn't like to talk much at all. Growing up, I thought Vern's reluctance about speaking was a choice, but something happened one time that made me wonder if there was more to it than that.

Your great-grandfather had agreed to be the assistant adult leader to J. D. Whybrew for the Green Township 4-H Club. The 4-H club is an organization for kids in the country that started out more than one hundred years ago to teach about better farming and homemaking techniques. Stan and I were members, probably beginning around the age of seven, but like most kids in the club in Green Township, we weren't farmers.

The country had already become an extension of the suburbs by then, no sidewalks but with fewer neighbors and a longer drive. Most farm kids were too busy farming for a club that taught about farming, but a few showed livestock, pigs and cows, at the Grant County 4-H fair in Marion. The rest of us were relegated to making extension cords and putting pictures on a piece of white cardboard. It was weird for me because I was always the smartest kid in my elementary school class. I thought I was something, some kind of leader just by being there, but the fact was that when it came to actually doing stuff, I wasn't good. I had the same experience in Little League baseball and basketball at school. I wasn't good.

It was fun, though. We met in the summer months at the little Soil Conservation Club building in Point Isabel. It was a boys-only club. The girls had their own. We played tag in the yard and basketball on a little gravel court out front, and then we'd come inside for the meetings. Before the county fair in the year's last meeting, we started in the morning and rode in a farm truck bed to the homes of all the club members to look at the exhibit projects we were getting ready.

We rode in the back of the truck on a sunny August morning, leaning out over the sideboards, throwing apple cores at road signs, joking around, and laughing. Oh, and using squirt guns. I was good at that. We'd end up at farmer-kid Phil Leisure's home, and we'd go swimming in what they called a pond, even though I'm pretty sure now it was the watering hole for the cattle. None of that would hold today, sorry to say for you, Vern. A dozen whooping-up-a-storm eight-to-fourteen-year-old boys in the open back of a 1963 Ford F700 grain truck kicking up gravel down the county roads and tar on the state highways at fifty-five miles per hour, followed by a swim in a mud bog we shared with cow shit and flies, was probably not healthy. But our parents knew from experience that losing the occasional runt-of-the-litter kid was not the end of the world.

Best day of the year!

J. D. Whybrew was the only grown-up at our meetings. We gathered in the regular meetings in groups by grade. Nobody had to be told where to sit. There was a definite routine to the meetings. A Pledge of Allegiance to the flag, a 4-H pledge to use our heads, hearts, hands, and health for the good of mankind. And was there a prayer? Not that I remember.

J. D. got the ball rolling, and we followed the script presented by Phil, who would have been club president, being the oldest member. Even though I did not know how to make a cow move the way that Phil did, club leader was a job I was most definitely sure I would have someday. How could I not, on my way to the United States presidency after being shortstop for the St. Louis Cardinals?

So anyway, J. D. said, "Time for the meeting," Phil said, "Paul, lead us in the pledge," and when it was over, J. D. said, "It's over," and we played in the yard until our parents drove us home.

Great club.

Somehow, I guess probably because J. D. asked him to do it and Vern liked J. D., my dad officially became Green Township 4-H assistant adult leader for the club that met five or six times a year in the Soil Conversation Club building in Point Isabel, Indiana, when I was a kid. Having one's dad be the club's assistant leader confirmed my conviction that I would someday attain two presidencies.

J. D. was devoted to the club, to being a positive role model for kids and a contributing member of his community. He never missed a meeting.

He never missed a meeting until once, when something happened that kept him away, and it must have been death-in-the-family kind of significant. So, and this is the point of this whole 4-H story, it was up to Vern, for the first time ever, to fill in.

We played in the yard. We played in the yard some more. Then we played in the yard some more. It was getting dark. We knew it was past time for the meeting to start, but if J. D. wasn't around to tell us, "It's time," and nobody else was, either, we were gonna play in the yard.

Finally, of our own accord, half an hour later, we meandered into the building and took our ordinary seats. Nobody had told us where. Vern, dressed in his ordinary short-sleeved white shirt with a pack of Camels in the pocket, sat in the farthest corner, in the back. He didn't say a word to anyone as we came in, and I don't believe anyone said a word to him. We sat and we waited for the adult in the room to start. He did not. We looked awkwardly at one another. Perhaps my brother and I should have just asked him, but we didn't speak, either. That would have been wrong.

Finally, Phil Leisure asked Paul to lead us in the Pledge of Allegiance, and I guess we learned we didn't really need anybody to tell us it was time to start the meeting. We all knew it was past time. Then, later, we didn't need anybody to tell us it was over.

Remembering this, I wonder if Vern's reluctance to speak was more than his decision. It seemed so odd. Stan told me it was. "Do you know why he never said much?" he said to me recently. "He stuttered when he was a child. Kids made fun of him. He never wanted to talk much after that. I never heard him stutter. I suppose he got over it at some point. It stuck with him."

Also, Stan said, "I thought that his mother's strictness, you know, in that Mennonite type of way, had a lot to do with him not talking, why he didn't say a whole lot. He was raised that way. 'You're a child. You don't speak.'"

7. LABELS

On Monday, January 23, 1933, Dad was back in class, a sixteen-year-old sophomore at Somerset High School, wondering why he hadn't started Friday night's basketball game. After the Shamrocks scored only two points in the first quarter, he came off the bench to score eight in a 26–19 win against nearby Lagro. He'd been a starter as a freshman on a team that beat Wabash in the sectional. That's nothing, though, Vern, compared to what happened in Wabash and Somerset that night. Bizarre, I call it.

After a speech in downtown Wabash to a meeting of a Communist Party auxiliary called the Unemployed Council, a Chicago organizer named Roy Larson "was run out of town," according to Wabash County historian Ron Woodward. Larson was "taken by car to Somerset and dumped out," Woodward told me. A headline in the next day's *Journal and Courier* of Lafayette called it a kidnapping, but in the story, "Police said he was not assaulted."[22]

The *Indianapolis Times* reported January 24, 1933, that around fifty men chased Larson from a building as the meeting ended. After that, Woodward said, the Unemployed Council would change its name and ban all Communists. That included Clarence Hamilton, who had been the Wabash County "Communistic candidate for Prosecuting attorney in the fall election"[23] according to the January 25 *Muncie Evening Press*, and Carl Hautt of Wabash and Milo Long from Somerset. Perhaps then, in a spirit of "send 'em back to where they came from," that could explain why Larson ended up in Somerset. I don't know how or when he made it back to Chicago.

A year later, Somerset's Communist Milo Long was in the Soviet Union. According to the April 11, 1934, *Indianapolis Star*, "Milo Long, farmer of near Somerset who has been actively interested in Communism left today for New York, where he will sail for London on the first leg of a trip to Russia. Long said he expected to be in Russia for some time in order to investigate conditions thoroughly."[24]

Long had come back to Somerset by 1938, we know, because he married in 1936 the sister of John Huddleston, the man who hooked up his windmill to his electric fence. Milo lived the end of his life in a town called Hope, south of Indianapolis. According to Milo's Find a Grave obituary, he "received a citation in the 1940s from the USSR for assisting Russia in production of corn."[25] Somerset. Communists. Who knew?

Union organizing was associated with communism back in the 1930s, and "strikes were not appreciated in Wabash," Woodward said. "Wabash men were often used as strikebreakers in the early days."

Strikebreakers were not appreciated by Vern. After his brief stint at Ball State Teacher's College in Muncie, where he had hoped to become a high school history teacher and a coach, he went to work at the General Tire and Rubber Company in Wabash.

He probably felt pretty good about being able to find a job after "homesickness" pulled him out of Ball State in 1935. That fall, the United Rubber Workers union first formed in Akron, Ohio, and began to organize in factories like General Tire and Goodyear all over the country. That's when Vern became a union guy. The tide had turned in the direction of workers' rights, with labor-friendly laws first initiated by the new Roosevelt administration in 1933 and a greater understanding in the courts, and more sympathy in the public at large. Still, the Great Depression continued to make life difficult for a lot of ordinary Americans and working people all over the world. There was a lot of resistance, though, too, from traditional political, economic, and social seats of power that encouraged people to feel threatened by the union movement's association with the American Communist Party in the 1930s. Some people then said people like my dad were Communists, even if they didn't know what that meant. My grandpa Fuller was like that.

According to family lore, Dad was fired from General Tire for unionizing, had to be rehired by virtue of the law, and then immediately quit as a gesture. My uncle Wayne has no memory of that, though, and I found no evidence to support the story Stan, Linda, and I heard when we were growing up. Dad was a union guy, but he was not a Communist. Dogma was not for him. But he agreed with the 1930s American Communist Party stance on things like collective bargaining, social security, racial equality, and socialized medicine. I know this because when I got to be around high school age and I began to consider how the things Vern talked about at the supper table compared to what I was learning on my own about socialism, it just made sense to me—briefly, like in a 1960s "Hey, this is cool" sort of way—that "Whoa, I think my dad is a socialist."

He wasn't a Socialist. It's fair to call him a socialist, but he was not a joiner. He ordinarily voted for Democrats. He liked Adlai Stevenson and Eleanor Roosevelt more than anybody else he talked about. He did not like Harry Truman. "Union buster," he said. At the table, passing the mashed potatoes, he said Republicans wanted to get rid of unions and Social Security. I hope you are reading the newspaper every day, Vern. That shit is still going on.

I think the experience he had living in a place that could accommodate socialist ideas and working at General Tire not long after he graduated from high school molded his beliefs about the importance of a strong labor movement in this country like a later time in Texas would cement his beliefs about equality. Dad complained more than once about how the young guys at his GM Fisher Body plant in Marion didn't understand the importance of a strong union, like the United Auto Workers, even though they were living with the benefits. They'd complain about paying dues, Dad said.

"They don't understand," he'd tell us, "what it's like to work in a factory and not have a union. Someday they'll learn." Nothing that's happened since has made me think he was wrong.

Vern's experience at General Tire made him "old guard," I guess, when it comes to unions and workers' right and what the "big shots" will do to you every time if they get half a chance. I know I heard that, but I don't remember how, or when, or where—just why.

Flood

8. BIG SHOTS

Dear Vern,

In a matter of weeks in 1939, an idea generated by Ralph Roessler's visit to an artificial lake near Lafayette had become a new federal law authorizing a Mississinewa River survey "from Matters Park to Conners Mill in Grant County, for flood control, for run-off and water-flow retardation, and for soil-erosion prevention."[26]

The project changed, though, when influential men from a wider area got involved, men that Roessler needed for support. They needed him, too. These men included the governor of Indiana, Democrat Henry Schricker; the Corps of Engineers captain in Louisville, Kentucky, Lester Rhodes; Republican Fifth District congressman Forest Harness of Kokomo; district Water Conservation Department supervisor Warren T. Lybrook; Rose Polytechnic Institute of Terre Haute professor R. E. Hutchins; Richard Bishop, the Indiana Department of Conservation planning director; and the Indianapolis Motor Speedway owner Tony Hulman. Big shots.

Roessler drove the Upper Wabash Valley Flood Control Project for thirty years. While his original idea to help Grant County with a big lake for recreation faded, Roessler's role with what the plan became remained central. After he presented an original idea for a reservoir park to his Marion Kiwanis Club, he helped create in 1945 a statewide organizing structure that could coordinate an expanded plan with the US Army. He privately counseled an influential congressman-to-be on the plan in 1958.

Roessler was on the podium for the Mississinewa Reservoir dedication ceremony with the fifth Indiana governor after Schricker, June 14, 1969.

Already, by 1944, he had proven that he was somebody who could lead. He remained, always, in a position to ensure that no matter what the plan grew into, a big lake for recreation, like Lake Shafer, remained on the table, even if not for Conner's Mill, Marion, and Grant County. When the focus shifted in 1943 to the entire state, Ralph led the effort.

Though not as bad as the 1913 deluge, heavy rain the third week of May 1943 created a Wabash River flood all the way from Wabash to Vincennes in southern Indiana, not far from where the Wabash empties into the Ohio River. The river was thirteen feet over flood stage in Lafayette, ten feet over in Terre Haute, and six feet over in Vincennes. In Wabash, the river was over its banks by twelve feet. It was described as "the worst flood in 30 years" for the area; the *Muncie Star-Press* reported that Red Cross officials said Peru was "about the worst spot in the state."[27]

A few weeks later, according to Roessler's diary, the Upper Wabash River Association formed, after he met with "official people . . . from Peru, Logansport, Marion, Wabash, Kokomo, and Delphi . . . in need of a more unified program . . . for managing the Wabash River."

Then, in August of 1943, he led the Upper Wabash River Association into a merger with the Lower Wabash River Association, and their officers began "calling for a survey of the whole state, Wabash and Ohio rivers," again according to Roessler's diary. A technical committee formed, headed by R. E. Hutchins, and one year later, the consolidated group reported that "a state commission should be formed to manage this work."[28]

Roessler explained the sequence of events in a report for that subsequent commission, the new Indiana Flood Control and Water Resources Commission (IFCWRC). He gave that to a January 1945 IFCWRC "public hearing" with the Army Corps of Engineers. That's a meeting that Governor Schricker said they needed to prepare for by forming the IFCWRC. The army wouldn't talk to just anybody.

According to notes he kept in his diary, Roessler gave the January 1945 hearing with the army a history lesson. In the "spring of 1943," he told the Corps of Engineers, "this territory suffered another very disastrous flood."

> A forward looking group of men led by Larry Vaughn, then Secretary of the Peru Industrial Association, called a meeting of representative men in Peru, Logansport, Marion, Wabash, Kokomo, Delphi and other communities, to be held in Peru in June of that year, mayors, city engineers and other interested men. As a result of this meeting an association was formed, the Upper Wabash River Association. Officers and directorate were elected, myself as president and Larry Vaughn as Secretary. Work was immediately started by these men to *further interest on the part of the federal Government* [my emphasis] in the need of a more unified program for the entire valley or the tributaries of the Upper Wabash.
>
> On August 9th, 1943, at a meeting of a group representing the area of the lower Wabash River and the Upper Wabash River Association, the two groups were merged. This action was based upon the idea that the problem of flood prevention and control was one of wide ramifications, taking in not only the construction of levees, the widening or deepening of channels, but that it could be made most effective by a general plan of detention and retention, of conservation as well as protection, of the creation of many small reservoirs at head waters, as well as larger ones nearer outlets, and conservation by including soil erosion prevention.[29]

In Roessler's foundational statement, I see five strategies for managing the river for "conservation as well as protection." They are 1) levees, 2) widening or deepening channels, 3) the creation of *small reservoirs* at head waters, 4) the creation of *larger reservoirs* nearer outlets, and 5) soil erosion prevention. In what would become the Upper Wabash Valley Flood Control Project, only one strategy was implemented, that being number four.

Why only one? There are no records to consult, but the available evidence suggests it was "to further interest on the part of the federal Government." The federal government had the money. "To further interest on the part of the federal Government" would mean doing what the federal government wanted them to do to get the public money controlled by the federal government. It was policy that the governing body of the federal government in flood control projects was the United States Army Corps of Engineers. The policy was made official in the authorizing language of the Flood Control Act that would be passed by the Seventy-Ninth US Congress in 1946.

The Army Corps of Engineers selected the sort of project with which they were familiar. That would keep the big-project big-money headed their way. It was what some came to call "the big dam plan." The Indiana Flood Control and Water Resources Commission, the newly authorized flood control governing body in the state government, went along.

Longtime Somerset resident Tom Snyder told me things changed when "Washington" became involved. "There was a lot of pressure put on politically to do something," Snyder said, "about widely reported flooding. The Army Corps of Engineers had started building dams for flood control all over the country."

In addition to growing up in Somerset, Tom Snyder worked for the Army Corps of Engineers for most of his adult life. "I was at Mississinewa Reservoir with Army Corps of Engineers from '82 to '84, the third reservoir I had worked on," Tom told me. He started with the corps at Springfield, Ohio, in 1976 and then started work at a reservoir north of Cincinnati in 1979. Tom, who became my best source of on-the-ground information for this letter, Vern, was chief of operations at the Upper Wabash Valley Flood Control Project's Salamonie Reservoir for twenty-one years.

"The Army Corps of Engineers," Tom said, "was motivated to create projects in order to rationalize their role in the greater scheme of things."

So backing up here to the start of this process, the big shots, led by our very own Ralph Roessler, got in touch with Indiana governor Henry Schricker, who agreed that, to move forward and deal with the army, they had to have the state commission. It needed a name, an official-sounding name, so the Indiana Flood Control and Water Resources Commission was born. It was one of Schricker's last official duties at the end of his term.

Roessler would then, not surprisingly, get a letter from Governor Schricker making him a brand-new IFCWRC member and setting a 10:00 a.m. "over by lunch time" November 9, 1944, organizing meeting that "needs to be done" because of that public hearing set for January by the United States Army Corps of Engineers.[30]

The letter from the governor named all its members and included that of Wabash Valley Trust Company president Carlos Life of Peru, Indiana. Peru is the town that had a major flood in 1913, an event that became the starting point for repeated opening arguments in favor of a major flood control project for the area. Peru, the seat of Miami County, was also the community in the area of what became the three "big dam" and three reservoir projects called the Upper Wabash Valley Flood Control Project that would likely suffer the most personal and material loss in the event of a flood. Peru had the biggest stake in getting the project done. No community pushed it more. No one in Peru pushed it more than Carlos Life. Life was a founding IFCWRC member. The commission was created to further the flood control interests of Indiana, and Life had a primary interest in the livelihood of Peru, the community that would benefit most from the Upper Wabash Valley Flood Control Project. Like Roessler, Life played a central role in the success of the project from the inception of the IFCWRC until the Upper Wabash Valley Flood Control Project was a done deal and the commission, in a remarkably telling moment, immediately disbanded.

No one from Somerset got a letter from Governor Schricker asking them to be an IFCWRC member.

Roessler reported in his papers that, the night before the November 9, 1944, meeting called by Governor Schricker, he met "in a secret session" with other unidentified members who also hadn't been appointed yet to make plans for what they planned to do at the meeting when everybody else would show up to be appointed, along with themselves, the next day.

The next day, Roessler was named vice chairman. Terre Haute businessman Anton Hulman Jr. was named chairman. He was better known as "Tony." Tony Hulman was the guy who, as owner of the operation, said, "Gentlemen, start your engines," to begin the Indianapolis 500 car race.

With the over-by-lunchtime organizing meeting over, everything was in order, then, for the January 1945 hearing with the Army Corps of Engineers where R. E. Hutchins, appointed the technical committee chairman, testified that a "preference for detention reservoirs" was the Indiana Flood Control and Water Resources Commission's position. That came, Roessler's diary says, after a yearlong study with the help of the engineering department at Purdue University in Lafayette. While detention reservoirs had included small reservoirs for Roessler in 1943, the strategy would ultimately settle on large reservoirs only, consistent with Roessler's big-lake-for-fun idea and the Army Corps of Engineers' area of expertise.

The "construction of levees, the widening or deepening of channels" and "conservation by including soil erosion prevention" were not noted in Roessler's report about the undocumented "yearlong study" that must have started in 1943 with the Upper and Lower Wabash Valley Associations merger.[31] Why the other strategies were discarded is not part of Roessler's diary report about the January 1945 meeting between the brand-new state agency and the army.

In February 1945, the Indiana legislature got involved with a hearing to begin implementing its support for the new IFCWRC and to consider mapping the entire state for perspective on flood control. As the war in Europe ended, the US Congress asked in May 1945 for a study on the Upper Wabash Valley flooding problems.

The Indiana Flood Control and Water Resources Commission had formed out of the army's bureaucratic requirement for the project to go forward. The project gave the IFCWRC its raison d'être. At every step, the loaded-with-supporters IFCWRC would provide cover for the project, a seal of approval. When the project was essentially complete and the organization's purpose was satisfied, it disbanded. Then and there. The Indiana Flood Control and Water Resources Commission no longer exists.

The IFCWRC met for the final time on June 26, 1965. The day before the last of three reservoirs in the Upper Wabash Valley Flood Control Project got the flag-waving, "big shot" standing-on-the-podium, dynamite groundbreaking treatment, the IFCWRC ceased operation. The day before the official groundbreaking for the Huntington Reservoir, the IFCWRC closed shop. Holy moly, Vern.

The 1965 closing-up-shop part was out in the open. What happened in the project-planning stage between 1944 and 1955, not so much. There weren't good records kept on that by the state commission or the army or the congressmen or even Ralph Roessler, who kept pretty good records otherwise. I filed a Freedom of Information Act request with the army for some help with that, and I got a reply that they didn't have anything to offer.

Is it possible that Ralph Roessler's 1939 Kiwanis Club idea story is an origin myth? When did the Upper Wabash Valley Flood Control Project really start? An October 19, 1961, editorial called "Benefits of Flood Control" in publisher Joe Nixon's *Wabash Plain Dealer* claimed that, for flood control, "in 1938 a comprehensive plan was developed and has been used ever since."[32] That predates Ralph.

According to Vern's little brother, my uncle Wayne, "We had stories about [the reservoir] way back during the war."

Dave Compton said his stepfather told him he started hearing about the Mississinewa River damming in 1942. That's evidence that the army had something underway even before the Roessler-led Upper Wabash Association merged with a downstate group in the middle of 1943 to begin the process that would connect a statewide group to the army. Tom Snyder said the army had river gauges installed in the '40s for all three eventual reservoirs that were right below where they built the dams.

Snyder told a group of around fifty people at a talk he gave at the Wabash County Museum on February 2, 2023, that "They put a gauge on the river in the '40s to gauge what happens to the river going up and down and up and down so they were already thinking, 'If we're gonna build a dam it's going to be between that hill and that hill and we're gonna see how high we gotta build the dam.'" Those gauges remain in service today, Snyder said.

Does early army activity belie a premise that it all began with Roessler's trip to Lake Shafer? Is there an Upper Wabash Valley Flood Control Project even without Roessler?

Perhaps, but local support would have had to come from somewhere else. The local support certainly started with Roessler. And I'll refer you, Vern, to the fact that Roessler would be later given the designation "Father of the Mississinewa Reservoir." No single person is more present in the process than Ralph, for thirty years, from 1939 until 1969. His track gave the army in the 1940s something to travel on.

"They had a lot of floods at that time," Uncle Wayne said. "The Wabash would flood. The Mississinewa would flood. They would cause a lot of trouble." Wabash County historian Ron Woodward told me that flooding had been a problem for Wabash as early as 1884 and that a 1909 flood was the city's biggest, forcing city officials to set up relief shelters for people who were forced out of their homes.

"Every time it flooded, there was articles in the papers," Snyder said. "People saying, 'Why don't somebody do something about all this flooding?'"

"Which politician could be elected and get it done?" was the common sentiment, according to Snyder.

Ralph showed that he was good at pushing the politicians, three congressmen among them, to "get it done." Mostly, he was behind the scenes, where his kind of help is most appreciated.

What actually happened remains shrouded in secrecy. Wayne remembered, "Before the war started, Bunker Hill [now the Grissom Air Reserve Base] was an air corps base. They put in a runway on the way to Converse, on State Road 513. It was a temporary runway for pilots to practice landing. We thought maybe the surveying that we saw was part of that, but it wasn't. It didn't have anything to do with that. They would do a lot of surveying. We would see them along the road, surveying and everything else. But we didn't know what it was for. They surveyed the whole area before they ever planned on the reservoir."

The best evidence for what happened is what happened.

With resignation in his voice, Wayne told me, "The only thing I heard from Mom and Dad was they didn't know what they were surveying for or anything else. We didn't know."

Vern

9. HOOSIERS

1.

Dear Vern,

Old Vern grew up on a farm so long ago that they still used horses where people later used tractors. I'm not sure that corporate factory farms have any more use now for what I'd call tractors that pull plows and discs and planters and cultivators and hay wagons. When I was a kid, they did, and that's how I remember farming around where I grew up. Farm equipment these days has come to look like the machines that build ten-lane highways and suburban strip malls called Heritage Square next to subdivisions with cul-de-sacs called Golden Harvest Lane. When every-day horses worked for a living, they were called *draught horses*. *Draught* is pronounced "draft," like the name of a light, late-summer wind coming in the house from under the door. Workhorses are draught horses.

The little river town where Dad went to high school, Somerset, was flooded by the Mississinewa Reservoir in something called the Upper Wabash Valley Flood Control Project. I think changing the name to Mississinewa *Lake* later is part of a cover-up, whether people meant it that way or not. The town two miles from the chickens and cows on Vern's family farm no longer exists. We can say it does, in the form of a transported village with the same name along State Road 13. It's up the hill from where Somerset lived along the Mississinewa River until 1966. But that's a lie, the kind that people tell to make themselves comfortable with being uncomfortable.

Vern's claim to fame was his success playing basketball from 1931 to 1935 for Somerset High School. After he graduated, he joined his big brother Maurice (pronounced "Morse") working at the General Tire plant in Wabash. His younger brother Burnell would enlist with the company a year later. His youngest brother, Wayne, told me over the phone from his home in Ocala, Florida, that Vern "worked there until he went into the service. All three of them did. He was living with Mom and Dad at that time. That was on the farm," Wayne said.

My first memory in life is that of sticking my finger into the twirling blades of a push mower on that farm when I was three. I can show you the scar. A little later, I touched the electric fence and felt it tingle in my toes.

A man named Tom Snyder knows about the farm where Vern grew up. His "Grams" was my grandfather's sister, Verna. Aunt Vernie lived across the road from the farm where Dad grew up, and Tom told me he "went over there all the time" when Tom was a kid. And he told me his father, Fred, told him stories about his uncle Charley.

"Uncle Charley" to Tom was Grandpa Shroyer to me. My dad called my grandpa "Pop." Tom told me a lot about Pop and Somerset and the Upper Wabash Valley Flood Control Project. A woman who still lives in the "new" Somerset named Helen Adkins had told me about Tom. I found out about her at a Lions Club meeting in the "new" Somerset I attended with an invitation from a woman named Lucinda Holderman whom I met through the Wabash County Historical Society Facebook page.

The best advice I got after I started this letter to you, Vern, was that I needed to talk to people. Tom Snyder was the best.

"Uncle Charley's house would not flood," he said.

Tom's dad, Fred Snyder, was adopted by Aunt Vernie and her first husband, who was also named Tom Snyder. "Everybody considered Dad Gram's son after she adopted him," Tom said.

"The Shroyers had an awful big influence on my dad's life and on my life, because of Grams being a Shroyer. She took Dad in and made him a part of her. I remember Aunt Evie [my grandma, Eva Arrick Shroyer] and Vernie talking, laughing." Tom told me about the farm where Vern grew up.

> The only good thing about that place was that it had a very good spring down by the barn. A natural spring. They milked cows for years when the boys were young. When they put the milk in the milk cans, they had to cool it down, so they took the cans to the springhouse and set them in that spring water that was constantly moving through that building. The cans sat in a concrete trough, and the water would run over them and cool the milk down. Goose Creek ran right through the center of the property. The springhouse was down the hill from the house. The creek ran behind the barn. It crossed the road and then turned west on the other side of the road parallel from the house.
>
> Goose Creek was right on the east end of the barn. And the barn was maybe ten feet higher than the creek, when the creek was fairly shallow. Goose Creek would overflow into the barn. The creek always had water in it. The creek was spring fed. The cattle went to the creek for water. They could just walk out to the creek and drink all they wanted. He never had to water his livestock because they drank out of the creek. That's why the barn was built where it was at.

When I traipse down the lane hill now to the reservoir's edge, on what was the road between Grandpa's place and Aunt Vernie's, I can see the remnants of Goose Creek.

"When the boys were older, he quit milking cows. Charley quit milking and then raised beef cattle," Tom said.

While Aunt Vernie and her second husband, John Knee, farmed, they also ran the Riverside Resort cabins and campground across the road from the home of Uncle Charley and Aunt Evie. Vernie also started the hot lunch program for Somerset schools in 1944, Tom said. "She had three people working for her"—Bessie Deeter, Hazel Garst, and Omma Sweet.

"Dad was all about Somerset High School, and he was on the varsity basketball team his sophomore, junior, and senior years," Tom said. "Dad was just enough younger than Vern and brothers Maurice and Burnell that he grew up watching them play ball. And my dad said, 'Well, I guess I kind of kept up the Shroyer tradition.'"

A writer named Pete Jones, Tom said, "did a retrospective article for the Wabash paper on the 1935 Wabash team that mentions Vern Shroyer. January 5, 2020, edition, it is. Vern hits the first of two free throws to win a three-overtime game against LaFontaine in the first game of the sectional."

Basketball was a big part of life around there. I heard Dad's cousin Kay Peas tell Aunt Vernie's son Larry Knee that she remembers her dad, Bob Shroyer, getting so upset watching a Somerset game that he lost his teeth. "It was probably when either you or Wayne were playing," she told Larry. "He yelled so much he blew out his false teeth, and they hit Guinevere Garst on the way down."

Her sister, Janet Schenkel, added, "People tried to get 'em before they stepped on his teeth."

At one point, Tom said, neighboring Somerset and LaFontaine had to quit playing.

> For two years, Somerset and LaFontaine could not play basketball together because of fights. It was too dangerous for them to play each other. The IHSAA [Indiana High School Athletic Association] banned it for two years. Neighbors got into fights. The parents in the towns would get into big brawls, and they'd have to send the sheriff's departments out from either Wabash or Grant County, depending upon where they were playing. It was a bitter rivalry.

In the old basement gyms, he said, "They were playing against those concrete walls down there. There were some players thrown into that wall from time to time, supposedly unintentional."

"At Uncle Charley's, they had a basketball goal on the barn and in the hayloft," Tom Snyder said.

Larry, the son of John Knee and Aunt Vernie, would become the leading scorer in Somerset High School basketball history before he graduated in 1956. Larry remembers playing ball with Vern and his brothers in that hayloft in the winters when it got too cold to play baseball in the farmyard. They were older men, veterans back home from the Second World War. Larry was born in 1938.

"The favorite thing I remember," Larry told me when I visited him in June of 2023, was that "every Sunday, all of Uncle Charley's boys would come home. I'd come down because I wanted to be with them. Over the hill in that flat land down there in front of the barn was a ball game every Sunday in the summer, and then in the winter, we went in the barn and played basketball.

"It was rough," Larry said. "I was the youngest guy out there but big for my age. They had no mercy."

In the hayloft floor, there was a hole to throw the straw down through, Larry said. "There was no guard on that. They shoved Mary's husband, Bud, and he went down that hole." Mary was Vern's younger sister. "It was bedding," Larry said, "but he never come back up."

"After a while, everybody's saying, 'You think he's mad?'

"'I don't know.'

"'Whadda you think?'

"We got to looking for him. He'd went to the house. He told somebody, 'I am never playing ball out there again.'"

Bud and Mary's son, Greg, was the best basketball player among the sons of Dad and his brothers and sisters. Grandpa Shroyer would become a regular at Greg's games at Windfall High School in Tipton County. Sports, meaning high school basketball and major-league baseball, were always a big deal for us.

"I remember Uncle Charley had to go to St. Louis all the time to watch baseball," Tom told me. "Uncle Charley would appreciate you and your son being Cardinal fans. I can remember my dad, he would go over there and come back saying, 'He's gonna go in that car, and that car isn't fit to go out of the county. He's gonna drive all the way to St. Louis in that thing.' Dad was scared of him going."

My understanding is that Pop became a Cardinal fan as a result of growing up in Kansas. Vern named my brother, Stan, for Stan Musial, the best St. Louis Cardinal baseball player of all time. I envied that name, but it was a burden for Stan.

Stan heard a story from Uncle Maurice about our dad's basketball playing.

Maurice told Stan that as Vern stepped to the free throw line in the 1932 sectional final against Wabash, Maurice heard referee Jesse Cage or Allen Klink say to the other, "This game is over."

With a few seconds on the clock and the scored tied at fifteen, Vern hit both.

Game over.

Then, Maurice told Stan, while the team celebrated with the crowd, Vern said, "Let's get out of here."

Beating Wabash was a big deal, the first of two basketball sectional championships ever for Somerset and one of those victories by the little school over the big school that made the Indiana every-high-school-together-in-one basketball tournament special at every level, from the sectionals in county seat places like Wabash through the state finals at the giant Butler Fieldhouse in Indianapolis. That lasted until "class" basketball started in 1997. Then school communities had to make it to the state finals in order for their fans, players, and coaches to experience that kind of excitement.

I saw four of those David-versus-Goliath games in 1964, sitting in the stands with 6,500 other people, next to Dad, when population 900 Swayzee beat population 38,000 Marion in the 1964 sectional first round and then won three more state tourney games. That 1964 team is the biggest thing that ever happened in Swayzee. Sixty years later, I remember stars Lennie Boswell and Burl Turner. Vern never mentioned 1932, but he had to be thinking about it, right? When the games were over, we went, as always, silently home, letting them speak for themselves and letting 1932 alone. "Let's get out of here."

Vern was a hero to me already, so what would it have hurt for him to tell me about 1932, something he was proud of? He never did. I had to find out about it on my own.

"Let's get out of here."

Vern got to whatever counted as a locker room in 1932 and got his fifteen-year-old self showered and dressed as fast as he could, or maybe he simply threw his pants and a coat on over his uniform and rushed out a side door into the quiet, cold February night. He never looked back, but he never left, either. I remember the letter jacket he never wore on a hanger next to the upright freezer in the kitchen after we moved into the new house thirty-two years later. Green with a white S.

He must have thought about that game every day until he died the week before Thanksgiving, Friday morning, November 21, 1986.

"We were gonna go see *Hoosiers* this weekend," Mom told me the afternoon after the morning he died. That movie was set twenty years after Vern played for small-town Somerset, but I think small-town Hickory captured the scene well.

2.

I can remember passing by a particular white-painted shed on the roadside west of Somerset on more than one occasion when Dad would point through the windshield and say, "We played basketball there." By "we," he meant, "our high school team, we played there."

That shed was home court to the Butler Township Tomahawks, Miami County. "Butler High School in Miami County was just west of where the dam is now, near Peoria," Tom Snyder said. "There were all kinds of stories about playing basketball at Butler." There were "big wooden rafters and two potbellied stoves at the center line on each side to heat it."

Kay Peas remembers, "They had a fence like you would put around a field that they put around the basketball court."

Her sister, Janet Schenkel, said, "There was a bump in the floor you had to be careful not to trip on."

Tom said, "One of the rules was the Butler players could shoot the ball through the wood rafters to make a goal, but the visiting team couldn't." Even for 1931, that last thing sounds unlikely to me, but I wasn't going to argue with my best source, and it's a good story. "Nobody wanted to play ball at Butler," Tom said. Nobody did after 1958.

Most of the little Indiana schools that centered their town and township identities disappeared into the consolidation craze of the 1950s and 60s. Maconaquah is the consolidated school students from Butler Township go to now, with children from Washington, Deer Creek, Pipe Creek, Harrison, and Clay Townships. In 1954, there were ten high schools in Miami County: Bunker Hill, Butler, Chili, Clay Township, Converse, Deedsville, Gilead, Macy, Mexico, and Peru. The Indiana High School Athletic Association membership history page lists as many as seventeen over time, beginning with Amboy and Peru in 1904. Now there are three. North Miami is the third, with Peru and Maconaquah. Maconaquah is the Miami Nation name of a woman famous in the area for being kidnapped when she was five years old in Pennsylvania. Named Frances Slocum when and where she was born, she came with the Delaware people who had attacked her family to live in the Somerset area in the Revolutionary War era. When the people from Pennsylvania found her, she did not want to go back.

Somerset, which is in neighboring Wabash County, dissolved into the Southwood school district in 1962. There are four public high schools now in Wabash County. Thirteen have disappeared. With declining enrollment, Southwood is close to shutting down now.

Vern played twenty years before the famous 1954 team from the little town of Milan that inspired mythical Hickory High School in the movie *Hoosiers*. I found a story in the January 7, 1933, *Kokomo Tribune* that says that V. Shroyer led all Somerset scorers in a game the Shamrocks lost to the Jackson Township Stonewalls of Howard County, 23–19. Dad had five points.

According to the box score, Burnell, "B. Shroyer,"[33] had six. Tom Snyder told me he could never tell those two apart, either. It was a different game then. Much like the hockey face-off, there was a center jump ball after every made basket until the rules were changed in 1936. Games were low scoring.

After high school, Vern briefly attended Ball State Teachers College in Muncie with the intention of becoming a history teacher and a coach. He was homesick, though, my sister Linda told me, and left in his first semester. I've seen some other coaches along the way, up close and from a distance. The Gene Hackman character, the coach in *Hoosiers*, could have been a Shroyer boy. In type, someplace between Maurice and Burnell. In time, that would have been Vern.

3.

Along with cousin Bob, all five Shroyer brothers played basketball at Somerset High School, starting with Maurice in 1929 and concluding with Wayne in 1951. Tom Snyder says they made an impression on "my uncle Larry," Larry Knee. I told you, Vern, Larry Knee became Somerset's all-time leading scorer by the time he graduated in 1956. Larry told Tom that being like a Shroyer boy had been one of his goals all along. "The Shroyer name in Somerset was pretty big," Snyder said. "They were neighbors, and they were good ballplayers at Somerset High School, and that was what Larry aspired to be." Like Vern, Larry played varsity basketball his freshman year.

"When you grow up in the Shroyer family," Larry said, "you gotta play basketball." Seventy-five years after the fact, he told me, "I couldn't wait to be a sixth grader, because you get to play ball with all the schools around."

It was basketball that kept him on the straight and narrow. A friend had encouraged him to start smoking when he was around the age of twelve, Larry said. "I had to do the milking on Vernie's farm," he said, after his father had died when he was eight years old. "I'd put the milkers on and sit on the barn beam and light me up a cigarette. I was sitting there trying to be big stuff when I look out the corner of my eye and seen the barn door slide open and Mom stuck her head in and seen what I was doing." She didn't say anything, simply turned around and left, Larry said.

"I put that cigarette down and looked up at that barn door, and I could see her going up the hill to get up to the house. I could tell she was crying. I mean, I knew she was crying. And I was crying, 'What am I going to do?'

"I washed the milkers; I rewashed the milkers; it took me forever to get in the house.

"I walked into the house, and she says, 'Sit down,' and I said, 'Okay, Mom,' and she said, 'I been figuring it out. I been worrying about how I was gonna get you to basketball practice,' she said. 'You just settled tonight. I'm gonna take up smokin', and you and I are just gonna sit around and smoke every night. We'll just sit and smoke and listen to the radio.'

"And I started crying," Larry said. "And I quit smoking that day. And that was the wisest thing. That was so profound, how she taught me. That was your aunt Vernie."

Your great-aunt Linda remembers feeling a bit like a princess when she attended Uncle Wayne's games at the Somerset High School gym before our brother, Stan, and I were born, 1950 or '51, when she was three or four.

"It was a very old-fashioned gym," she said. "The windows were above the bleachers. There was a giant scoreboard and a stage where they held graduation. It was also the auditorium. It was green and white, and it smelled sweaty. It was hot.

"It was packed with people. People couldn't get in. Six hundred maybe. Everybody knew our dad. Everybody spoke to him. It was the gym that Dad played in. Shroyers were a big thing.

"I had a green-and-white outfit, and I cheered. I sat with the cheerleaders. I was hot stuff. I was Vern's kid, and I was Uncle Wayne's niece. We never missed his games."

"The brothers would show up for them ball games," Tom said.

"Wayne was really good," Linda said. "All the brothers showed up. It was like a family get-together every Friday night." Wayne's senior year, the school opened a new gym, and it remained a source of pride for the community until it closed in 1962 and then was demolished for the reservoir in 1965.

"When Wayne was a senior, I was a seventh grader," Larry said, seventy-four years after the fact. "I was the first seventh grader to make a basket in the new gym." When Vern and Burnell came to his high school game against Marion St. Paul, he remembers now, "They were not impressed with my ball playing."

"Impressed or not impressed," I replied, "it wouldn't much matter," and he sort of chuckled, like he was glad I understood.

"When I talked to 'em afterward, I wouldn't know if I'd scored a point."

"I should have been happy they were there," Larry said, in a way that sounded like he still would have liked a bit more. And then he changed the subject.

"Your dad was handy," he said. "When he lived in Marion, he built a TV tower out of pipe. What I knew about Vern and Burnell, they were quiet, but they were also deep thinkers. Your dad didn't talk much. More action than talking."

4.

For my brother, Stan, being Vern's firstborn son, the expectations of Shroyer basketball were a burden. "I felt like I disappointed him in the end," he said. "He wanted me to be like his brothers. Like his brothers' sons. They played, and he would have really liked that for me."

When I told my cousin Greg Hoback at a family funeral that I can remember watching him play for Windfall High School in 1964, he spoke like he could barely remember it himself. "Why would you remember that?" he asked.

It seemed really important at the time, and it never occurred to me then that Stan simply didn't like it. How could he not want to be a basketball hero?

"I do remember going to a basketball game one time," Stan said when I asked him about what Shroyer basketball meant to him. "He [Dad] took me when I was pretty young. I remember his hat. I was so young. I was more interested in his hat than what was going on in the ball game. I just remember that hat sitting there on that bench where we had our seats. It was one of those 1950s-style hats that guys wore back in those days, and I guess I kind of associate that with Dad way back when. His hat."

My brother golfs and rides a bicycle. He has the look of a movie star–handsome, fit, and tall–but for competitive sports, he never had the drive. I could see that myself when I watched him play on the junior varsity team at Fairmount High School. He didn't want the ball.

"It occurred to me that the only reason he had anything to do with me was that I was intended to play basketball or baseball," Stan said. "He bought me contact lenses so that it would help me see better at night for a baseball game in the outfield. I had complained about the glare. So, he said, 'Okay, we'll get you some contact lenses.' That seemed unnecessary to me. Dad was always trying to train me. Talk to me? What do you mean, talk to me? Wanted me to go out and hit or shoot more baskets. 'You gotta do this. You gotta do that.'

"I do think he gave up. He never gave up, though, on wanting me to get my grades. 'I want you to get your grades up,' he said. I always got that.

"Sports for me wasn't what it was made out to be. I never played with a bunch of people who acted like they wanted to be a team. It was always individuals. I never cared much for it. I remember being on the bus, sophomore year, I was on the B team. The guys in the back of the bus. They didn't give a shit anymore. The team wasn't doing that well. Sullivan and Hasley would yell up at the front of the bus. They called the coach 'Harpo.'

"'Hey, Harpo!' they'd yell. 'What about you and that nigger up there?'"

That slur was directed at Stan's Black classmate, Sid Wilson.

Like ours, Sid Wilson's family lived "out in the country." In my memory, Sid belonged to the only African American family with kids in the school, and there were no Black families in Fairmount then, even though it had been an outpost for the Underground Railroad 120 years before. More recently, it had been an area that was home to the men who fomented the infamous Marion courthouse lawn lynching in 1930. I remember that the violent revolts against racism of the 1960s usually associated with larger urban areas also hit Marion and Kokomo. It was front-page news in the Marion newspaper when, in July of 1967, 150 members of the Marion National Guard were sent to South Bend to quell rioting.

In 1967, Sid was the only Black kid and the best player on the Fairmount High School team already as a sophomore.

My brother had had enough. That was the last straw for Stan. He said, "I thought, *I don't want to be a part of this. I don't want to do this anymore.*" His friendship with Sid grew.

Perhaps Sid considered a transfer to nearby Marion and their state-finals-caliber team, but he continued to play for Fairmount through his senior year. I remember that he later played on the junior varsity team at Purdue. After college, he worked with Dad at Fisher Body, and Stan said Vern was also among his friends there.

You're going to have to get used to the idea, new Vern, that being right won't necessarily bring you the joy you deserve. No matter what he achieved for the community team, Sid was called "nigger" on the team bus.

Stan suffered the sorrow of disappointing his father.

"Dad didn't have anybody that he could brag about in sports. He thought he had me, and it just didn't turn out that way," Stan said.

I envied my brother. I never realized how difficult Vern's expectations were for him until I started writing this letter to you and we talked about Dad.

I've always been a little guy, and although I love basketball and baseball, it was clear to me by the time I was in seventh grade that I would not be good enough to play for a high school team. I cried, but it was a clean break. I only disappointed myself.

Vern's perspective was much easier for me, and it continued to evolve, I can see, to the point that we were on the verge of friendship when he died twenty years later. Linda's son, Arrick John (A. J.), and Vern were close, only a mile apart when he was a kid and happy in one another's company. I listened when Linda told Stan the story of when A. J. didn't make the eighth-grade basketball team:

"He was crushed. It broke his heart. I don't think that A. J. could have ever been cut from a team without thinking that Dad would have been so disappointed in him. So A. J. felt some of what you are saying," Linda told Stan. "But Dad handled it better with A. J. than he did with you.

"They had had two teams, the Summitville team and the Fairmount team, and it was when the new junior high started. It was then a single Madison-Grant team. Dad told A. J. that it was okay, that being in sports was not all that it was cracked up to be. 'It's just a game,'" Linda said. "Dad died a couple weeks later."

That day, A. J. sat alone in the car in Dad's driveway for a long time.

At his funeral home visitation, Sid Wilson told Stan that Vern was "great to me" when they worked together at the Fisher Body plant in Marion. Phil Leisure, J. D. Whybrew, and a third farmer, Stan Downing, told me separately that day that Dad would not accept payment for his welding help repairing broken-down equipment in the field. Money would diminish the value.

"I'd see him all the time walking along the roadside since his last heart operation a year ago," J. D. told me that day. "I can't believe he's gone."

10. TALK

Like his brothers, Uncle Wayne worked at General Tire after high school "for a year and a half," he told me. "Then I went in the service in September 1954." Wayne's service was the navy.

The service is what we called the military when I was growing up because that's what my folks called it when they talked about the men who joined the United States' effort to defeat the Germans and the Japanese in World War II, no matter if they were drafted or if they enlisted. *The service.*

Good word, *service.*

People back then weren't encouraged to be all puffed up with themselves about having been in the army, the marines, and the navy, like they were after the United States lost the war in Vietnam. Before the war in Vietnam, servicemen of Vern's generation did what they had to do, and most of them came home. They didn't spend a lot of time demanding acknowledgment of their service on their everyday clothes or at community sporting events. They weren't standing up between the second and third periods of a college hockey game dutifully acknowledging the dutiful applause of a dutifully appreciative crowd who hadn't made it yet to the concession stand for their service.

Back then, giant football-field-covering flags and jet flyovers and seventh-inning-stretch renditions of "God Bless America" were not a thing. That didn't come along, I guess, until we needed to pump ourselves up after we'd lost a war. I saw an overhead photograph of players and coaches lined up for introductions at the 1966 All-Star game in St. Louis, and it immediately struck me that the only things on the field were the teams and the umpires. You wouldn't see that now.

We didn't see Wayne a lot, because he made the navy his vocation. Wayne was a lifer.

"I come home on leave once in a while, but that was it. Of course, I would see Vern and all the boys and everything." Public displays of affection were not a thing in the Shroyer family, either, so I mistook what I saw when I was growing up for unconcern. Wayne's absence at most family gatherings never struck me as an absence because I didn't know any different. I didn't miss someone who was never there to begin with. I don't know why he stayed in the navy. I don't know if he talked to Dad about it. I don't know how much his absence bothered Wayne's brothers and sisters and his mom and dad. He was a good guy, and I think he paid more attention to his nieces and nephews than they did when he was home. He wasn't all that much older than we were, being seventeen years younger than Vern. Maybe he saw his parents the way I saw mine, as part of an older generation, like grandparents. He was gone, and the flood came, so a chance to talk about any of that with a bunch of people who didn't talk anyway never had a chance. I never talked to him as much as I have lately, because I'm writing this letter to you. Thank you for that, Vern.

From before the war, Wayne said, "I remember Vern being at work and Vern coming home from work. General Tire had an independent basketball team. Vern was quite a basketball player–and a softball team. The softball team was bigger. He also played a lot of softball. Everybody knew about the softball team. The basketball team wasn't that good."

When I told Uncle Wayne, Vern's last surviving sibling, that you had been born and that your parents had given you the name of his big brother, he said to me, "Good. That's very good. The world needs another Vern." You're Vern. I hope that isn't harder for you than being named Stan.

"All of Dad's brothers thought a lot of him," my brother, Stan, said. "I remember at his funeral, Uncle Wendell came up to me and looked at me and said, 'He was the best of us.' And I agreed with Wendell. I said, 'Yeah, I think he was.'"

After high school and before the war, when the boys and sister Lenore were working but still living at home, Vern made sure that they paid their mother "rent money." That's what my sister, Linda, said. He was the enforcer, I guess, telling his siblings, "It's the least we should do," Linda said. After the war, Vern was the guy who took up a collection to buy their parents things they could not afford, like a television and a new refrigerator. I did not treat my parents that well.

"I loved him. I thought he was the greatest," Wayne said.

"I remember growing up, him and Burnell and Maurice would come home from work and they would take me anywhere they were going. They were going to the store or going to get gas, something like that, I'd ride along with them.

"On Friday night and Saturday night, they'd come home and get all dressed up, and I'd say, 'Can I ride with ya?'

"'No,' they'd say. 'We're going to Jalapa, the street fair.'

"Well, I never knew this until my mom passed away." That was 1958, four years after Wayne started his career in the US Navy.

"I came home, and we drove around quite a bit. And we'd end up in Jalapa. And it was two county roads that came together. At that time, they were probably gravel. There was a Caution sign there, when you come up to it. You had to stop for the Caution sign. The intersection had a filling station on one side, a store on the other side, and a church. And that was it. There wasn't anything else."

Big brothers did not spend Friday and Saturday nights in Jalapa, after all.

11. FREE STATERS

There was no greater day for me for a long time in my life than the day every summer when we went to Amboy, Indiana, for the Arrick family reunion. The maiden name of my grandma, Vern's mom, Eva, and her sister, Aunt Emmy, was Arrick. It was a picnic and a cookout, and we played baseball with the men and women of Vern's family. It was July, and it was hot, but there was shade around and a cool breeze and iced tea and lemonade. That's just background noise, though, to the best people a person could ever hope to meet in a long, long life. There were some long lives there, too, going back to the point where it seemed like some of them could remember the Civil War. That's not actually true, but some of them could remember people—parents and grandparents—talking about the Civil War. In fact, in looking at some family research, I learned that Eva Arrick Shroyer's great-uncles fought for the Union side together at the 1862 Battle of Shiloh in Tennessee. Benson Arrick was injured there, and further on, George Arrick would die of dysentery at a hospital in Memphis. Their father, also named George, volunteered for the Union cause at the age of fifty-five in October of 1861 but left the service "for disability" the following May. Your great-uncle is Stan, so your presence makes that more real to me.

Everybody called my grandfather, Vern's dad, "Pop," and Pop grew up in Kansas. After Grandma Shroyer died in 1958, Pop spent some of every year traveling to Kansas on a Greyhound bus to visit the people and places where he grew up. Going back to Kansas every year was a chance for him to visit an innocent place in his heart.

The Kansas that Pop visited was, in my memory, unimaginably far away. Now, I think, I could have been, I should have been, on that bus with him. That would have been cool. This letter is the bus for you and me. There are things I want you to know that I will not always have the chance to tell you. By writing them down, I'm giving you the chance to listen when you have the chance. I'm your "Pop."

Pop's dad's name was Isaac Asberry. I've only ever heard him called Asberry. I'm surmising that the love of Mary Beck of Miami County, Kansas, was what led him to leave the Shroyer family home near Somerset to settle in Kansas, where they were married in 1887. Mary Beck Shroyer, Pop's mom, died August 1, 1899. I don't know why. Their four-year-old son, William Cyrus, died one week later. I don't know why. Asberry and Mary had by then already suffered the loss of two other children, three-year-old Cordia in 1895 and two-month-old Roy in 1897. My grandfather witnessed all of that as a child between the ages of seven and eleven. His mother died when she was thirty-one. Mary Beck Shroyer is buried in Miami County, Kansas, and so those trips for Pop must have included melancholy visits to the Fontana Cemetery. It wasn't so sad that he stayed away, though. He looked right at it. Her gravestone reads MOTHER.

Pop stayed with Asberry when they came back to Indiana after Mary died. Pop's sister, Verna, moved in with Asberry's sister Mary and her husband, Milo Stitts. Asberry's third living child, Henry Dee, two years younger than Pop, stayed with relatives in Kansas.

About the only thing I ever heard about Asberry growing up was that he was an alcoholic. My dad never took a drink of alcohol that I knew of, and we never had alcohol to drink of any kind in our homes when I was growing up. Somehow, I learned that Dad's experience of growing up around Asberry was connected to that. I didn't give Asberry much thought then; now, I think of him sympathetically. All I know about that is what I know about myself, about grief and loss, and that his wife died when she was thirty-one and he was forty-four and Pop was eleven and Dee was nine and Vernie was three, and that all three of his other children died. I can imagine that circumstance setting me off on a downward spiral that would be hard to get out of. I wonder if he had someone to talk to. I hope so. His thirty-one-year-old wife died on one Tuesday, and his four-year-old son died on the next one.

When Vern was growing up, Asberry lived with Vern's family two miles from Somerset, with some embarrassment, I guess, and while I'm sure they understood, there wasn't enough understanding. They must have felt it difficult to acknowledge him a whole lot to the outside world or even to a succeeding generation. Isaac Asberry died the year Vern graduated from high school, 1935, the very month that Vern left for Ball State, where he never really even got going because, the story goes, he was homesick. Homesick? He could have handled being away. It's more likely that he felt that he had a greater responsibility at home. He saw college and decided there was something more important for him to do. Maybe he figured there was time for him to go back to school, but he never did. "I'll get to that later" became "It's too late for me," as he had to have the money he made at General Tire to help his mom and dad and the war came and he met Mom and they were married and the war ended and Linda was born, and before he knew it, he was thirty years old working at the Malleable, a foundry in Marion. "Life is what happens to you while you're busy making other plans," Vern.

Dad would have been a great teacher and a great coach, one of those quiet guys who knows what he's talking about and who people would be eager to please. I think people would have walked through walls for him, and I think he knew he would have been better at it than other coaches every time he watched a game and saw what they were doing. He had a way of seeing what was going to happen before it happened, and he'd tell me what to look for when I watched a game with him. "Don't watch the ball. Watch number six," he'd say when we were watching the Celtics. He knew which players did the most to help their teams and why. "It's not a good pass if your teammate can't catch it."

"Hank Aaron is better than Willie Mays."

"Here comes a homer," he'd say, and, sure enough, homer is how I remember it.

"Watch out for the Republicans trying to get rid of Social Security," he'd say, even though it seemed absurd.

I've already told you how quiet Vern and mostly everybody was back where I grew up, and so what I know comes from snatches of talk like that that I overheard. Asking questions was frowned upon, too, especially from somebody as young as I was then.

I overheard snatches of conversation that the reason Pop grew up in Kansas had to do with the Civil War, but the Civil War wasn't fought in Kansas. Once, Vern made a pronouncement to no one and to anybody and to everybody all at the same time about John Brown. Vern said, "Don't let them tell you a bunch of nonsense about John Brown," and I remember where he was standing when he said it. It's odd, that way. How often do you remember where someone was exactly when they told you something? Big things, maybe, but this was more like an offhand comment. Anyway, Vern was standing in the old house living room in the space between the front door and the door to his bedroom. "John Brown was right," he said. It popped out. And that was the end of it. Four words. "It's our flag, too," came later.

From putting together conversations at places like the Arrick reunion and at Grandma and Grandpa's house in Waltz Township with what I learned about history, I developed the notion that Pop's family, before he was born, had migrated from Pennsylvania to Kansas to be with the abolitionists who wanted to prevent Kansas from becoming a slave state in the 1850s.

The Kansas-Nebraska Act of 1854 provided that Kansans' vote would determine if that new addition to the United States would be a place where, like down south, Black people could be enslaved. Lots of people moved out there after the law was passed so they could vote, one way or the other. I heard often growing up that our family was among them. There were violent fights between the two sides. Frederick Brown was killed by proslavery fighters in a town called Osawatomie, and then those slavery-supporting men burned down the town looking for Frederick's dad, John Brown. I know the places Pop visited on the Greyhound bus were right there where that had been going on. Osawatomie is eleven miles from the cemetery where Pop's mom is buried.

John Brown was the most famous antislavery abolitionist leader out there in Kansas. In places where the Civil War cause is attributed to "states' rights," he's portrayed as a crazy guy stirring up trouble. Vern wasn't buying that. That puts us on the right side of history but in opposition to pretty much all the people who had anything to say about the matter in the place where I grew up.

If you want to see the wrong side of history, watch a movie called *Santa Fe Trail.* That movie made the people who wanted to stop slavery look like troublemakers. When it came out in 1940, Vern was twenty-four years old. Twenty years later, he told me not to believe the bad stuff you hear about John Brown.

There wasn't much talk of politics or current events at the Arrick reunion, but in my mind, it was a place where, in addition to great games of baseball with Vern and his brothers and his cousins and my cousins and Vern's aunts and uncles and their kids whom I didn't really know and hot dogs and lemonade, people didn't talk shit about John Brown. He coulda been there for all I knew. One of those Civil War old-timer ZZ Top–lookin' guys.

Full-time pitcher.

My grandfather's wife was an Arrick. That's why we were there.

My grandfather's father, Isaac Asberry Shroyer, was one of eleven children born to Henry D. and Elizabeth Shroyer, residents of Ohio until no later than 1860. Isaac Asberry was born in 1855. Henry's residence changed to Butler, Indiana, in Miami County in 1860. Henry's father, George, does show a residence in Urbana, Illinois, where he died in 1858, but there's no sign of Kansas in any records I found for the Shroyer family from around 1850 to 1860.

However, for the family of Vern's grandma, Mary Beck Shroyer, it's a different story. Vern's youngest brother, Wayne, told me that the Becks were involved in the Underground Railroad in Kansas, in the area near where John Brown was active in the late 1850s. Wayne said he'd visited there once with his parents and had a look around, but he couldn't tell me much more than that. Later, though, in some papers that my sister had gathered up after Mom died, I found some relevant family history on a couple of typed and copied pages inside a booklet about the Arrick family.

According to the account that Mary Beck's sister Cordie Beck Johnson wrote for her family in 1957, active abolitionism was entirely possible.

She wrote that their parents, Henry D. Beck and his wife, Elizabeth, "came to Kansas and homesteaded in Miami County in 1858, along with her father [Cyrus Tuttle] and family and his brother William Beck."[34] I don't know if they voted, but in 1859, a free state constitution would pass 2–1 in a statewide referendum. Again, Vern, they settled in Miami County, which had been the site of an attack by proslavery forces on the abolitionist settlement town of Osawatomie in 1856 that killed John Brown's son and four others.

After the four hundred proslavery "Border Ruffians" routed the "Free Staters" in that attack, they burned to the ground every building in the town but three. It's unlikely that when the Becks decided that Miami County was where they wanted to go that they did not know about the conflict. Henry Beck enlisted in the Union Army in 1862 and, according to his obituary, served for three years. Osawatomie is today home to the John Brown Museum State Historic Site. My grandfather's visits to Kansas included visits to the nearby Fontana Cemetery, where his mother and many members of her family are buried. We are descended from abolitionists, Vern, the Beck family.

Dad's folks and everyone else in his family but him were Republicans, but "Lincoln Republicans," I'd heard. My mom's dad, who was every bit as bigoted as they were not, was a Democrat. Like George Wallace and Lester Maddox and Strom Thurmond. We're descended from him, too, Vern. We're Americans.

12. NOT TALKIN'

After Vern died, Mom stayed in the new house he built in the backyard of our old house until she couldn't drive anymore. My sister, Linda, called me up to tell me to drive down from South Bend because somebody other than herself needed to tell Mom not to drive anymore. I gave Mom a driving test, and while she made it off the highway and down the driveway, when she pulled into the garage, she was so close to the side wall that she couldn't open the driver's-side door.

"That's it," I said.

She moved into a Century Fields Retirement Community apartment in Greentown, the place where I went to high school. Your aunt Lily and I visited there one afternoon when Dad's sister, Mary, was also living there. We visited her, too.

Aunt Mary was seven years older than Wayne, same separation as Linda and I. Mary was spry, like her aunt Emmy. She told Lily and me stories that I regret I didn't record. From my memory, Aunt Mary said:

"One Saturday, Aunt Emmy came over." She didn't say when that was exactly, but it must have been before the war. In 1939, she was thirteen, Vern was twenty-three, and Burnell was twenty-one. That sounds about right. Aunt Emmy, Vern's mother's sister, was what somebody back there might have called a "live wire." She liked to needle people, especially people who were getting "too big for their britches." But she wasn't mean. Everybody liked her. She just liked to laugh and have fun.

Mary said, "When Emmy came in, the screen door slammed. Everybody was always so quiet, and she liked to make some noise. The folks were gone. It was just Vern, Burnell, and me in the house."

Wayne told me once that the only noise among eight or nine people at the breakfast table was the tinkle of Vern's spoon inside a coffee cup. "And that was stretching it," he said. "No one talked. No one dared talk."

Linda remembers Vern and Burnell hanging out together on our visits. "You'd never see them talk to each other, but you would get in the car to go home, and Dad would know everything about him. You never saw them talk."

So anyway, on this day in a life in a year we're calling 1939, Mary says, "Emmy slammed the door and walked through the kitchen past the table where Vern and Burnell sat. 'Howdy, boys,' she said, and then we talked in the living room for a couple of hours getting caught up and laughing at I don't know what, about anything, I suppose. In that whole time, we never heard a peep out of either one of 'em. As far as I could tell, they never moved, either. Never so much as moved. Not a sound.

"Then Emmy got up to leave; it was a pretty summer day, you know, a light breeze making the curtains shake, and we said, 'Bye.' On the way out through the kitchen, like I say, Vern and Burnell were sitting exactly like they were when she came in. Never moved.

"'Nice talking to you boys,' Aunt Emmy said, and then the screen door slammed.

"That's your grandpa, right there, Lily," Mary said.

Dad's cousin Larry Knee said that Vern and Burnell were "quiet. But they were also deep thinkers. My mom and I went down to Uncle Charley's. Aunt Evie and Mom talked. Maybe your grandpa did and maybe he didn't. Your dad and Burnell had their noses in books. We got ready to leave. Your dad said, 'Aunt Vernie, glad to see ya,' and she said, 'You sure didn't act like it.'"

"You know," Mary told Lily and me that day in Greentown, "Vern always made sure that nobody ever said a negative word about Aunt Emmy." A man named Ancil was Howard and Emmy's son, but he seemed distant, somehow, at family gatherings. "Maybe nobody told you, but I'll tell you now," Mary told us. "Her husband, Howard, wasn't Ancil's father.

I can't tell you who Ancil's father is. Nobody never told me."

"All it took from Vern was a 'look.' He didn't have to say anything. Aunt Emmy knew it, too, and she loved him for it. She loved all of us, but especially she loved Vern. You know Maurice was the oldest, but Vern was the leader. Everybody looked up to Vern. He didn't have to say anything." Mary laughed. "And he didn't."

I remember Mary and Emmy for being people who were nice to be around.

13. THE FAMILY

Vern's best friend was his brother Burnell. Burnell was two years younger than Dad. Burnell was married to my mom's sister, also named Mary. About thirty years ago, Mary and Burnell had a little family party for their fiftieth anniversary at the home of Vern's sister Lenore and her husband, Pete. That was in the same house Pete and Lenore lived in when I was a kid, near the Somerset farm where Vern and his family lived when he was growing up. Pete and Lenore lived in conservative accordance with the rules of their Church of the Brethren faith, without the trappings of modern life like a television. That was noticeable to a kid. We couldn't watch baseball after dinner over there. They had a car, but it had to be the most basic model possible, no radio and no whitewall tires. Lenore always had a head covering. Pete's top shirt button was always buttoned, but he never wore a tie.

Their two-story brick house was up the hill from the Mississinewa River, so it survived the flood that wiped out the town and a lot of what was around it. Pete and Lenore's son, David "Butch" Lorenz, joined the marines after he graduated from the new Southwood High School in 1964, and he was wounded pretty badly in Vietnam. Pete had been a conscientious objector during World War II as a member of a so-called peace church. That's a little tidbit of something that helped me understand the difference between how the world is portrayed in the "conventional wisdom" scheme of things and reality. Butch, whose picture among others carrying a dead comrade up a hill in Vietnam appeared in *Life* magazine, rebelled against his father by enlisting. It's only ironic insofar as it's not what other people might expect. We typically associate objection to war with Vietnam and compliance with war with World War II. Swimming with the Shroyer tide meant not swimming with the tide. Going along with not going along. Butch bought a Corvette when he got home. He was around a lot of Agent Orange defoliant in Vietnam, and he died at the age of fifty-four.

Back at Pete and Lenore's for Mary and Burnell's fiftieth anniversary party, somebody had put together a little picture book of Mary and Burnell's life and made enough copies for everybody. When I looked through it, even things I'd never seen before were familiar. But, about halfway through the twenty or thirty pages there was a picture of Burnell taken when he was in the service; that was a picture that did not ring a bell.

I knew from hearing a little talk that the family lost track of Burnell during the war. "Any word from Burnell?" friends and family would sheepishly ask anyone but Burnell's parents for over a year at the height of their war, and the answer was always a headshake. Nope.

Burnell was in the South Pacific. The news from the South Pacific, always with an undercurrent of stereotypical racism, was rough. He might be captured and tortured, with fingernails torn out for some caricature's sick fun. He might be dead. That might be better. Why don't we hear?

That's what I knew, what I'd heard, and what I'd imagined other people imagined had happened to Vern's brother and best friend somewhere in the back of my mind as I was turning the pages in the Mary and Burnell anniversary book. Then I came to a picture of Burnell. In the driver's seat of MacArthur's jeep. General Douglas MacArthur, the commander of all the Allied forces fighting the Japanese army in the South Pacific in the Second World War, was sitting next to him, shotgun. Nobody'd ever mentioned that. That's where Burnell had been. It was a secret they'd just kept on keeping.

It's not hard to imagine the joy in the little farmhouse by Goose Creek the first time all four Shroyer in-the-service boys were home together with Wayne and Mary and Lenore and Pop and Mom after the war. I suppose they felt that again, every time they were together after that. That's what Stan remembers. "Dad was never happier than he was when he was with his brothers and sisters. They would all sit around and talk and laugh about the old days, and that was something that always struck me."

Stan told me, "*Wow*, I'd think, even back then. *He's really happy when he gets together with his brothers.*"

I found a letter Vern wrote to his parents when he was in the service during the war, at the Army Air Forces Combat Crew Training School at Tarrant Field in Fort Worth, Texas. If something happens to me before I can give you that letter, make sure you find it. The postmark on the envelope is May 6, 1943.

Wed. Eve.

Dear Folks

I received your letter today and I was glad to hear from you. I got a big kick out of Wayne getting his fishing pole caught in a tree. Also laughed when I read about you thinking Wendell's legs would keep him out of the Army, after all.

Yes I received the preacher's letter he's probably ok. I haven't answered Mrs. Sweet's yet. Edward wrote me this week but didn't say much. Aunt Emma used to answer my letters so quick but haven't heard from her for a long time. Lenora sort of got on me about not writing but I've been answering all your letters haven't I.

I hope you get this before Sun. which is Mothers Day. I'll be thinking of you. You know I was never much on shopping but I do want you to know I appreciate every thing you have done for me. A person isn't in the Army long till he learns just how much his mother does for him. You don't throw your dirty clothes down and find them hanging up clean when you want them. Nobody cooks you something else to eat if you decide you don't want what the rest have. I could name much more but I do want you to know I think a lot of you and think you are tops as a mother. I wouldn't want you to change any.

Did I tell you the Wacs have moved in they are a dizzy looking bunch.

I must close now but will be looking for your next letter.

Yours,
Vern

14. MOM

Not long before she died, my mom told your grandma Shroyer that the war was a hard time for her. Her own mother, my grandma Fuller, told her that Vern wouldn't care much for her if he ever really got to know her, and if they did get married, it wouldn't last very long. Judy and I were visiting at the Century Fields Retirement Community in Greentown when Mom began to tell us things that I had never heard about her life. Some of it was pretty sad, and it made me feel bad for not being nicer to her.

Patty and Vern were married August 30, 1943. Mom told us that for her wedding, there was a justice of the peace and there was the justice of the peace's wife and there was Mom and there was Dad and that was it. No family at all. Vern went back to his army air corps base a couple of days later, and Mom stayed back at home. She told your grandma that she wanted to go with him, but he didn't want her to. He didn't think it was a good idea. Patty got a little apartment in Marion and worked at the Farnsworth radio factory. During the war, they made shortwave radios for the war effort. She said she liked it, that she was a good worker, that she was promoted, and that she even dealt with the resentment of some other women who thought her hard work made them look bad. It's hard to imagine Mom being anything other than Mom, but that story made me think about some other kind of life she led. She didn't get much encouragement for anything. I can see that more clearly now. That time when she was on her own and Vern was away, she must have felt some measure of accomplishment that she didn't get anyplace else, other than feeling, maybe, like her kids turned out okay.

That's all I had known already when Uncle Wayne told me that Vern told him that Vern and Patty met at a movie theater in Marion. My sister, Linda, told me later that she understood it was in Kokomo.

"They went to a movie," Wayne said. "They happened to sit beside each other. They met, and they started dating after that. Until they got married, he lived with Mom and Dad.

"That was about it. Vern told me one time that's how they met. He was quiet. He didn't have much to say.

"I remember when Vern brought Patty the first time to meet Mom and Dad. Your mom was little and short. We all talked about how small she was. She sat at the kitchen table, and her feet didn't even hit the floor.

"Your mom, Patty, was a wonderful, wonderful, wonderful person," Wayne said to me. "I can't say enough about how great she was. Vern was very, very good to her. Vern was always very proud of her. He couldn't do enough for her."

I wondered if Wayne was thinking about the wife of a different brother. Vern didn't show Patty a lot of respect at my house. I knew what the word *divorce* meant when we lived in the old house, and it scared me. I remember fearful circular arguments, but I don't remember what they were about or how they ended. Stan told me about an ending that he heard. Stan was living at home my first year at Indiana University.

"I remember him and Mom. It was a Saturday night and I had to be home because there was no car for me to drive, or something. I was twenty years old or so. You remember how they would argue," he said. "It just got louder and louder. I'm in the bedroom listening to music or something and then, you could just hear it.

"*Slap, slap, slap.*

"Something happened. Somebody hit somebody. Then I heard, 'Oh, Vern.'

"Like that.

"And it was over."

My memory says that Dad ridiculed Mom.

My family was set up like the two sides of the Civil War. There was the Vern side and the Patty side. I was on the Vern side, and Stan was on the Patty side. At Mom's funeral, Stan told a story in which Mom told him that any girl would be proud to go to prom with him right before he asked a girl who said she wouldn't go to prom with him. My story was about how I couldn't tell if she was messing with me or not. I never talked to her about a girl. She would have laughed at me.

I told her funeral gathering a story about our last time together before she lost her faculties, there at the assisted living center in Greentown. When I think back on that, it's funny to me that those visits there were always the same and, in the moment, felt like they were permanent. The drive down, walking from the car to the front door, this would now be where she would always be. The last place.

Mom wouldn't answer the phone when I called. Somehow, she knew it was me. "I don't always hear it ring," she told me. It could ring twenty times and she would not answer. Like Vern, back home, except for the fact I know that she liked to talk on the phone. On those occasions when I was with her in the assisted-living one-bedroom apartment and the phone would ring, I could see that she heard it and she would answer. It was odd.

On my last visit, I stood, as I always stood, in the little glass booth area between the outer door and the locked inner door, wondering how I would get in. There was a phone on the wall there with instructions to call the person you wished to see and request them to buzz you in.

The idea was, "Hi, Mom. It's Sid. Can you buzz me in?"

And Mom would say, "Sid! Yes, of course."

That would presuppose, though, that Mom heard the phone, or acknowledged the phone, or that she didn't know in her weird supernatural way that it was me, and answered it and hit the right button to let me in.

The phone would ring and ring and ring, and I'd stand in the glassed-in area between the outer door and the inner door, berating myself for falling for the same sick joke every time I went down there. "How am I gonna get in?"

So as I told the people at the funeral that February day in Converse, 2014, my story concerns the last time this happened, a cold, sunny day in January.

Linda had called me for a meeting because Mom had fallen, and

Century Fields Retirement Community administrators wanted to move her into Century Villa Health Care and Rehabilitation.

"When's a good time for me to come?" I asked.

So there I stood like an American journalist on Russian trial, berating myself for even trying to get Mom on the phone, when at that moment, I saw Mom on her little red old-person scooter scooting down the hallway from the cafeteria area on my left toward me on the way to her room on my right. I began to yell, "Mom, Mom, Mom!" and wave at her on her way by. I know she glanced at me, but she did not stop. A kindly resident stranger a few moments later smiled as he violated the door-lock policy the Century Fields Retirement Community enforces at the Department of Homeland Security's behest by opening the door.

"Thank you. I'm here to see my mom," I told him in anticipation of a visit from the inspector general. "Really, just tell them I deviously convinced you that I'm not a terrorist."

Thirty minutes later, in her room with Linda and me, after some discussion about her situation and the recommendation from two of her children that she not move to Century Villa Health Care and Rehabilitation, Mom turned to me suddenly and said, "Was that you standing in the doorway when I came by on my scooter?"

"Yes, Mom. That was me."

"I thought so," Mom said.

Mom was hospitalized not long after I was born, and I'm told I stayed with Mary and Burnell for a few weeks. I couldn't understand who Patty was when it was time to go home, I'm pretty sure, and Patty probably thought, *Well, you know, little buddy, I don't much feel like hanging out with you, either. I've got two kids already, and the noisy one seems to like me.*

Is it possible that stayed with Mom and me all the way through? There was a lot of time when I was a kid when I wished Mary and Burnell were my parents. But I always thought that was because they lived in a town and had a red single-piece phone with the dial on the bottom.

Flood

15. THE FIX

Dear Vern,

According to a July 24, 1956, story in the *Indianapolis News*, 1946 was the year the Army Corps of Engineers began work on the Upper Wabash Valley Flood Control Project. The 1956 story about US Senate approval of the plan says that the project "will require relocating the town of Somerset in Miami [actually Wabash] County 10 miles southwest of Peru."[35]

The Seventy-Ninth Congress passed the Flood Control Act of 1946, amending a 1936 law, "authorizing the construction of certain public works on rivers and harbors for flood control, and for other purposes"[36] to support building flood walls and levees in Wabash, Peru, and Logansport by increasing the money and making the Army Corps of Engineers the gatekeeper. The 1946 law says, "No project or any modification not authorized, of a project for flood control of rivers and harbors shall be authorized by Congress unless a report for such project or modification has been previously submitted by the Chief of Engineers, United States Army, in conformity with existing law." That put the Army Corps of Engineers in charge. Individual members of Congress were even more likely then than they are now to go along with whatever the army said was the right thing to do, Democrats and Republicans. "These army guys know what they are doing" was the 1946 zeitgeist, of course, coming off the most successful military campaign ever. Congressmen have better things to do than study water flow. Their focus was generating support for the next campaign.

What to do with the new authorization came next. On the evening of October 23, 1946, the Army Corps of Engineers, according to that morning's *Indianapolis News*, was to meet in Logansport with the Indiana Flood Control and Water Resources Commission (IFCWRC) "for a discussion of the flood control requirements of the upper Wabash vicinity."[37]

The story, on page 26 of that day's *News*, is headlined USE OF TRIBUTARIES MAY CUT FLOOD CONTROL COSTS. In it, David H. Harker, the chief engineer of the IFCWRC, said four "sites for reservoirs had been observed, on the Mississinewa river south of Marion; between Marion and the Wabash River near Peru; on the Wabash River two miles southeast of Huntington; and possibly on Eel River near Logansport."

Harker also said, "Sites had been found which could store inches of rain and provide flood control barriers for many areas. 'If these sites can be utilized to the fullest extent . . . less expensive local protective works will be required.'"

What Harker had to say to the newspaper in 1946, as the IFCWRC's chief engineer, on the eve of a meeting with the army, differs from what Roessler reported that the IFCWRC technical committee chairman, R. E. Hutchins, had said the year before. Harker had noted the feasibility of "less expensive local protective works." Hutchins, according to Roessler, had limited his recommendation to a more general "preference for detention reservoirs."[38]

Whatever studies the IFCWRC and the Army Corps of Engineers did between 1943 and 1950 on using tributary control to cut costs, on what became known as the "small dams" plan, are hidden. By the time the people in Somerset, and Wabash, and Peru, and Logansport found out about what the IFCWRC and the army had in store for them, the only "reasonable" question was the choice between "big dams" or floods. The "small dams" plan never got a proper hearing, not in public, anyway, not so the general public knew about it. A less evasive, less expensive strategy was not an army priority. They had the money.

That October 23, 1946, the Army Corps of Engineers met in Logansport with the IFCWRC "for a discussion of the flood control requirements of the upper Wabash vicinity" that the *News* reported on which would later be described as one of two "public hearings." That self-serving description appeared in an Army Corps of Engineers September 12, 1955, "interim report" on the Upper Wabash Valley Flood Control Project.

The other "public hearing," the 1955 report said, was in Crawfordsville, Indiana, on March 27, 1950, ninety-six miles southwest of Somerset. Neither of these "public hearings" gathered input from the public. After the fact, both would be used as examples of a proper procedure to satisfy a bureaucratic checklist. Nowadays, Vern, it's weird—some people call even pretending to care about the public "political correctness" and "woke." Back in 1955, the unstoppable forces of development, at least, were putting on a show.

For the 1950 "hearing," unlike the 1946 meeting, there was no mention of a less expensive use of tributary control or a small dams plan. By then, the March 28, 1950, *Lafayette Journal and Courier* reported, the Indiana Flood Control and Water Resources Commission was only recommending to the army the construction of three reservoirs that would be up and running twenty years later. Those would be, it said, "near Huntington on the Wabash, at Dora on the Salamonie, and at Peoria on the Mississinewa."[39] This is the first official public evidence I found of precise locations for where the dams would go.

The locations recommended in the 1950 meeting were exactly where the dams would be built. That's where the army wanted them, and that's where the IFCWRC told the army they should be. To be honest with you, Vern, I think the army told the commission to tell the army in 1950 what the army wanted the commission to tell the army to say. That's my guess. It's not a guess that in the four-year interim, something had changed between the eve of the first meeting between the commission and the army and the second meeting.

Despite what those two meetings were later called for public consumption, neither was actually a "public hearing," so we don't know how things came to change. "What" had changed, we can gather. "Detention reservoirs" had become big dams only. Mention of a small dams plan had officially disappeared. "Use of Tributaries [That] May Cut Flood Control Costs" had gone away. So had David Harker, who was no longer chief engineer of the IFCWRC.

The commission, whose spokesmen were not identified in the 1950 *Lafayette Journal and Courier*, told the army that the reservoirs were "vital" in controlling Wabash River floodwater as far south as Vincennes. "They are described," the story said, "as the key links in a system of 19 proposed reservoirs between Marion and Turkey Run State Park," which is on Sugar Creek, between Crawfordsville and the Wabash River. No alternative flood control solutions were reported to have been mentioned this time. Whatever chance the small dam alternative had to supplement or replace the big dam plan had disappeared. The nineteen reservoirs would become only the three the commission recommended to the army, "near Huntington on the Wabash, at Dora on the Salamonie, and at Peoria on the Mississinewa."[40]

While the story suggests that the state commission was making a 1950 recommendation to the army as to how best to proceed with flood control, there's evidence that the army's "proceed" had begun some time before. There's the mention of a 1938 "comprehensive plan" in an October 19, 1961, *Wabash Plain Dealer* editorial.[41] There are stories from his stepfather that Dave Compton heard about dams in 1942. Larry Knee said that before his father, John, died in 1944, "he knew the reservoir was coming. I knew of the reservoir coming for as long as I can remember anything, " Larry told me. Larry was born in 1938.

Wayne Shroyer remembers surveying that happened during World War II. Tom Snyder said dam site river gauges were installed in the '40s.

Karen Stouffer still lived, seventy-five years later, on the farm where she witnessed army reservoir planning activity in 1948. She told me at the Wabash History Museum on February 2, 2023,

> In the spring of '48, there was a guy in our backyard with surveying equipment. I'm three years old, and I went out and asked him what he's doing there. He picked me up and told me to look through his scope, and he told my mom that I could tell people that I surveyed for the reservoir. That's the first we'd heard that they were even thinking about a reservoir.

The spring of '48, Vern. That's between 1946 and 1950, isn't it?

The Stouffer farm, Karen told me, was a mile east and a mile north of my grandparents' land. I later found the "R. & L. Stouffer" label on a ninety-acre plot of land designation on the same map that Dave Compton helped me use to find Pop's property. It's two miles due north of Somerset, bordering the land that would be confiscated.

"My dad started asking around in '48, but nobody knew anything," Karen said. "It was a concern to think that nobody had ever heard of this, and they're out there surveying our place. There were rumors, you know, that there was going to be something, but the government was pretty quiet about it." In 1950, the Indiana Flood Control and Water Resources Commission recommended to the army that the place the army had been surveying in Karen's backyard in 1948 would be a good place for a reservoir. That then, in 1955, was described as a "public hearing."

Vern

16. NECESSITIES

Dear Vern,

During the war, Vern dreamed about what would make him happy, and when the war ended, he found a farm where he could live near Marion. My sister, Linda, was conceived on that farm. Linda was born October 20, 1946, three days before the Indiana Flood Control and Water Resources Commission and the Army Corps of Engineers met in Logansport.

Linda says she doesn't remember the farm because, she supposes, she was two or three years old when they moved away. The nature of Vern's situation in the postwar American shift toward a factory-model agriculture industry made it clear to him that he couldn't make enough money to get started farming for himself and support his wife and his daughter, so he gave up. "I heard Dad talk about the farm," Linda told me. "The owner was a big, rich farmer, and he didn't like Dad."

Uncle Wayne remembers that time, after the war and before I was born in 1953. Wayne graduated from Somerset High School in 1951. "When I was in school, during the summer, I stayed with your mom and dad," Wayne told me, "maybe about two weeks. They were living in a farmhouse that was for rent. This was right after the war was over, right after he came back. It was an old farmhouse, and it was rickety, wasn't that great a place," Wayne said, "kinda south of LaFontaine, north and west of Marion, between Swayzee and LaFontaine. That was the first place they lived after they come back from the service. They lived there maybe a year."

"I was born when they lived there," Linda told me. "We moved when he got the job at the Malleable. We couldn't stay there because we were living there as part of Dad's pay. He was a hired hand. After that, he always helped Grandpa Shroyer. On the weekends. He would help him get his crop out. And he would help him harvest."

Nine years later, he found seven acres at Normal, where he could turn the soil, plant some corn or beans, and take a crop to the elevator in the fall. That was real. The draught horses stayed all that time, I can see now, in his imagination. It was the part of him that he wanted to go back to, to recapture what he had before conditions forced him off the land.

Vern never gave up on the draught horses. That last year of his life, he started talking about them again, and Linda and I dismissed the idea pretty openly in a way we would have never done when we were younger.

"That's crazy. You don't need to do that," we told him, and now I'm sorry that I didn't help him figure out a way he could.

"It's just not necessary," was my mom's favorite saying, and we learned in my house while Vern was out in the barn, or out in the field, or welding something together than no one else had ever made before, or building us a new house in the backyard, that reaching for something beyond, like the decent pay he got as a skilled union worker for a General Motors factory job that he hated, was "just not necessary."

"You'll fail," was what I learned inside when he was outside. Better not to be disappointed.

Outside, he made dreams come true. He really did take six years to build a house in the backyard, a good house. He took some old pipe and a lawn mower engine and made a go-kart for the son of a man with whom he shared a ride to work. He gave my mom's brother some of our land so he could have a house.

Vern had a dream. Of course, he didn't "need" to re-create the innocence of his youth behind a team of draught horses plowing a field. I'm sorry that in the last year of his life his children had learned to stifle his dream, too. Vern deserved better. It wasn't about "need."

"Under the GI Bill, there was a lot of money given to veterans to buy a house," Wayne said. "That's when they got off of that farmhouse and moved into Marion. All the houses were alike. It was a small house."

In 1948, the Muncie newspaper reported that a fifty-two-year-old former city cop named Paul Stevens died of a sudden heart attack and that he'd be buried in the Pleasant Grove Cemetery near Somerset.[42] That's where Pop and Grandma went to church, the place where she'd be buried ten years later. In 1948, Congressman Forest Harness lost his bid for a sixth term to a Democrat named John Walsh, who wouldn't be around very long. Vern left somebody else's farm in 1948 and got a job in a loud, smelly, dirty ironworks foundry called the Malleable in Marion, Indiana.

In 1950, the new Somerset High School gym opened, and Walsh lost to a Republican by the name of John Beamer from the Somerset-size Wabash County town of Roann. During Beamer's campaign, back in May, he'd gotten a letter from the National Rivers and Harbors Congress executive vice president congratulating him for his nomination and offering advice.[43] Beamer sent a thank-you.

In 1951, Uncle Wayne graduated from high school, the Arrick reunion was held at Matter Park in Marion, and some pretty awful Kansas and Missouri River flooding killed seventeen people and drove over half a million out of their homes.

In 1953, I was born in Marion, where we lived until 1957. I was only four when we moved to Normal, in Green Township, Grant County, but I remember a little something about that Marion life, the first of many lives for me.

I remember Stan and I would walk with Mom down to the Malleable foundry and sit with Vern under a tree in the factory yard and eat lunch with him. "Sometimes," is how Stan remembers it, "Mom would fry up bologna with catsup on it, put it into a sandwich, and take it to him. Linda was in school."

"There was the administration building," Stan said, "with a lawn where we could sit." Other workers did the same. "Dad would come out and have lunch with us. He was black, so dirty. There's no telling where he had been. Maybe he'd been crawling through some furnaces. He was a maintenance worker."

"I don't even know what they did at the Malleable," said Linda. "Tore metal apart?"

My sister remembered walking to the Malleable for lunch, too.

"Our mother was sick a lot. I would walk to the Malleable for lunch because there was no cafeteria at Lincoln School. I would go into this little bitty restaurant that was right by the factory, and Dad would meet me there and make sure I had my lunch and then send me back to school. I don't remember Dad talking to me, but everybody knew me. They knew who I was, so evidently they'd talked about me.

"I remember going in the Malleable. It was extremely dirty," Linda said.

"When he'd come home in the evening, he'd be covered in soot, black dust, I guess," Stan said.

Wayne said, "He would come home covered with dust, black dust, lookin' like a Black person. He'd get cleaned up." In spite of the tenor of the time and the place in which we lived, Vern being Black seems like an appropriate memory to me somehow. Later, when I saw an interview with Negro League baseball's Buck O'Neil, I caught a glimpse of Dad. I'd point you in that direction if you are interested in knowing what the man for whom you are named was like. He had a quiet dignity and respect for people. Think Bill Russell, the basketball player. Dad was more like those men than anyone famous I can think of. Quiet, dignified, and not letting on he knew that he was the smartest guy in the room. Until he had to.

"He'd take a bath," Stan said, "and we'd all be in there with him while he was taking his bath, and we'd talk about how dirty the water was."

I remember that.

"He was a hardworkin' man," Wayne said. "He never changed that."

He worked at the Malleable for eight years. If you work someplace you don't like for eight years, you're probably going to wonder if you'll be there forever. From the age of thirty-two to the age of forty.

I remember that sometimes Vern drove home a rusty-brown flatbed foundry truck.

I kind of remember the time Stan got in trouble for running away, but he remembers it better.

"I was four or five," my big brother said. "I had taken off, gotten away from Mom and she couldn't find me. Mom was the keeper of the kids. Dad was the breadwinner. She called him home from work, which would have angered him, to find me. I had walked from our house on Butler for about three blocks east down the alley to a very busy street, which we knew simply as 'the bypass.'

"I wanted to get a look at a new shopping center—today, we'd call it a little strip mall— that had just gone up there.

"I crossed the bypass somehow. There wasn't a traffic light or anything, just the alley emptying out onto a very busy street. I remember a drive-in restaurant there, and I remember standing on the curb. I saw a car coming around the corner and into the bypass against the traffic right at me. It pulled right up on the curb and stopped. Out popped Dad. He didn't bother to shut the car door, and I remember thinking, *I'm gonna get it.* And I did. I remember my arm going up, and he gave me three smacks right there and put me in the car."

Flood

17. HARD RAIN

Dear Vern,

The Indiana Flood Control and Water Resources Commission (IFCWRC) chief engineer who had recommended methods other than the big reservoirs to solve the Upper Wabash Valley flood problems resigned in 1949. David Harker left for political reasons, he said. Purdue University alum Joseph I. Perrey, a former assistant engineer with the Water Resources Branch of the US Geological Survey, replaced him.

The new Fifth District congressman, John Beamer, began to get involved with the project when he got a February 19, 1952, letter from executive secretary Robert Kellum advising him that IFCWRC members were coming to Washington. The letter said the group of them would

> appear before the Army Civil Functions Subcommittee of the House Appropriation Committee at 1:30 p.m., February 22, 1952, to present our request for survey funds for fiscal 1953. We are asking for $75,000. Ralph Roessler, Vice-Chairman; John C. Mellett, Member; Joseph I. Perrey, Chief Engineer, and myself are planning to appear before the Committee. If there is anything you can do to help us along on this, we would appreciate it.[44]

Beamer wrote, in a letter dated February 25, 1952, that Kellum visited Beamer's office and that Beamer said he'd try to be helpful "for the state of Indiana."[45]

Ten months later, in November 1952, the IFCWRC sent Beamer a copy of a report[46] they'd authorized in August saying that they'd created a "priority list" of major projects. The dam that would drown Somerset, "Peoria," is number one on the list, followed by those at Salamonie and Huntington. That reflects what the commission had recommended at their meeting with the army in Crawfordsville in March 1950. Nothing had changed or would change after that. The precision of the locations suggests to me they knew what it would mean to the people above the dams in 1950. It would take five more years for the public to know.

There had been a lot of flooding again in 1952. This time, the upper Midwest mostly, the Mississippi River in Minnesota especially, and it was major news. President Truman did an aerial survey of damage in Illinois, Iowa, Minnesota, Wisconsin, and Nebraska, and according to an International News Service report in the *Palladium-Item* newspaper of Richmond, Indiana, "Truman said that a federal plan for control of the major rivers and their tributaries of the whole central U.S. should be completed without delay."[47]

In December 1953, Congressman Beamer received the first of many flood project constituent letters that I could find at the Indiana State Library. Johnny Burnes of Peru wanted to know how much money would be spent on the project. Also, he asked that the river be dredged so they "don't have to clean trash off the banks all the time."[48]

The flood control project moved along through official channels in 1954: Ralph Roessler and the IFCWRC, the Army Corps of Engineers, Congressman Beamer, and Congress. Not much had changed since the 1950 "public hearing" in Crawfordsville, when the IFCWRC recommended to the army the construction of three reservoirs that would be up and running twenty years later:[49] "near Huntington on the Wabash, at Dora on the Salamonie, and at Peoria on the Mississinewa." That is precisely what happened, after all. The surveys were done; the data had been collected, the studies completed, and the plans made. Before the residents of Somerset knew, before the residents of Somerset had a chance to offer an opinion about losing their town to save someone else's town, Somerset had been deemed dispensable for the "greater good." I can tell they didn't know, Vern, because in 1954, Congressman Beamer got only one constituent letter on the matter. That would change when the residents of Somerset did find out in 1955.

In 1954, information on the Upper Wabash Valley Flood Control Project ran only through official channels. In February, the IFCWRC sent a memo to the US House Civil Functions Subcommittee chairman, Glenn Davis, saying the commission was

> working with the Corps of Engineers, U.S. Army, on these and several other projects in Indiana. Members of the commission regard the projects listed as the most urgently needed at the present time. The cities of Huntington, Wabash, Peru and Logansport are vulnerable to serious damage by floods and the proposed projects would eliminate much of this danger. We urge that the funds listed be made available to the Corps of Engineers for the designated projects.[50]

A July 1954 letter informed Congressman Beamer that at a May meeting, the US Army assistant chief of engineers for civil works, Brigadier General E. C. Itschner, informed the IFCWRC vice chairman, Ralph Roessler, and its chief engineer, Joseph I. Perrey, that an "interim report on the headwater reservoirs [is] now under consideration."[51]

As it turned out, the "interim" report was the final report. The word *interim* implying that the army was at a midpoint in the process is misleading. Looking back, we can see it was "what we're gonna do" rather than "what we're thinkin' about doin'." The "interim report on the headwater reservoirs" would take no account of the four additional flood control strategies laid out when the Upper and Lower Wabash Valley Associations merged in 1943 before morphing into the IFCWRC. Those were 1) levees, 2) widening or deepening channels, 3) the creation of small reservoirs, and 5) soil erosion prevention. "Headwater reservoirs" was the fourth item on the list, and that was an army specialty–creating large reservoirs. Not levees, not dredging channels, not small reservoirs, and not soil erosion prevention. At some point between 1943 and 1954, upper Wabash River valley "flood control" had been reduced to only the creation of large reservoirs. What happened to make it so in those years is a mystery because neither the army nor the IFCWRC preserved any records of what went on. When I filed a Freedom of Information Act request with the Army Corps of Engineers for their records of meetings with the IFCWRC and their congressional correspondence on the Upper Wabash Valley Flood Control Project for those years, I got the same for those meetings and letters as I got from the Indiana State Library, the Indiana State Archives, and the archives at Indiana University: nothing. Cincinnati assistant division counsel Ryan J. Albrecht was nice about it, and he referred me to some other possible army sources when we talked on the phone, but nothing. "No records responsive to your request have been located,"[52] he wrote on May 3, 2023. One other possible army source did not respond to me at all.

Recordkeeping Ralph Roessler created a limited account of the period in his usually detailed notes on the Upper Wabash Valley Flood Control Project. Those notes were with his picture and a title page that reads "Last Living Charter Member, Marion Kiwanis Club, Presents a Documentary and Autobiographical Record of a Kiwanis Dream and a Seventy Million Dollar Reality, 1939 to 1968." For the 1945–1955 period, he only wrote:

> 1945–1955 - First project under study by the Indiana Flood Control and Water Resources Commission was a continuation of the studies of the Mississinewa River project started in 1939 by the Army Engineers, bringing the Corps and the State Commission in continuous coordinated study for ten years with a final report submitted by the Corps recommending a complete project for head water

> control in the upper Wabash River basin that would consist of building three reservoirs, one on the Mississinewa, one on the Salamonie, and the third on the upper Wabash River near Huntington, Indiana. The combined capacity and coordinated operation would furnish flood storage and flow retardation to the extent of justifying what is now a project exceeding Seventy Million Dollars in cost, 99% of it to be paid by the Federal Government, 1% by the State.[53]

What happened specifically in the ten-year period of "continuous coordinated study" is not available for study. We know the army and the IFCWRC met because correspondence references meetings more than once. If someone kept minutes, someone didn't make them available.

Back in 1954, on the same day Itschner announced the coming interim report in the July letter to Beamer, Itschner wrote a more detailed letter that was not on army stationery to Roessler.

> I am informed that field work for engineering and economic studies by our District Engineer, Louisville District, is essentially complete and that office studies are nearing completion for the sites on the Mississinewa and Salamonie Rivers, and on the Wabash River above Huntington, Indiana. These reservoirs are understood to be in the part of the basin of primary interest to your Commission. I understand, also, that your agency has cooperated with our District Engineer in these studies by making flood damage surveys, and in providing topographic and subsurface information. The District Engineer expects to complete an interim report on the three reservoirs mentioned above about 1 October 1954. Funds to be available for the Wabash

> River study from fiscal year 1955 appropriations for such investigations will, I am pleased to inform you, be sufficient to complete the interim report and to start studies on the remainder of the Wabash River above the mouth of the White River. After review of the interim report, the Division Engineer, Ohio River Division, will submit the report to this office and will issue a public notice on his recommendations.[54]

"All interested parties will have an opportunity to state their support or opposition formally before the Board of Engineers for Rivers and Harbors," Itschner told Roessler.

Then, he wrote, the Corps of Engineers administrators would set review with the IFCWRC, acting for the governor, other federal agencies, and the bureau of the budget, before it went to Congress for approval.

Process. Approval.

The pie was in the oven, July 1954. Ten months later, the people in Somerset would get a look, when it was ready to eat.

18. GONNA FALL

On July 30, 1954, the Indiana Flood Control and Water Resources Commission (IFCWRC) led a before-the-heat-of-the-day morning-highway this-is-where-it's-gonna-be Mississinewa and Salamonie dam sites tour. According to an AP article that appeared in the *South Bend Tribune* that evening, the city officials from Peru, Wabash, and Huntington numbered one hundred persons in forty-two automobiles.[55] A caravan. What a sight!

The next day's *Indianapolis Star* reported that "heavy flood losses from 1913, 1943, and 1950 [were] emphasized in a pamphlet distributed to tour participants." With an update, it was the standard, recycled Roessler accounting that he first delivered to the Army Corps of Engineers for the IFCWRC in 1945. The *Star* included a picture of IFCWRC chairman Tony Hulman, Louisville district engineer for the Army Corps of Engineers Colonel W. D. Milne, Indiana lieutenant governor Harold Handley of LaPorte, and Mark C. Honeywell, the "Wabash industrialist who donated the Honeywell Community Center where an IFCWRC meeting was held."[56] Honeywell was also the stepfather of John and Joe Nixon, publishers of the Peru and Wabash newspapers. Lunch was served after the tour.

Congressman Beamer wasn't there, saying he had business in Washington, but he had asked Robert Kellum, executive secretary for the IFCWRC, that "John Duffey, Wabash, and J. A. Schmalzried of Lagro be included in the plans for the 'group' inspection of the Upper Wabash River Valley in order that they could report to me some of the program that is proposed."[57]

The *Star* story mentioned that the "Mississinewa River Dam would create a permanent lake covering about 1,300 acres."[58] Seems to me like engineers at the Army Corps of Engineers and the IFCWRC would have known that included Somerset. The *Star* story doesn't say. I wouldn't expect an Indianapolis reporter to know to ask.

Both the *Star* and *South Bend Tribune* stories reviewed the kind of procedure General Itschner had mentioned in his letter to Roessler, and interestingly, in one, when someone mentioned to IFCWRC chairman Tony Hulman that water levels were currently low, Hulman said that simply proved that a big rain was coming. Dam if you do and dam if you don't get rain.

The next month, Beamer got a letter from Colonel Milne complaining that they hadn't gotten as much money from Congress as they wanted for surveying the upper Wabash River, but that they'd make do.[59]

When Beamer responded with a request for drawings and plans, Milne said the "field work for these reservoirs is essentially complete," but the drawings and plans hadn't been completed. Expect now the interim report in November, he said.[60]

We know the report issue deadline then changed again because of a letter Ralph Roessler wrote to Congressman Beamer's office in December 1954.[61] In it, Roessler said that Milne told an IFCWRC meeting that month that the report wouldn't be ready until February or March of 1955. More importantly, but not for publication, Milne had told them, Mississinewa and Salamonie were a go—Huntington, not so much.

The following month, on January 10, 1955, Robert Kellum passed along that December meeting information from Colonel Milne to the *Wabash Plain Dealer* publisher Joe Nixon.[62] The handwritten note had advice about how to report it without attributing the information to the army. The hush-hush army report to the IFCWRC details by how many feet the project would reduce 1913 flood levels, he told Nixon.

The army engineers had calculated by that time how many feet the proposed reservoirs would have reduced the 1913 flood river overflow at Logansport, Peru, and Wabash, Milne had told the IFCWRC: six feet and more. That's some good calculating. Seems to me like engineers at the Army Corps of Engineers and the IFCWRC would have known that day by how many feet of water Somerset would be covered under the proposed Mississinewa Reservoir. It's not, though, something that Joe Nixon's *Wabash Plain Dealer* passed along to the people of Somerset without attributing the information to the army.

Roessler had also written in his December note to Beamer that the fact that Milne hadn't gotten all the money he wanted for surveying was a "matter of immediate concern." Then, after a meeting with Roessler, Kellum reiterated that concern in another letter to Congressman Beamer eleven days later.[63] It sounds to me like Congressman Beamer was in the US Army Corps of Engineers/IFCWRC/Upper Wabash Valley Flood Control Project doghouse.

Vern

19. REFUGE

Dear Vern,

You might want to dog-ear the next two pages for future reference. Perhaps you'll want to do a family tree diagram.

Vern's best friend was Burnell, his brother, Charles Burnell Shroyer. "Burnell" is what the people in our family called him because Pop's first name was Charles. Charles Burnell Shroyer was called by his middle name because Pop's name was Charles even though nobody in his immediate family called Vern's dad by any name other than Pop. Pop was Grandpa Shroyer. Burnell was my uncle.

The person we knew as Charles was the son of Vern's oldest brother, Maurice, which everybody pronounced "Morse." The character Drew Carey played on a TV show set in Cleveland looked like Uncle Maurice.

The person we knew as Charles was my cousin, the same age as my sister, Linda, Vern's daughter. Charles was the son of Maurice and Julienne. There was never a problem for me. Burnell was Burnell, Pop was Pop, and Charles was Charles. Every one of them had a wry sense of humor and a twinkle in his eyes, but I could tell them apart. Some outsiders had issues.

My sister, Linda, and Charles and Butch (Aunt Lenore's son) and Greg (Aunt Mary's son) and Larry (Uncle Wendell's son) were the real baby boomers, born in 1946. They were the original thirteen states. The rest of us cousins were places like Indiana and Iowa. I was Wisconsin. Lenore's daughter, Nancy, was the oldest cousin, born during the war. I guess that makes her the Massachusetts Bay Colony. Nobody was Texas, and all the Southern states were part of my mom's family.

Pop's sister Verna, "Aunt Vernie," and her first husband, named Tom Snyder, adopted a little boy named Fred, whose mother died in childbirth on her tenth go-round. That little boy grew up to be the father of a man who is Linda's age, a man also named Tom Snyder. The second Tom talked to me a lot about the world that my dad grew up in.

"We went over there, to Uncle Charley's, a lot," the second Tom Snyder said, "because they lived just across the road" from the home of Aunt Vernie, who was the woman that the second Tom Snyder called "Grams." Tom said he had a hard time keeping the boys' names straight. Vern, Maurice, Burnell, Wendell. "They were always together," he said.

Vern had an older sister named Verna, but she died in infancy. Any confusion about your name that might require us to call you by your middle name, Scott, was cleared up a long time ago. Baby sister Verna died in 1913. Aunt Vernie died in 1983. Vern died in 1986. All those Shroyer Verns are gone but you. One time when we were at the family plot at Pleasant Grove cemetery, Vern nodded at me with his foot on baby Verna's gravestone to cover the *a*, I guess to give me a glimpse of what's out there. I knew he wasn't dead. He had a wry sense of humor and a twinkle in his eye, if you were paying attention.

Aunt Emmy was Vern's mom's sister. My clearest memory of Aunt Emmy was the time we got caught in a big snowstorm on the way to a basketball game in Marion. I don't know what year that was—1963, 1964, 1965? We were headed to the county tourney, the Grant County high school basketball tourney in Marion, in the second or third week of January, and State Road 22/US Highway 35, heading east across the flat farmland plain of north-central Indiana, was already drifting into impassability. Linda could have been on the fan bus. Or with John. Or at Ball State already.

There were so many tourney games over the years, it's hard for me to remember that night at Marion's Veterans Memorial Coliseum in particular. The building was always full. Did we make it to the game and then afterward decide we couldn't make it home? Did we try to turn around on the way in but then decide we couldn't make it through to back home?

Stan remembers that "the Swayzee basketball team couldn't make it. Their bus got stranded."

A deep nighttime snowstorm on a rural highway is a frightening danger. The car radio is off because it's a distraction. Taillights on the car ahead are invisible until it's too late to do anything about it. Headlights on the low beam are pointless, and the high beams magnify the snowflakes into a million dancing critters, laughing, "We got you now!" Dad was trying to contain the panic in Mom's voice as I looked out the passenger window and counted the cars in the ditch. "We could die." No, really, we could die.

Aunt Emmy and Howard lived in a house in Marion that I thought about the first time I visited your house on Thirty-Ninth Street, in Minneapolis, the place you came home to from the hospital. Warm. Rugs, wood paneling, and a place upstairs that felt like it had been patiently waiting for a hundred years for us to arrive. Aunt Emmy could not contain her joy. "Come in. Come in. Oh, of course. Look at you. Come in."

Joy. Vern had found for us refuge.

That's what I remember about Aunt Emmy, that she seemed to be always laughing and that she made everybody feel better by being around her. I know that Vern found the perfect place for us to go. He loved Emmy, and she loved him. They were a pair. I could see that. That night, while we were tucked in and I was on my way to sleep, I could hear Emmy downstairs laughing. At a kitchen table, they talked. That's what I want to remember.

Flood

20. YOU COULD SAY

Dear Vern,

It's clear that by 1950, a policy had been settled. Three dams, three reservoirs: Peoria, Salamonie, and Huntington. By 1954, a campaign strategy was in place; the issue would be a choice, without alternatives, between big dams and reservoirs or floods. In 1955, the army and the state of Indiana revealed themselves to the doomed people of Somerset.

Moving things along was the idea in 1954. General Itschner's July 6, 1954, letter to Roessler detailed the necessary steps leading to congressional approval. In the middle of those seven steps was step four: "All interested parties will have an opportunity to state their support or opposition formally before the Board of Engineers for Rivers and Harbors."[64]

Understanding how once again the public input "opportunity" did not happen begins with some focus on the interim report that Itschner told Roessler in the July 6 letter that an Army Corps of Engineers Louisville district engineer "expects to complete . . . on the three reservoirs . . . about 1 October 1954."[65]

That deadline changed to November in the August 27, 1954, letter to Congressman Beamer from that very engineer, Colonel W. D. Milne.[66] Milne then changed the due date to "February or March of 1955" in a December meeting with the Indiana Flood Control and Water Resources Commission and to "early 1955" in a January 21, 1955, letter to Beamer.[67] That note said it was delayed "due to the need for additional flood frequency studies." As it turned out, the report came out, sort of, in

September 1955, but it was never really released to the public.

Two people who knew anyway what was happening without needing the release of an interim report were the *Wabash Plain Dealer* publisher and sometime correspondent Joe Nixon and the IFCWRC executive secretary Robert Kellum. In the files at the Wabash County Museum, there's a January 1955 "not for publication" note from Kellum to Nixon that mentioned a summary of a report that the army had given the IFCWRC in December 1954. That summary was favorable to the three dams. Kellum did not say it was the interim report.

Kellum advised Nixon about how to report the information they wanted revealed without attributing it to the army, information like how many feet the project would have cut from 1913 flood levels. "You could say," Kellum wrote Nixon, that, among other things, "the need for expensive local protective works would be cut sharply."[68] Critics of the plan, like Huntington County's Ivan Funderburg, would later complain that an unstated purpose of the project was to retard the need for city sewage treatment facilities by giving the river water more room to run.

Kellum does not advise Nixon how best to tell people by how many feet Somerset will be underwater. An army that knew by how many feet the project would have cut from municipal 1913 flood levels could have known certainly, and the IFCWRC could have known, too, unless they simply didn't care enough to inquire. "Any valuable property going under?" someone among the twenty members of the IFCWRC plus the executive director and the chief engineer might well have said in December 1954 when they met to look things over with the army. We're not privy to what actually went on that day.

There's a large, detailed 1955 army project map that Milne said wasn't ready for Beamer in 1954. That map labels Somerset as "Town to Be Relocated" and Red Bridge as "Town to Be Purchased." I saw it, with Colonel Milne's mimeographed signature on a line just above where it says "Col. Corps of Engineers, District Engineer."[69] It's folded up nice and neat now in the fourth-floor Indiana University Herman B Wells Library archives in Bloomington, where, I must say, Vern, the people are pleasant and helpful. Its connection in my mind is to the interim report I keep going on about. I do not know that that map was available for the December 1954 meeting between the army and the Indiana flood commission group. But.

But, US Army Corps of Engineers Louisville district engineer Colonel Milne had been dotting the i's and crossing the t's on the report since July of 1954. It's hard for me to believe that when the big reveal came, the big map was an afterthought. It looks to me like what you'd want to have at a big reveal. Maybe I'm wrong, Vern, but I see these big-shot guys pointing pool cues at a rolled-out map on a giant table in the "situation room," a highlight for everyone at the December 1954 meeting. If he was there, maybe H. Earl Capehart, the guy on the commission normally known as US senator Homer Capehart, would've-could've-should've noticed his constituents down there. Under. Water.

What we know, Vern, is that the army told the IFCWRC to tell the publisher of the Wabash newspaper that served the affected community what the army wanted known, and the executive director of the agency that was created to make a big lake where people could run their boats, under the guise of flood control, told the publisher of the local paper how best to word that.

"You could say . . ."

Being a helpful guy, the publisher of the Wabash paper, who was the stepson of Wabash industrialist Mark Honeywell, the publisher who occasionally wrote in the paper about the project, followed the commission instructions for the hush-hush army directive. Believing in the "greater good," I suppose, *Wabash Plain Dealer* publisher Joe Nixon neglected his primary duty to the people in the community that his newspaper served to tell the whole truth, not just the part that suited his agenda. Community members did not get a chance to weigh the positives against the negatives, because the negatives were omitted from the information the army gave the Indiana flood commission to give to the newspaper. No negatives. No alternatives, except floods. Nixon did not need to acknowledge the fact that he had a role in the story. Plainly, though, he was acting as an agent for the army and for the state commission to enhance the public reception for a project plan that had yet to be made public. Also plainly, it's a project that would destroy a town and chase your great-great-grandfather off his land.

In April 1955, Congressman Beamer wrote Ralph Roessler, IFCWRC vice chairman, that he'd learned that the highly anticipated interim report might not leave Cincinnati until May. It was not out yet, though, on May 25, 1955, when the fate of Somerset was revealed in a letter to Beamer. A week later, the note was partially repeated word for word in the *Indianapolis News* and the *Muncie Evening Press*, but not in the Wabash newspaper.

In Milne's letter to Beamer, the big news is like an afterthought. Not until the third paragraph of the May 25, 1955, letter did Colonel Milne for the first time mention to the congressman who represented Somerset in the US House of Representatives that Somerset would be going underwater. "Reference is made to your letter of 17 May 1955 in which you request information on the proposed flood control dam on the Mississinewa River," Milne begins.

He continues,

> An interim report on Wabash River at and above the mouth of White River has been prepared by the Louisville District in accordance with the resolution adopted 9 May 1949 by the Committee on Public Works, United States Senate. Investigations of the flood problem indicate that the most favorable plan of protection would result from the construction of three reservoirs in the upper Wabash basin. These reservoirs would be located (1) in the Mississinewa River with the dam site at Peoria, Indiana; (2) in the Salamonie River with the dam site near Dora, Indiana; and (3) in the Wabash River with the dam site near Huntington, Indiana. The top of the proposed flood control pool on the Mississinewa River is elevation 779 which would require a dam about 137 feet in height. The reservoir at elevation 779 would cover 12,800 acres and extend up the Mississinewa valley about 28 miles.[70]

When the Mississinewa reservoir is complete, he then mentions, "The height of the flood control pool at Somerset, Indiana would be approximately 75 feet above the stream bed and would cover the present site of the community."

Next, Milne says, *all* the buildings in Somerset will be removed and the community of Somerset relocated "above the flood control pool." He adds, "The plans and recommendations by the Louisville District for construction of the reservoir are subject to review by higher authority and are not necessarily the final views of the Corps of Engineers."

In Milne's letter, which was a response to a forwarded inquiry from Somerset Hardware owner Gene Smith, the army colonel noted that there were bureaucratic hurdles that were yet to be cleared.

What Milne revealed was news to the Fifth District US congressman in whose district the Upper Wabash Valley Flood Control Project had been planned. It became public knowledge the next week, when on June 1, 1955, the *Indianapolis News* and the *Muncie Evening Press* identically reported from their shared "Washington bureau" what Milne had said. In the same story, Beamer said that he was only just now hearing from the Army Corps of Engineers about relocating Somerset and that "he would oppose any far-flung plans to move the community."[71]

The interim report, meanwhile, was still being reviewed, the Louisville-based Milne told Beamer on June 9.[72] Information trickled from it, but it remained sealed.

The interim report would finally be released in a limited way at the end of August 1955. That's thirteen months after General Itschner told Ralph Roessler it was coming. That's nine months after the army told Roessler's commission what was in it and eight months after the commission's Robert Kellum told the Wabash newspaper publisher how to make the information look good. It was three months after word got out about Somerset's fate.

As you might imagine, there was a lot of talk generated by the Somerset's-going-under news as May became June in 1955. The "lot of talk" proved that people wanted to talk about it, but a closed "procedure" that led to the "interim report" meant the talk didn't really amount to much. By the time the people of Somerset and all the Mississinewa

Reservoir area found out in June of 1955 what was planned for them, "a lot of talk" wouldn't change anything. I'll come back to how people reacted when newspapers reported Somerset would be sacrificed in the Upper Wabash Flood Control project. Right now, Vern, I want to stay on the trail of the interim report.

Congressman Beamer received a letter, dated August 30, 1955, from Colonel J. L. Person, the Corps of Engineers division engineer, Cincinnati, with word that "inclosed [*sic*] for your information are advance copies of a notice of issuance of an interim report on Wabash River and Tributaries, at and above the mouth of White River, Indiana, for flood control and allied purposes. General release of the notice is scheduled for 12 September 1955."[73]

The interim report is here!

The interim report is here!

The interim report is here?

No, wait. It's not the report. It's an advance notice to the congressman that there is a report, with everyone getting a chance to get the notice that there is a report on September 12. Actually, seeing the report would take a bit more effort–a trip to Cincinnati–unless somehow someone violated procedure and gave you a copy. The notice also said that the Army Corps of Engineers liked the report from the Army Corps of Engineers on the project that the Army Corps of Engineers was creating that the public was now getting the chance to hear officially for the first time existed.

It had been almost fourteen months since the US Army assistant chief of engineers for civil works, Brigadier General E. C. Itschner, on July 6, 1954, notified Congressman Beamer about the report. Remember, he said then, "all interested parties will have an opportunity to state their support or opposition formally before the Board of Engineers for Rivers and Harbors."

In that time, some carefully guarded, limited information favorable to the plan passed from the army to the IFCWRC to the *Wabash Plain Dealer* to the public. The three worked together to create a positive first impression. First impressions, Vern, are the most difficult to dispel.

That January 1955 first-impression information did not include the fate of Somerset. Colonel Milne revealed that in May, in an offhand, matter-of-fact sort of way to Congressman Beamer, without mentioning that it was "just between you and me."

Robert Kellum, IFCWRC executive director, didn't have the chance to tell Beamer, "You could say . . . " He didn't have an in with the *Indianapolis News* and the *Muncie Evening Press* before they revealed the news. What Milne wrote Beamer in response to a question from the owner of Somerset Hardware turned up partially word for word in the *Indianapolis News* and the *Muncie Evening Press*, not the project's purveyors of choice, like Joe Nixon's paper. It appears the information about Somerset being held forcibly underwater wasn't guarded closely enough. And Beamer didn't know at first that he'd made a mistake when he told the outlier papers that he'd try to protect Somerset. He'd learn, though.

21. COOPERATION

The notion that the public would have a chance to see and respond to what the army was doing to Somerset conflicted with the August 30, 1955, interim-report-is-here letter from Colonel Person in Cincinnati to Congressman Beamer in Washington. It said that "copies of the report will not be furnished or loaned for use outside of these offices"—*before September 12*—"but interested parties, including the press, will be permitted to make such notes of the contents as they desire."[74] The public did not have genuine access, but a newspaper that favored the project did. Before anyone.

A September 7, 1955, *Indianapolis Star* report details the interim report contents favorably.[75] ARMY TO RECOMMEND 3 HOOSIER RESERVOIRS is the headline. It says that Congressman Beamer knows about the recommendation, but he's not clearly the story's source.

The reporter is from the *Star*'s "Washington Bureau," but Beamer isn't quoted or paraphrased once in the story's sixteen paragraphs. By rights, the Washington, DC–based reporter must have traveled to Colonel Person's Cincinnati office to look at the report that "will not be furnished or loaned for use outside of these offices." Or else someone who got a look told him what to say. Based on what executive director Robert Kellum told the Wabash newspaper publisher to say about what the army told him in 1954 about the plan, I'm merely speculating here, Vern, that the source is Kellum or somebody else on the Indiana Flood Control and Water Resources Commission. It's clear the army and the

IFCWRC had, with cooperation from the *Star* and the newspapers in towns along the Wabash River, tried to keep a firm handle on controlling the information about the Upper Wabash Valley Flood Control Project.

The September 7, 1955, *Indianapolis Star* story mentions, of course, what the dams would have done to prevent the 1913 flood. Attributing the information to "the engineers," it says, "The flood control and water conservation dams would provide substantial benefits along the Wabash River." It says, "The recommendation will be based on studies that go back as far as 1946."

Reporter Ben Cole's page 1 story does not mention the Indiana Flood Control and Water Resources Commission. Cole's story does not mention Somerset, Red Bridge, Dora, or the people and graves that, would be displaced by the project. You wouldn't know there would be any of that if all you knew about the plan was this story. The story does say that "interested parties" had until October 12, 1955, to let the Board of Engineers for Rivers and Harbors in Washington, DC, know what they thought about the plan. It does not say that if you wanted to look at it, you had to go to Cincinnati.

The office Person mentioned to Beamer where the report would be held, the Army Corps of Engineers office, was in Cincinnati. That's 173 miles from Somerset.

The September 12, 1955, interim report general release "notice" said, "Notice is given hereby that an interim report on that subject has been completed by the District and Division Engineers and is favorable to such improvement."[76]

So, beginning September 12, the interim report was available in Cincinnati, where "interested parties" like, say, Pop and Somerset Hardware owner Gene Smith, who happened to somehow find out about it, were "permitted" to travel 173 miles in the car Fred Snyder thought shouldn't leave Wabash County to look and to make notes. Pack a lunch.

Oddly, Beamer appears to have sent the actual interim report on to one person, Robert Dawes, who was a student at Manchester College. Dawes had asked in late September for information for a paper he was writing. On September 30, Beamer sent the report with a note that said floods were a problem and "it is hoped that those people who will receive no benefits and who, naturally, would have to move will be properly and fully reimbursed."[77]

There's nothing in Beamer's correspondence from the period to indicate he sent it to anyone else.

Thirty days after the notice went out, October 12, 1955, was the deadline for "all interested parties [who] will have an opportunity to state their support or opposition formally before the Board of Engineers for Rivers and Harbors."

"Written communications should be addressed to the Board of Engineers for Rivers and Harbors, Washington 25, D.C." the notice says, "and should be mailed to be in possession of the Board on or before 12 October 1955."[78]

And if you got your written communication about the interim report being held in an office in Cincinnati sent in on time or successfully filed for an extension, the next step was a meeting for the Board of Engineers for Rivers and Harbors in Washington, DC, to consider public comments about a report that, quite frankly, the public had not seen. It was set for November 28 and 29:

> CORPS OF ENGINEERS, U. S. ARMY Board of Engineers for Rivers and Harbors To Consider Report on November 28, 1955.
> For Immediate Press Release:
>
> Interested parties may attend this meeting as observers and listen to discussions on the report by Board Members. The meeting will open at 9:30 a.m. EST on November 28 and at 9:30 a.m. on November 29 for the consideration of other reports. Anyone desiring to be present during the discussion on the other reports will be welcome.[79]

Observe and listen. Seems like a long way to go for that. The public comments designed to be sparse from interested parties would be digested and then regurgitated by the Board of Engineers for Rivers and Harbors of the US Army Corps of Engineers. That's a division of the organization that created the plan.

"All interested parties will have an opportunity to state their support or opposition," indeed.

While he missed the October 12 deadline, the Wabash Chamber of Commerce manager, Sam Hubley, nonetheless took time to send a telegram to the Rivers and Harbors Board at the end of November. "The Wabash, Indiana Chamber of Commerce Board of Directors with supporting resolutions from its Retail and Industrial Divisions favors your recommendations for location of three flood control reservoirs in the headwaters of the Wabash River Basin."[80]

And he got a nice response, with a copy to Beamer and Kellum. "Got your telegram supporting the project," a River and Harbors Board member wrote, and "made it part of files on the report."

Deadlines, I guess, are made to be broken.

Colonel H. S. Miller then also responded to Hubley:

> I am pleased to inform you that the Board, when the report was before it for review and consideration at the meeting held in this city on 28 November, concurred in general in the recommendations of the Division and District Engineers report and recommended the construction of the three reservoirs for flood control on the Wabash River.[81]

Well, then, Vern, that's that.

Also, under the heading, "It's a done deal," allow me to go back a few months to the written report that Ralph Roessler prepared after a March 26, 1954, IFCWRC meeting. That's a couple of months before Roessler told Beamer that an Army Corps of Engineers interim report was just about ready.

Roessler told the IFCWRC in *March 1954* that it was time to move on from the details of the Upper Wabash Valley Flood Control project. Matters are settled, he told them. Let the engineers handle that.

"I believe," Roessler said, "the commission members should graduate from the matters of preparation to the acts of accomplishment and these acts require broad policy, sound salesmanship and good publicity."[82]

March 1954.

Roessler told them, then, that the time, now—in *March 1954*—was for project promotion and that "we should inform members of Congress of benefits and of what they should be doing," specifically with money appropriations, and that Congress should be doing it. We should be helping the Army Corps of Engineers, not critiquing their work, he said. Fourteen months before the citizens of Somerset learned that their town was doomed, "we should inform members of Congress what they should be doing," Ralph Roessler said. That's nineteen months before the deadline for which "*all interested parties will have an opportunity to state their support or opposition formally before the Board of Engineers for Rivers and Harbors.*"[83]

How shitty is that?

22. SEVENTY-FIVE FEET ABOVE THE STREAM BED

Early in 1955, three and a half months before the big Somerset-is-toast reveal, Congressman Beamer got a letter from a Huntington County farmer named Rolland Bozarth. Bozarth said he'd been spending money on a farm he bought three years before. "Now I hear my farmland will be taken in the project," the Salamonie reservoir, he means. "Should I quit spending money?"[84]

Beamer said he didn't know, and he referred the question to the Army Corps of Engineers' Colonel Milne in Cincinnati. Milne replied, it depends on what land it is, can you ask him? Beamer did, and Bozarth answered, "I am enclosing the description and a plat of my farm. I would like to have it returned to me when you are finished with it. I want to thank you for your cooperation in getting this information for me. It has cleared up a lot of rumors around here."[85]

After Beamer forwarded that to Milne, Milne replied to Beamer that the part of Bozarth's land in the "creek valleys"[86] would be flooded. I did not find a letter from Beamer back to Bozarth with that information in the John V. Beamer collection boxes 10 and 11 files in the rare books and manuscripts section at the Indiana State Library in Indianapolis.

In the spring of 1955, after Congressman Beamer wrote letters to the Wabash and Huntington newspapers and testified before the House Appropriations Committee in support of funds for three dams and three reservoirs in the Upper Wabash Valley Flood Control Project, he got another constituent letter on the topic. This was the one from Somerset Hardware owner Gene Smith. Can you tell me, Smith asks, May 10, 1955, what it means for Somerset? "Lots of rumors," he wrote.[87]

"Rumors," again.

Like for Bozarth, Beamer forwarded Gene Smith's question to Milne, who replied on May 25, "The height of the flood control pool at Somerset, Indiana would be approximately 75 feet above the stream bed and would cover the present site of the community."[88] That, Vern, was the first acknowledgment that I came across that Somerset would drown. That's why I'm mentioning it again.

I did not find a letter from Beamer to Smith with that information in the John V. Beamer collection boxes 10 and 11 files in the rare books and manuscripts section at the Indiana State Library in Indianapolis, either.

Milne also told Beamer that the town would be moved to a place above the flood control pool, which prompted Beamer to then ask Milne for a map in a letter dated June 1 and more specific information about the move "as promptly as possible." And, oh, by the way, he inquired, "may I ask whether or not there is any possibility of the report being expedited in order that it could be reviewed by the Chief of Engineers, the Board of Engineers for Rivers and Harbors, the Governor of Indiana, and other agencies during this present session of the Congress."[89] Where's that interim report, anyway?

The day after June 1, 1955, when the Somerset-moving story made the *Indianapolis News* and *Muncie Evening Press*,[90] the *Kokomo Tribune* and the *Bedford Daily Times-Mail* ran an Associated Press story that said Beamer said he would oppose moving Somerset and that he planned to investigate.[91] Saying he would investigate was as far as the investigation would go.

23. INTERESTED PARTIES

In 1971, a woman named Florence (Bowman) Roby wrote a twenty-eight-page mimeographed account for distribution at reunions and family gatherings that she called "Spotlight on Somerset High School and the Surrounding Community." I got a copy from Dave Compton, the long-time Somerset resident I met at the Lions Club meeting.

Florence graduated from Somerset High School in 1923 and taught second grade at Somerset Elementary for forty years, until it closed, and then for three years for the consolidated Southwood Elementary. Dad was too old by two years to have had her, but she was there in the building with him, and his younger siblings would have been in her class. She knew of him, I know, because Vern's name appears when she includes the 1932 sectional championship basketball team names in her writing. Brother Maurice and Pop's cousin Robert are there, too. Maybe Florence was at the game. Like the Barbara Hershey character in *Hoosiers*. That's a nice way to imagine it.

Brother "Wendal" [*sic*] is among the 1941 sectional winner roster names she transcribed. Aunt Vernie ran the cafeteria. Wendell and Wayne and Mary and Lenore, and maybe Burnell, and Bob's daughter Kay were Florence Roby's students. How could she not know the Shroyers?

Bob's daughter Janet was not her student, Janet told me, because Mrs.

Roby took a year off from teaching because she lost her only child in birth in 1946. That's the year your great-aunt Linda was born. Rebecca Ann and Florence Roby are buried in the same cemetery as Vern. Florence Roby is a person I want my account to do justice.

Florence Roby's account of Somerset is the best one I've come across. She speaks straightforwardly about what the Upper Wabash Valley Flood Control Project meant to the people who lived in Somerset.

"The people at once became disturbed and despondent." She writes that 1958 was the year in which they found out Somerset "would be under water."

> Fear gripped their hearts, fear of losing their homes. What should they do? Where could they go? How could they go and leave their homes and neighbors that they had loved so long? Their lives were torn asunder. How cruel to be driven from their beloved town to perhaps new and distant places so foreign to them. Some became ill and it is thought were hastened to their death by this terrible experience. Some became angry. Still others did not believe that such a tragedy would ever happen. But that was only wishful thinking.[92]

That's what "75 feet above the stream bed" meant, you see, Vern. That's what a seemingly offhand third paragraph matter-of-fact comment from an engineer in an office 180 miles away meant. It meant there were victims. You can't judge whether or not the Upper Wabash Valley Flood Control Project was worth it without taking them into account. I suppose there are a million of these stories of people not being considered. This is the one I have to tell, Vern.

I wonder if the Upper Wabash Valley Flood Control Project made a victim of John Beamer, too. John Beamer, the man from little Roann who was Somerset's congressman from 1951 to 1959, had a heart attack in April 1957 from which he was still recovering at his home in Huntington that July. In November 1958, he lost his bid for a fifth term in Congress. He died in 1964 at the age of sixty-seven. I wonder if in service to the Upper Wabash Valley Flood Control Project he made victims of others, and I would wonder if he were a bystander if I believed bystanders are something other than low-level perpetrators.

We know that Beamer overstated his support for the project. We know that Beamer overstated his opposition to the project. We know that both sides blamed him for whatever they didn't like about the policy and the process by which the Upper Wabash Valley Flood Control Project came to be. We know he had a heart attack in the middle of all of it. We know he refused to "campaign" for the project. We know he voted in Congress for the Upper Wabash Valley Flood Control Project at every opportunity. We know that after the matter was settled, he was not reelected to office. And after that, we know he claimed he deserved more credit for making it happen than he got.

What have I observed? In his correspondence with persons who supported the project, the general tone was businesslike and sometimes contentious. In his correspondence with persons who objected to the idea, his general tone was friendly and cooperative. Given a choice, I think he'd rather hang out with the small-town, down-to-earth folks than the big shots. He was conflicted.

We know that twice in the month between the interim report notice and the deadline for responding to the interim report, Congressman Beamer steered constituents away from the avenue that was available for voicing concerns about the project.

Soon after word that Somerset would be flooded became public, Beamer received several letters opposing the project. Unlike the back-and-forth correspondence regarding procedure he had been receiving from plan supporters, these notes are generally heartfelt, genuine, and well written, with the care of people remembering how they were taught in school to express themselves.

Here's an early September 1955 one from a resident of nearby Converse, Inez Highly:

> I am much concerned about the Army Corps of Engineers and the Flood Control Commission plan to remove Somerset on the Mississinewa. It is a small, beautiful and peaceful place where the inhabitants are contented and many are retired citizens. The Christian religion is taught, preached, and lived. In the school children and young people are taught to become useful and upright citizens. Can't you use your influence to stop this ruthless project.
>
> Respectfully Miss Inez Highly.[93]

Beamer responded September 7 that he was also "concerned" but that it was not a done deal yet, and that

> the suggestion has been made that all who are interested in expressing their opinions for or against the project, do so in writing to:
> Corps of Engineers,
> U. S. Army
> Office of District Engineer
> 830 W. Broadway
> Louisville 3, Kentucky,
> before October 12th.[94]

Perhaps that was an oversight, but in fact, the October 12 deadline mentioned in the interim report notice was "that all interested parties have the privilege of presenting their views on the subject matter of the report to the Board of Engineers for Rivers and Harbors, a permanent body sitting at Washington, D. C. to which all examination and survey reports of this character are referred."

It seems less like an oversight when it happens a second time, in response to a letter from D. R. Dragstrem, an *Encyclopaedia Britannica* salesman from Wilmette, Illinois, who wrote Beamer that the flood control project was "not in best interests of Somerset community."[95]

Beamer responded October 3,

> May I suggest that you and all of your friends who
> either support or oppose this program write to:
> Corps of Army Engineers
> U.S. Army
> Cincinnati, Ohio.
>
> This should be done before October 12.[96]

The date is right, again, but the correct address is Board of Engineers for Rivers and Harbors, Washington 25, DC. Not Cincinnati or Louisville.

On the day after the newspaper reports that said he said he would oppose moving Somerset, back in June of 1955, Beamer wrote a letter to Roessler disavowing the accounts. "Mischaracterized" was how he put it. Inquiring only, Beamer maintained, about what's happening to Somerset in all of this, he wrote on June 2.[97]

Still waiting to hear what's happening, he said to Roessler, even though he had the May 25 letter from Milne that made it clear Somerset was going under.

June 2 is also the day that Ruth Rudicel of Nineveh, Indiana, wrote Beamer referencing the AP article as it appeared in the *Indianapolis News*. It's apt and worth mentioning that Nineveh is the unincorporated little town about twenty miles south of Indianapolis where parts of *Hoosiers* were filmed. Rudicel asked Beamer about moving the Somerset cemetery. Relatives are buried there, she said, among them her grandfather Asa Ross, a Civil War veteran and two-term sheriff of Wabash County.[98]

In replying June 6, Beamer again deceptively maintained, "I do not have the information in regard to the areas that will be flooded if the proposal is accepted. Consequently, at the present time I am unable to advise in regard to the cemetery to which you referred."[99] That's simply a lie. "Seventy-five feet above the stream bed" would obviously cover the cemetery on the west edge of town along the riverbank. He added, then, what also became his stock answer to upset citizens of Somerset and the surrounding area.

"It may be several years," he told Ruth, before the matter is settled. It's going to take time to get this through the bureaucracy.

That's what he told Glenn Henderson of Elwood, who wrote he was worried about his cabin at the Riverside Resort owned by John Knee, Aunt Vernie's husband.[100] "This program is merely in the proposal stage," Beamer wrote, "and, consequently, would not become effective perhaps before five years even if it is approved and funds appropriated by the next session of Congress."[101]

That's pretty much what he told Willard Oppy, Riverside Power and Development Corporation president, who wanted to know if the dam of Salamonie at Dora would affect his project.[102] That's what he told Fernie Trigalet, a Somerset man who said he could remember that when a new school opened in 1924, it had indoor restrooms.[103]

To Ira Roby, the father of Florence Roby's husband, he said it was only a proposal. "The first proposal is merely one that was submitted by the Corps of Army Engineers. There is nothing special that can be done at the present time until other agencies and the people themselves have had a chance to express themselves on this important subject."[104]

Also, Beamer often takes the "I'm on your side in this, looking out for you" angle. In his July 21 reply to Trigalet, he said, "I certainly agree with you that this entire matter should be resurveyed and reconsidered before any such drastic moves are made as proposed by the Corps of Engineers."[105] There's no evidence that he did anything to make that happen, though.

To Lawrence Scheffer, self-described "farmer, taxpayer, voter" from rural Wabash, with three years of military service, "fighting in foreign lands" who "gave three of the best years of my life that I and others might live in peace,"[106] Beamer responded, "You may be assured that I shall do everything to protect your interests and the interest of all of the people in the district."[107]

What I know now about all of this, Vern, because I started writing a letter to you about Dad, makes me cringe.

Scheffer's critique: expense, waste, and destruction of good land; "a scheme to get a recreation center near this Slocum park . . . backed by conservation clubs and a few rich men who don't care for anything except a few more dollars. Do everything in your power to put a stop to this."

As letters from opponents increased after the flooding of Somerset became, in June of 1955, a well-known Upper Wabash Valley Flood Control Project feature, as fashioned by the Army Corps of Engineers with the Indiana Flood Control and Water Resources Commission, supporters sensed that they needed to step up their information-control efforts. This harkened back to what Roessler said in his March 1954 report to the commission: "I believe the commission members should graduate from the matters of preparation to the acts of accomplishment and these acts require broad policy, sound salesmanship and good publicity."[108]

The "Somerset's going under" news was not good publicity—*bad optics*, they call that now—and Beamer's equivocation was not helping the situation. Plan proponents perceived that he had forwarded what Milne told him would happen to the town to unsympathetic newspapers and with that had said that he was going to save Somerset.

Roessler, IFCWRC member and Peru banker Carlos Life, and IFCWRC executive secretary Robert Kellum needed to get busy with the "sound salesmanship."

Quickly, they organized an opportunity for the press. The *Marion Leader-Tribune* reported on an IFCWRC press briefing June 3, 1955, at which Life was the spokesman. He said that Congressman Beamer had been "very cooperative" in forwarding the flood control plans, and in fact, the paper reported, "in referring to the allegation that Rep. John V. Beamer would fight the proposed relocation of Somerset, commission members said they had learned that the congressman had denied this report and had said in fact that his remarks had been misunderstood."[109]

Somerset would be moved, Life confirmed, but residents would be reimbursed. Kellum said that $700,000 set aside for the town was more than it was worth, in a *Wabash Plain Dealer* article covering the same day. They could build an "ideal, model town,"[110] Kellum said. Backtracking from his backtracking in the same article, Beamer now said, "I do not have enough details to make a definite statement" regarding his position on intervening on behalf of Somerset's fate.

The busy week continued as, in a June 5 letter, Roessler told

Congressman Beamer that he needed to tell Somerset residents that moving the town was the best thing that could happen for them.

> Many of the buildings are very old and there is considerable sentiment involved, but once the residents understand they will be well taken care of, they will be paid for any damage incurred, and will end up by a replaced village on high ground and in an admirable location to become a revived lakeside resort village, then they will see the benefits against the disturbance incurred. With the funds allocated to take care of Somerset, it would seem to me you will have little trouble convincing your constituents that relocation means a great improvement to Somerset and of great value to each individual involved.[111]

All you need is some of that "sound salesmanship."

Later that week, Kellum and Life assembled reporters from Wabash, Miami, and Grant Counties to tell them that the heretofore mentioned interim report wasn't quite ready yet, but some details were "out" and that it looked like a winner, a great plan that would stop floods, save money, and provide recreational opportunities. There's money in it to move Somerset, and, you know, while we're at it, they say, Beamer is denying he said he'd fight the plan to destroy the town where Vern went to high school.

There was another Kellum and Life Show article in the June 10 *Peru Republican* newspaper adding "water flow" and "sewage removal" as benefits.[112] While it provided interim report details that again favored the project, the article said "text of the report" from the army wasn't public because it hadn't yet cleared all the procedural hurdles that "call for such release to be made from the chief's office in Washington." The subhead on the article acknowledged Kellum, saying, "State Secretary Says Project Up to People." The "people" aren't allowed to see the report while the people who created the project are cherry-picking it to create support.

"Project up to people." I sigh.

Write your congressman, Joe Nixon's *Wabash Plain Dealer* said in an editorial June 11 supporting the project, whatever it is, for the same reasons Kellum and Life had been giving all week.[113]

One thing I've noticed in looking at the Beamer and Roessler letters is that there was a tendency for people opposed to the project to write letters to their congressman because of something they saw in the newspaper about it or something they heard from a neighbor or friend. People who favored the project were more likely to write letters to their congressmen because someone in a position of authority had told them to. Something I noticed, Vern.

24. THE SMALL DAM PLAN

A different kind of letter from a person in a position of authority came to Congressman John Beamer, dated June 3, 1955, just days after the news got out about submerging Somerset. It came from Wabash Circuit Court judge Byron Kennedy, and it made me think of that very first "public hearing" that the interim report notice would say was held in Logansport on October 23, 1946. In a page 26 advance story that October 23, 1946, the *Indianapolis News* had reported that Indiana Flood Control and Water Resources Commission chief engineer David H. Harker said that "utilization of Wabash River tributaries . . . may lessen the need for artificial flood control projects." Harker said sites had been found that could store inches of rain and provide flood control barriers for many areas.

"'If these sites can be utilized to the fullest extent, then the upper Wabash River cities from the city of Wabash down to south of Logansport will be aided materially on flood crests,' he said, 'and less expensive local protective works will be required.'"[114]

Judge Kennedy's letter, like Roessler's March 1954 directive to the IFCWRC, called upon Congress to act, but in a very different way. And Kennedy shows he knows more than we might expect about the Army Corps of Engineers Upper Wabash Valley Flood Control Project for the IFCWRC, given the lack of public notice about the plan at that point.

This is the letter:

Honorable John V. Beamer
House Office Building
Washington, D.C.

Dear John:
Everyone agrees that whatever steps are necessary to alleviate the flood damage which occurs along the rivers of our state should be taken. Let that be understood at the outset. There are, however, two very distinct and divergent schools of thought on how this may and should be accomplished.

On the one hand, the Army Corps of Engineers, whose thinking and philosophy have been adopted for the most part by the Indiana Flood Control Commission, believe that flood control should be accomplished by the building of large dams and the creation of huge impoundments of water, with the inundation of whatever land happens to be in basin, including towns, productive farm land and other lands. This type of flood control gives no consideration to the loss of soil and the dissipation of the water resources in the upper reaches of the drainage areas upon which the rain originally fell. In fact, impliedly at least, it encourages those in the drainage area to continue to denude the land which should be in trees and cover crops and in effect encourages these people to seek and install additional drains to speed up the run-off. This all will ultimately have a devastating effect in dry seasons and is already appearing in many areas in both northern and southern Indiana where, even now, irrigation measures are being sought.

On the other hand, there is the philosophy of engineers of the Soil Conservation Service, who contend that flooding can and should be controlled in the upper reaches of the drainage areas where the rain falls and before it reaches the rivers and streams. They contend (and this makes real sense to me) by the building of many small impoundments on submarginal lands or the least valuable lands throughout the upper reaches of the watershed, the excess waters may be trapped and held for the dry season and will not reach the rivers to create floods. This program, they say, and it was only last year, I believe, that Congress gave USCS a small amount and authorized it to try it somewhere in the west will cost about one-fifth of what the Army Engineers' program will cost and will do the job better. For a rather comprehensive comparison of these plans, probable results and costs, may I suggest that you read (if you have not already done so then review) an article by a very respected authority entitled "Big Dam Foolishness." May I suggest, therefore, that before the dams on the Mississinewa, Salamonie and Wabash Rivers are built and the great impoundments created and vast sums of money spent, engineers of the USCS be directed to survey the watershed and make their report and recommendations and then let Congress decide.[115]

Judge Kennedy signed it, "Very sincerely, Byron K."

Congressman Beamer responded the next day. He wrote Kennedy that he'd follow up with the Soil Conservation Service (SCS) and "Congressmen Ralph Harvey, who is on the Agricultural Committee," whom he said vouched for the SCS. Also, Beamer told Kennedy, "I am wondering whether or not you might contact Mr. Charles Beckert, Chief of the Water Resources Division, Department of Conservation, State House, Indianapolis" to give him the judge's opinion."[116]

It was the Indiana Department of Conservation director Hugh Barnhart who objected in an Indiana legislative hearing in 1945 to "the fact that the Indiana Flood Control and Water Resources Commission wished to take over everything connected with flood control."[117] It was at that hearing, on Indiana Senate Bill 174, that the Senate Rivers and Waters Committee considered the legislative approval for creating the IFCWRC. That's the group that Governor Henry Schricker had to create in November of 1944 to properly meet with the army about flood control for the entire state: Roessler, Kellum, Life, Tony Hulman.

According to the hearing notes from that day in February of 1945,

> Mr. Barnhart said that the engineers in his department have given much study and thought to the matter of flood control. It was their opinion that their department would be one of the most helpful agencies to the Flood Control Commission because of their past experience in water resources and surveys and would be willing to cooperate in making any information available. However, they objected to the fact that the Commission wished to take over everything connected with flood control.[118]

Between that 1945 hearing and Judge Kennedy's 1955 letter, we know hardly anything about the army and the IFCWRC work in creating the Somerset flood. We don't know of any impact the "most helpful willing to cooperate" Indiana Department of Conservation Water Resources Division had between 1945 and 1955 on the Upper Wabash Valley Flood Control Project. There are no meeting records in the Indiana State Archives or the Indiana State Library from the IFCWRC between 1945 and the March 1954 Roessler address to the group, when he tells them their "phase one, preparation" work is over.

The army responded to my request for information on the "phase one" period by telling me that no such information is available. That leaves me with the impression that in 1945 there was a struggle for the control of Indiana water management policy between the Indiana Department of Conservation and the newly created Indiana Flood Control and Water Resources Commission. The IFCWRC won, they followed the money-rich army's lead, and the army wanted the Upper Wabash Valley Flood Control Project, the three big dams and reservoirs.

Story.

On the day of Judge Kennedy's letter, then, the Upper Wabash Valley Flood Control Project proponents—the army and the IFCWRC—had not permitted for ten years for there to be a publicly considered alternative to three big dams and reservoirs. They'd controlled the language so that the choice, in 1955 and beyond, was their plan or more floods.

Period.

My way with a spillway. Between the years of 1945 and 1955, we can surmise that there must have been questions and answers and information that they kept to themselves. But we don't know. There's no record.

Congressman Beamer wrote to the Soil Conservation Service in the Agriculture Department a few days after he got the letter from Judge Kennedy. It sounds sympathetic, open-minded, and like, maybe, just maybe, the army's Upper Wabash Valley Flood Control Project created cooperatively with the IFCWRC is not a done deal. Beamer wrote:

> Inasmuch as the villages of Dora and Red Bridge and the town of Somerset would have to be relocated on nearby higher ground, numerous questions have been raised in regard to the feasibility and necessity of these three high dams that are proposed by the Army Engineers. In fact, one proposal has come to me that the Soil Conservation Service experience in other areas might be of value in the Upper Wabash River area. Am I correctly informed

> that in numerous instances a series of many small dams would serve the same purpose as the three larger dams at less cost and with less permanent inundation of land?[119]

The response he gets is a pass-the-buck bureaucratese sort of letter suggesting again that it is too late to stop the IFCWRC and the US Army Corps of Engineers and the Upper Wabash Valley Flood Control Project. The alternative needed to be presented years earlier, for further study, and in discussion with the "interested parties," as administrators like to say. Maybe back in 1945.

There are instances where the small dam plan has been effective, the Soil Conservation Service's Donald Williams responded to Beamer, but "we" haven't looked at the area you are talking about. Local organizations could apply to the Department of Agriculture for study. "If the local people in Indiana desire more information concerning the assistance available under this Act," Williams wrote, "we suggest that they contact Mr. Charles E. Swain, State Conservationist, Soil Conservation Service, 215 E. New York Street, Indianapolis 4, Indiana."[120]

Beamer forwarded Williams's response to Kennedy.

This won't be the only time the "small dam" alternative is referenced by constituents opposed to the three big dams and three big reservoirs plan. In August 1955, Beamer got a postcard from A. G. Allen, a self-described farmer and high school teacher. Dams on small streams are the answer, he said, at one-tenth the cost.[121]

Beamer had forwarded the Kennedy letter to W. D. Milne at the end of September, and the army colonel's response was quick, within a week, with detail that suggests that he didn't have to search long for answers.

> It would require more than 100 small reservoirs each controlling 20 square miles of drainage area to provide the same volume of flood storage as would be provided by the three recommended reservoirs. A greater area will be flooded if reservoirs are made

> smaller because the average depth of water stored becomes smaller. Based on past experience and assuming that sites were available, cost of a system of small retention type reservoirs in the upper Wabash basin would exceed the cost of a system of large reservoirs with equivalent control. The three reservoirs recommended in the interim report are preferred over a system of small reservoirs because of lower costs and more positive control of floods than would be obtained by a system of small reservoirs.[122]

This makes a lot of sense, Vern. Also, it carries the weight of 1955 US Army authority. But none of it was documented. It referenced no study that provided the statistics cited. Nobody got a chance to question it.

Also, in this period, the pro-project public relations campaign continued. Roessler, Kellum, and Milne had a meeting with Somerset "folks" and Beamer at the high school on August 26, 1955. That elicited a note from Beamer to Milne saying, "I also hope that the people of that community can understand the problem."[123]

A travel article in the October 18, 1955, *Kokomo Tribune* about the Frances Slocum Trail mentions that Somerset and Red Bridge are headed under.[124] It's a fact, that's all.

Mrs. Charles Shelley of Huntington addressed a November 7 letter to both Mr. and Mrs. Beamer generously thanking the congressman for the Soil Conservation Service's information on the "small dam" plan. However, "the feeling we have of impending disaster still remains," she said. "Drive up some Sunday morning and see us. Our pastor is a prince."[125]

Three weeks later, Beamer told Kellum, "I want to keep everybody informed in order that there will not be too much resistance and that you perhaps can get the support that is desired."[126] My concern for the people being negatively affected by this plan is a ruse, he was telling the IFCWRC executive director, designed to deflate resistance and help the Upper Wabash Valley Flood Control Project come to fruition.

Were I still a smoker, Vern, and you could see me, you'd see me take a long drag and twist the cigarette out in my ashtray. That's what smoking was for.

Beamer appeared to have gone over to the dark side, but in 1955, many of his constituents still believed that he was their best hope, their only hope, for stopping the Upper Wabash Valley Flood Control Project. The most vocal were two of them named Funderburg.

25. REPRESENTATIVE

Cliff Funderburg was a Huntington County superintendent of schools for eighteen years and a state school board member who served one term in the state house, 1939–1941, and two terms in the state senate, 1943–1951. His nephew was Ivan Funderburg, the son of Cliff's brother. Ivan also lived in Huntington County, the location of the Huntington Reservoir and the Salamonie Reservoir, which, with the Mississinewa Reservoir of Wabash County, were designed and built by the US Army Corps of Engineers for the Upper Wabash Valley Flood Control Project in north-central Indiana. The Huntington Reservoir name would later be changed to Roush Lake for Congressman J. Edward Roush, who followed John Beamer into the Fifth District of Indiana seat in 1959.

Cliff Funderburg regarded Roush with personal animus.

The two Funderburgs corresponded meaningfully and in a personal manner with Congressman John Beamer several times between November 1955 and March 1958. On May 14, 1957, Ivan testified on his opposition to the "big dam" project before the US House of Representatives Committee on Public Works hearing on the Flood Control Act of 1957, "a bill authorizing the construction, repair, and preservation of certain public works on rivers and harbors for navigation, flood control, and other purposes." Those public works included the Upper Wabash Valley Flood Control Project. Congressman Beamer arranged Ivan's appearance.

Cliff Funderburg was a farmer, educator, and lawmaker. He was born in Huntington County in 1884, and that's where he died in 1965.

John Beamer left the farm he grew up on after he graduated from Roann High School in 1914 to attend Wabash College in Crawfordsville, one hundred miles away. After serving in the US Army as a PFC with an artillery unit during World War I, he settled back in Wabash and worked as a salesman and an executive. Immediately before he became a US congressman in 1951, Beamer served a single term in the Indiana house of representatives.

Cliff Funderburg returned to Huntington after graduating from Indiana State University in Terre Haute and doing graduate work at the universities of Michigan and Chicago. He continued to farm while working in education in his home county.

Beamer's two years in the Indiana legislature coincided with Cliff Funderburg's last two years in the Indiana senate, 1949–1950. They were both Republicans. His correspondence with both Cliff and his nephew Ivan over the contentious flood control project issue between 1955 and 1958 suggests a relationship of respect, with the strength of a friendship between people who agree to disagree but one that would end in resigned disappointment. "We can look for no help from you. You have forgotten your duties to us,"[127] Cliff would ultimately write Beamer.

The first letter to Congressman Beamer from the Funderburgs came from Ivan. It's dated November 28, 1955. That was, coincidentally, also the first of two days an Army Corps of Engineers press release set for its Rivers and Harbors Board to hear about public comments on the interim report. While the army moved the incontrovertible process forward, the people and the people's representatives sat together on the sidelines. The Funderburgs were among the people who mistakenly thought the people's representatives could still do something about it.

Ivan wrote Congressman Beamer, "Help kill the measure,"[128] when it was brought up in the next session of Congress. He called it a "useless project" that "would force us to evacuate our homes and farms." The "little Wabash was dredged several years ago to make the water flow faster," he said. "Now dams are proposed to hold the water back."

"People who live in flood prone areas knew the risk when they settled there," Ivan said. "We speak for the majority of landowners involved."

The letter included a signature from an Albert Sheets with no additional comment and a note from Ivan's mother.

"I am Ivan Funderburg's mother, Charlotte Funderburg and am hoping that through this letter that we might have some influence in avoiding what you might do to my farm and Ivan's."[129]

Before Congressman Beamer would respond on December 5 in the manner we have come to expect, that he was "looking out for the interests of everyone in the district"[130] and that there was a long way to go before the project was finalized, the Rivers and Harbors Board had finalized its November 28 hearing response.

In a December 1 letter, Colonel Milne of the Army Corps of Engineers wrote the Wabash Chamber of Commerce manager that the board "recommended the construction of the three reservoirs for flood control on the Wabash River."[131] Ivan and Cliff were just getting started, but it was already, clearly in retrospect, a done deal.

In January, Indiana governor George Craig announced his "full support" for the project, and Beamer began making inquiries with the army as to how people forced out were to be paid. Before Congress could move, Milne had told the Indiana Flood Control and Water Resources Commission in a meeting for which there are no records except for a Roessler letter to Beamer that several federal agencies had to approve. Roessler told Beamer to get busy. Beamer replied, "Be patient."

Beamer heard from Cliff Funderburg on February 14, 1956. Without needing to explain, he told Beamer that the ambitious Democrat, "young Roush, has never been defeated in an election." J. Edward Roush, the Huntington County prosecutor and the county's only elected Democrat, was running for Beamer's seat.

The "people of this district" were "not happy with having our homes and farms and work of a lifetime destroyed by these foolish and unnecessary dams," the former school superintendent said. They "want you to get that 35 million dollars for the proposed dams eliminated from the budget."[132]

There's nothing like what you are talking about in the budget, the congressman responded in a letter two weeks later.

> Cliff, I think we know each other well enough to be frank with each other, since we served together in the State legislature. I have not proposed this program nor have I opposed it at any time. At the same time, I also have told the people whose property will be damaged that I feel that they should be especially well paid if the program finally is accepted. . . . had hoped you would not bring politics into the matter. I hope we can sit down and chat.[133]

The next day, Beamer wrote the *Huntington Herald Press* editor and publisher, Howard Houghton, about Cliff. "Tell him to be a good party member. He wrote me a rather challenging letter."[134]

Cliff responded to Beamer's patronizing immediately. Handwritten. Fountain pen blue ink. Seven pages. He didn't propose a date to "chat."

> Saying you neither favor nor opposed the project? If the budget is pushed up to you with that attitude, you will then most likely vote for it, just like we used to in Indianapolis when we were confronted with a budget we hadn't help make or didn't understand.
>
> That's what we are afraid of; and that will result in ruining our beautiful country. Dam the small streams coming into the rivers. The whole thing is wrong, the propositions themselves are wrong and the rights of individuals are neither looked into or considered.[135]

A Republican Party that is philosophically opposed to government bureaucracy and wasteful spending is hypocritical on this matter, Cliff told Beamer. Schools, hospitals, and roads need financial support.

"This plan is wasteful," Cliff said. "Politics is part of this." Roush is "ambitious, vain, conceited, crazy for power and position. He's no good!! . . . You are a good man. We need your help."

It's hard not to feel a little sorry for Cliff and Ivan and the people around Somerset who were so full of energy, writing letters to their congressman and the newspapers thinking that there was something in 1956 that they could do to stop the Upper Wabash Valley Flood Control Project. It's sad to know what I know, now, about what was going on and to read the letters that signal naïveté. It signals to me the roots of today's widespread cynicism.

Beamer's follow-up letter to Cliff Funderburg refers to the October 12 Rivers and Harbors Board deadline for feedback, again erroneously and misleadingly when he says, "People should have let the Army Corps of Engineers know of opposition last October, as announced in the press. Apparently, the supporters were very active because their letters far outnumbered the protests."[136] Beamer mischaracterized the process and shifted blame to the victims. The process purposely kept opponents away.

The congressman continued to blame the victims in response to more letters about the project.

Somerset

26. MINNICK

Dear Vern,

While residents of Somerset were awakening in early 1956 to a reality that the state and federal governments were removing their homes from the map, they were shaken further March 12 by the fatal shooting of sixteen-year-old James Minnick.

The *Elwood Call-Leader* was among many statewide papers that carried the Associated Press story the next day, March 13, 1956.

> One bullet left in a gun he thought he had emptied killed a 16-year-old Somerset High School junior Monday as he waited for his cue in a class play.
>
> "Look it won't fire," James Minnick said to companions at the school after taking several shells from a .32 caliber revolver. He put the gun to his temple and pulled the trigger and it fired. He died three hours later at Marion General Hospital.
>
> Coroner Henry Alderfer ruled death was accidental. The gun was to have been used in the play but was not to have been fired.
>
> Presentation of the play, set for Friday night, was cancelled. Somerset is in Wabash County, northwest of Marion. The boy's father, Russell S.

> Minnick is principal of Gilead High School, in Miami County. The parents, a brother, and two sisters survive.[137]

"The school was a center of the community, so naturally an incident like that took a toll," longtime Somerset area resident Tom Snyder said when I reminded him about it. Tom's uncle Larry Knee graduated there that spring. "In a small community," Larry said, "a young man dying at the high school was very shocking."

In the den at Kay (Shroyer) Peas's house north of Wabash on a rainy late morning, our conversation about Vern and Somerset led to her sister, Janet Schenkel, remarking that while Kay graduated in 1962, Janet had graduated from Somerset High School a few years earlier, in 1957.

The shooting at the play, I immediately thought.

"I'm sorry," I stuttered. "But I feel like I have to ask. The shooting. The boy who was killed. At the play practice. Do you . . ."

"It was my gun," Janet said. "I was the one the sheriff interviewed when he came to investigate."

"Somewhere in the play, somebody was supposed to shoot somebody," Tom Snyder said later.

"It had a round in it," he said. "He had pulled the trigger several times and it wouldn't fire, and then he pointed the gun at his head. And it did."

Janet remembered, "We'd pulled the trigger on that gun a hundred times, and it never fired."

"When they opened it up, we didn't know it, but there was a bullet in every chamber and every bullet had an indentation to show it had been hammered," she said. "That gun never fired."

"They figured that it had to be the angle. That Jimmy had to hold it at just the exact right angle for it to fire that one time," Janet said.

What Tom knows about it, he heard from his father, Fred, whom he said was the school parent-teacher organization president.

"Dad went over there. It was outside the girls' restroom in the gym at the far end, the opposite end from the stage, where he [Jim Minnick] was showing other class members, members of the cast, the gun.

"Dad said when he got down there, there was still blood all over the gym floor in that corner."

The very next day, Janet said, they were back in school. "There weren't any grief counselors back then. We walked by a constant reminder every day. Back then," Janet said, "you sucked it up and you went on."

"I don't remember anybody even talking about not having school," Tom said.

"We did get the afternoon off for the funeral," Janet said.

Larry remembered that the funeral closed the school.

Tom told me that the Minnick family left town soon after the accident for a new home in Florida.

"Minnick," longtime Somerset resident Helen Adkins said softly when I mentioned to her the shooting at the play. She paused. "You know the house that he lived in? His mom never changed anything in that bedroom, and it was moved up to the new town and finally somebody bought it and I think probably they've done away with that room, but it was that way, they said, for years after he got killed."

Classmates "got together for lunch once a month for a number of years," Janet said, "and we've talked about how in today's world they would have brought counselors in. It was traumatic," Janet said, but "life went on. We probably could have used the counseling, but we survived." When we last spoke, she said it had been "two years since our graduating class got together. There aren't as many around here anymore."

27. OPPOSITION

Also in March of 1956, the US House of Representatives Appropriations Committee held a hearing on the public works funding for 1957 that was to include the Upper Wabash Valley Flood Control Project. In it, Congressman John Beamer testified that Indiana governor George Craig and the Indiana legislature had sent their support for the measure. Indiana Flood Control and Water Resources Commissioner Carlos Life provided the committee with a plan overview and said that the three reservoirs would hold an amount of water equal to the "worst on record"[138] 1913 flood. Huntington, Wabash, Peru, Logansport, Lafayette, Terre Haute, and Vincennes were cited as cities that would be protected.

When Beamer testified that "a very very large majority of the people in the area involved will be very much in favor of the flood control program," Appropriations Committee member T. Millet Hand, a Republican from New Jersey, continued with a question.

> Mr. Hand: Is there any substantial opposition to this project?
>
> Mr. Beamer: I would not say substantial opposition. I will say that the opposition will come, if it is termed opposition, from the people who will be relocated in this particular area. There is the village

> or town of Somerset. The entire town will have to be relocated. Some of the people are resigned to it; others welcome it, and some will raise objections.
>
> Mr. Hand: How large a community is that?
>
> Mr. Beamer: I understand it is approximately 280 people, 50 or 60 houses. Dora and Monument City, too. Small. Also water storage is part of the benefit of the program.[139]

"I would not say substantial opposition." What do you think, Vern? Would that be a better title for a book? *No Substantial Opposition.*

IFCWRC executive secretary Robert Kellum continued testifying to the committee that day that the plan would aid the region's economy. Transcontinental railroads passed through the area, he told them. "The Wabash is the last major tributary to the Ohio River which does not have flood protection and it is just as vulnerable now as it was in 1913 to serious flood damage."[140]

With that, a discussion continued off the record, and then the hearing ended.

Congressman John Beamer chose the words: "I would not say substantial opposition."

Beamer chose not to advocate that day on behalf of Lawrence Scheffer, the Wabash County "farmer, taxpayer, voter" who had written him to oppose the project back in July, as "a scheme to get a recreation center near this Slocum Park [that] is backed by conservation clubs and a few rich men who don't care for anything except a few more dollars."

Beamer chose to categorize a man as "not substantial," who had written Beamer that he "gave three of the best years of my life" to his country, "fighting in foreign lands [so] that I and others might live in peace."

"I would not say substantial opposition," Beamer said that day. Before a congressional committee. Under oath.

The next day, March 21, 1956, the *Indianapolis Star* Washington Bureau reported that the public works appropriations request included $100,000 for planning construction of "the first of three reservoirs in the Upper Wabash River Flood Control System."[141]

On March 22, there were two flood control issue letters in the *Huntington Herald Press.* One of them was from Ivan Funderburg. "Write your congressman," he wrote. It's wasteful, "all of this to benefit the residents of the lower Wabash valley who have had 43 years since the 1913 flood to move."[142]

The other came from Lucius Sheets, and when I read it, I was reminded of the subsequent writings of noted rural Kentucky writer Wendell Berry about the threat of "modern" farming techniques. It's a long letter, and in it, Sheets said, "It is a shame that so much of our topsoil is being eroded and washed away down the rivers." He blamed the federal government. "With one hand it builds dams and dikes and levies. With the other it channels and dredges and drains and ditches."

Heavy machinery is packing down the soil so tightly that water can't get through, Sheets wrote.

> If water cannot readily soak down into the sub-soil to replenish the springs, wells, and underground water supply, it runs off the top of the ground causing erosion, gullies and great loss of rich top-soil. It causes floods which would never happen if the water could go down to where it belongs. Then in dry times there is no reserve underground water to feed the springs which in turn feed the better level during the hot dry months.[143]

Sheets suggested that "implement manufacturers, politicians, Mr. Beamer, agricultural experts, Chambers of Commerce, Kiwanis and other do-gooders" are irresponsible. "Attack this pressing problem and forget about dams until this thing is solved. If it can be solved maybe we won't ever need a dam."

Why am I picturing Sheets as a quiet man who speaks only when he has something to say?

Sheets added in a quick follow-up letter March 25 that "basketball games get more press coverage."[144] The same day, the paper published an editorial saying he was wrong about that.

Cliff Funderburg sent a letter to Congressman Beamer that day quoting Louis Bromfield, a popular American writer of the 1920s and '30s, who, according to his Wikipedia page, later "became one of the earliest proponents of sustainable and organic agriculture in the United States."

"'Floods and erosion aren't stopped at the bottom of rivers but upstream in the forests, fields, and low pastures.'" Cliff quoted Bromfield's *From My Experience: The Pleasures and Miseries of Life on a Farm*, published in 1955.

In his own words, Cliff added, "The small dams plan is better. The property belongs to the people, not the bureaucracy. We do not intend to be pushed aside. No amount of money the government may give us can pay for the things taken away, homes, buildings, farms." He wrote Beamer that "we have farms to maintain" and that it was hard for people to get to Washington. The opposition from three districts was meeting on March 29, he said. "You should meet with us."[145]

That willingness to speak made Cliff Funderburg a target.

A constituent from Andrews, near Huntington, wrote to Beamer on March 26 that Funderburg was making trouble, "insulting the intelligence" of people at a meeting in Huntington. Mark Fisher wrote, "I would like to call to your attention, that a small but noisy bunch of people around Huntington are opposing the proposed construction of the Flood Control project in this area." Some bitter discussion was provoked at the courthouse last week, Andrews wrote, "by a heated, one-sided speech given by a former state senator Funderbug [*sic*]." He "even got to reciting poetry."[146]

Fisher suggested to Congressman Beamer the possibility of calling a meeting at Huntington "with some of the top brass present, especially the Army Colonel, to explain the project and answer questions. I thought that the boys did a wonderful job in their meeting at Somerset selling the dams to the people."

Beamer got a note near the end of March from *Huntington Herald Press* editor and publisher Howard Houghton that said that the letters the paper had been getting about the project were frequent and some of them were from people who were not reasonable. "Clifford is included in this category," Houghton wrote, "nor does he intend to be a good party member if that means keeping quiet."[147]

Stifling the opposition to the Upper Wabash Valley Flood Control Project continued in what appears to have been an organized fashion. There's no indication in the Beamer papers at the Indiana State Library from where the congressman gathered that he should do so, but John Beamer wrote to Carlos Life, Peru banker and founding member of the Indiana Flood Control and Water Resources Commission, after Beamer received a petition against the project from mostly Wabash and Somerset area residents. For Life, Beamer wrote, "I am enclosing a copy of the 200 names that are on the one petition in opposition to one of the reservoirs at Peoria, Indiana, for the Upper Wabash River Flood Control Program. I also have numerous letters that have been received and I shall be glad to check these at an early date, if you would like to have these additional names."[148]

He's handing over the names of citizens who oppose the project to the purveyors of the project for investigation. As a congressman, who speaks to the interest of all the people in his district in their seat in the federal government in Washington, DC. Maybe Beamer never understood the significance of his job. Volunteering letters.

The petitions and the letter-writer "additional names" are in the files in the boxes at the Indiana State Library, Vern.

The letter-writer "additional names" are on two sheets of plain paper, titled "Against" on one and "For" on the other. The names match the letters from constituents that I found elsewhere in the files in the boxes. Some I have mentioned. Dragstrem, Highly, Allen, Scheffer, and Ivan Funderburg, but no Clifford Funderburg, are among the eleven "Against." Maybe Cliff's "Against" went without saying.

Hubley and Fisher are among the five "For," but not Roessler and Life or various US Army Corps of Engineers employees. Maybe that went without saying, too.

Life wrote Beamer on April 2, 1956, to say thanks for the petitions. "I hope to contact some of these people and try to determine their reasoning. I think a great many of these names were placed on these petitions when the program was originally announced and before they learned what the full details were."

What full details were those, do you suppose, and when did "they" learn the full details, Vern?

As for the letters, Life wrote, "I don't need the letters, just the names."[149] Peru banker and IFCWRC founding member Carlos Life does not want to waste his time reading what opponents are saying.

"Just the names."

The petition signatures are on fourteen sheets of paper titled, "We the undersigned firmly oppose the proposed construction of the reservoir at Peoria, Indiana, affecting property in Miami and Wabash Counties."

It's the Peoria dam, Vern, that backed up the water over Somerset and created the Mississinewa Reservoir that's now called Lake Mississinewa.

In looking at the signatures for familiar names, I saw those of James Minnick's grieving grandparents, Lawrence Scheffer, Florence Roby, Fernie Trigalet, and Robert and Mary Shroyer, Kay and Janet's parents. The names of my parents and grandparents, aunts and uncles, are not among them. Some writing is faded and difficult to read, but I counted ninety-six signatures from Wabash, six from Peru, and thirty-two from Somerset. By Beamer's calculation, that's 18 percent of the town. No substantial opposition.

Cliff Funderburg was back in the Huntington paper with an April 4 letter that said, "We are told to relax and forget about being drowned out, while the opposition goes forward in high gear with all the force at its disposal."[150]

The tone had become more contentious.

Beamer, on April 10, wrote that supporters outnumbered project opponents "100 to 1"[151] in response to Mark Fisher's warning about the Huntington County opposition led by Cliff Funderburg. Opponents should have written earlier, Beamer said.

Life's friend, Peru attorney Frank Dice, wrote Beamer a week later, it was "2,000 to 1" in favor and no one in Somerset was opposed, and in

Huntington County it was just "Thunderburg [*sic*]" and one other person "with personal axes to grind."[152]

Dice's April 19 letter suggested that in talking to Life, he had gotten the impression Beamer was not as project supportive as he should have been. "I was shockingly amazed to hear you tell Mr. Life that if you were forced to take stand on this measure, you would oppose it. I surely trust that you will re-consider and openly support and vigorously fight for this highly desirable and imperative project for your entire district before your Democratic opponent is nominated and does so." That would be J. Edward Roush, the Huntington County prosecutor that Funderburg warned Beamer about.

A letter from Life, like that of Dice, dated April 19, creates a sense of shared conversation.

"I was very much surprised," Life wrote, "and disappointed yesterday when you advised me over the phone that if you were forced to make public statement regarding the proposed flood control program in your district that you would not endorse the plan."[153]

"Clifford Thunderbird," as Life called Funderburg, and one other Huntington County farmer were stirring up trouble, he said. "Wishing to check further on your statement that the people up and down the Wabash were organized solid against the program, there," Life wrote Beamer. "I talked with several and [was] surprised at the attitude of the people. John, these people are almost 100% for the project." The names on the "Against" petition from the Wabash and Somerset area were bogus, Life said. "Someone went around with the petition and apparently told the people a wild story that was about the way the bodies in the cemetery would be handled and persuaded the people to sign to protect the cemetery." The people who were against the big dams and reservoirs were selfish, he wrote, "the type of people who are against everything."

It's a long letter, from Life, three pages, and it closes with a threat to Beamer's political future. "I also shudder when I think what the people of this district would do to a person who would object to this project, if we should have another flood similar to the one experienced in 1913, 1937, 1943 and other years."

It's hard for me to read through the letters and notes and newspaper articles and comprehend the animosity with which Beamer is treated by Upper Wabash Valley Flood Control Project proponent leaders. He was, in fact, making it happen with them, as their representative in Congress. I said earlier that he seemed to be in the doghouse for not attending some meetings and events, like the big motorcade tour back in July of 1954. He showed concern in a newspaper article when the Army Corps of Engineers publicized the destruction of Somerset, but he didn't do anything to stop it. He publicly acknowledged the existence of plan opposition, but he downplayed it. He also often maintained publicly that he was neither for nor against the plan but that he was weighing its benefits carefully on behalf of "all" the people he represents. That sounds good, but his actions obviously belie that sentiment. Clearly, though, Life and Roessler and Kellum were on his case.

I remember again, Vern, Roessler's March 1954 address to the IFCWRC when he said that matters had been settled, that it was time to move past the details and let the engineers have that, that the present time was for project promotion, that the commission should inform members of Congress of its benefits, and that members of Congress should do what the IFCWRC told them to do. And what they should be doing was funding the plan.

I think Beamer's problem, in their eyes, was that he wasn't campaigning for the project. They wanted someone who would, as Roessler had put it, "graduate from the matters of preparation to the acts of accomplishment and these acts require broad policy, sound salesmanship and good publicity." They wanted Beamer to campaign for them. In their eyes, the time for debate had passed. For the Funderburgs and the two hundred people who voiced their concerns in letters and petitions, no debate had ever occurred.

Vern

28. A '57 CHEVY

Dear Vern,

Your grandma Shroyer lost relatives in the Holocaust from both sides of her father Ray Firestein's family. Since I came to live the rest of my life with her in 1975, I've found that most of the Jews I meet have similar lineage. When I was at New Prairie High School, a big step I had to take in teaching the Holocaust was in conveying the fact that the perpetrators were humans, too. It's not an easy lesson, but if we only see ourselves as the good guys in the story, in history, we will not learn.

I got to ride in our green 1957 Chevy that replaced the gray-blue '53 model before Stan and Linda did because they were in school. That would have been a fall day in 1956 not long after the nationwide excitement of new car models in magazines and showrooms. Maybe Nat King Cole or some news about the Montgomery bus boycott was on the radio, or maybe there was talk about the court order that desegregated Marion's Matter Park swimming pool. I remember it as the day when Mom leaned back over the passenger seat as we drove past Lincoln Elementary and told me that by moving out to the country I wouldn't have to go to school with "colored" children. A new car makes people feel superior. Vern was driving.

A bad thing we learned from Vern growing up was to keep our mouths shut when we should have said something. I would have remembered if he had said something then, even though I was only three years old. Maybe he said something to Mom later.

What I came to know about us seems to have come mostly from what my brother told me that Mom had told him. One time, he told me about when Vern was in the service at Fort Worth, Texas. Your great-uncle Stan said that a comrade who invited Vern home for some friendly homestyle Texas cooking attacked an African American man walking down the street because the "colored" man didn't pay them the proper deference. I don't know the attack specifics. I bet it was ugly. I don't know how best to characterize the man I love dearly or if there ever really is such a thing as a "bystander."

I do know from my own experience that Vern hated Texas. Irrationally.

Or maybe not irrationally.

"Nothing good ever comes from Texas," he'd say, and that was even before President Kennedy was ambushed in Dallas. Loudmouthed bullies. Self-serving, self-satisfied bigots. Lying politicians. Big shots.

Say "Texas" and watch what happens.

Maybe he carried around some disappointment in himself that he associated with Texas. He didn't say anything to me about what Mom said to me, in the car, that day when I was three, about Black people as we drove by Lincoln School. I would have remembered it. I remember what Mom said. Maybe he said something later when I wasn't around. Maybe he held it against her and didn't say anything to anybody, ever. Maybe he held it against himself.

Like you, Vern, the man who shares your name was not perfect. Be conscious. "In the end, we will remember not the words of our enemies, but the silence of our friends." Martin Luther King Jr. said that.

I told you already that, when I was a kid, there was no greater day for me than the day every summer when we went to Amboy for the Arrick family reunion. I have a picture that shows the Arrick reunion at Matter Park in Marion from two years before I was born, but I only remember it being in Amboy. I don't know why they moved it. Amboy is ten miles southwest of Somerset, just a little closer than Marion. Amboy is a little place like Somerset. It seemed to me that when we were there, we pretty much had the park to ourselves. Marion was probably a lot more crowded. Maybe Amboy was closer to where more people in our family lived.

Maybe we moved the reunion because the swimming pool had been desegregated by a court order in 1954. That's possible. I'm not really part of "we" yet, Vern. I was born in 1953. "We" fits, though.

The 1951 reunion picture shows that "we" didn't seem to have any problem being there when it was segregated. People look happy. Some cities in America filled in their pools with concrete after they were desegregated. I know that from reading a book called *The Sum of Us* by Heather McGhee.[154]

Marion—well, the whole area I grew up in really, Vern—was racist. Maybe that "whole area" is the United States of America. We like to think the bad stuff in history was somebody else and someplace else, but it's us and it's here. Two men were lynched on the courthouse lawn in Marion in August of 1930, and no one was ever held accountable. None of that was taught to us in school in Grant County, Indiana. Many perpetrators of that act came from Green Township, but that didn't keep Vern and Patty from moving us there from Marion in 1957. There's a book called *Our Town* by Cynthia Carr that I gave to your dad. You have to read it. Most people who lynched Thomas Shipp and Abram Smith were still around in 1957. Twenty-seven years ago is nothing, now, to me, in my old age.

It's possible that the utter joy I felt in Amboy is connected to some awful shit. Maybe the Arrick clan just wanted to avoid the chance that there could be "trouble," more "trouble," in Marion. Maybe some of them let some others know they didn't want to be around colored folks. Maybe some others accommodated their relatives' racism. I wasn't born yet.

I visited the Bergen-Belsen concentration camp memorial grounds with a group of twenty-five American Holocaust educators in 2010. That's where Anne Frank and her sister, Margot, perished in 1945. Fifty thousand other Jews, Sinti, and so-called anti-social elements . . . "others" . . . died, too, at that camp . . . people . . . from places like the Netherlands, Greece, and Poland . . . Earth. Carola Rudnick was among several German educators we met with that day, July 13, 2010, and she told us, "We are not responsible for the Holocaust. We were not born yet. But"—Carola Rudnick said this to us from inside the Bergen-Belsen commemoration museum building in a moment I will never forget—"our fathers and grandfathers were perpetrators. The younger generation is not to blame, but they do have a great responsibility to acknowledge and to teach."

I wasn't born yet when the Arrick reunion was held in 1951 in a park where people who were called "colored" weren't allowed to swim in the "public" pool. I know we swam in a segregated gravel-pit members-only "club" pool three miles from my house, though, for years after that, without giving it a second thought. I wasn't around when two men were lynched on the Grant County Courthouse lawn in Marion in 1930. But I know the perpetrators organized themselves not far from where I later lived.

What Carola Rudnick said to me that day made a lot of sense.

Flood

29. CONSCIENTIOUS OBJECTION

Dear Vern,

Your great-grandfather Vern Shroyer was in charge of everything. But he was never in the house very much.

In 1956, we lived in a three-bedroom bungalow on Butler Avenue, a little residential street in Marion, walkable, just a few blocks from the Malleable iron foundry and a few blocks from Lincoln School and a few blocks from the A&W root beer stand on Baldwin Avenue. It was when Vern added an attached one-car garage to that house that he learned he could build an entire house if he wanted to.

Vern was among the first workers hired when the General Motors Fisher Body plant opened in November of 1956. He'd learned to weld at the Malleable, so with that, he hired on as a skilled laborer in a United Auto Workers shop, a big step up. "He quit the Malleable before General Motors was finished," my sister, Linda, told me. "He helped build the plant. He thought if he was working there, he would get a job quicker. He was like number ten to be hired. He was there the day they started hiring. It was a job to make money so we could have it better."

"Vern was a very, very hard worker, very hard worker," Uncle Wayne told me. "He was dedicated to whatever job he had."

Even so, my brother, Stan, said, "He hated the factory. He didn't like having a boss." He didn't want to be a boss, either, so he turned down chances to be a foreman. Stan said, "He kind of resented it, but it was the best way he could make a living. The last thing he ever wanted to see was one of his kids in that factory.

"It was a mystery to me. He would go in there and come home. You never heard nothin' about it. What does he do there all day long? He didn't speak about it; he didn't care to."

The bigger-is-better forces of postwar American industrialization that drove folks like Vern off the farm and into factories in cities and towns closed small-town community schools, too. Students in little three-story brick high schools in towns like Swayzee and Fairmount and Converse and Somerset would be left behind by students in consolidated school districts with vague names like Oak Hill and Southwood and Eastern.

By 1956, it was clear that all the small-town schools near Marion would soon disappear, and so Vern and Patty began making plans to kill two birds with one stone, move us away from the urban jungle and take us close to where one of these brand-new sparkling white consolidated schools would be built. Plans to unite Franklin, Sims, Liberty, and Green, the four remotest townships in Grant County, into one school district were to include a high school in or near a little town called Cole.

We moved to Normal, another tiny town, around twenty-five people, five homes, a church, and a country store with gas pumps, three miles away from Cole. Not too close.

An article in the *Marion Chronicle-Tribune* on January 8, 1956, had informed the public that the Indiana Flood Control and Water Resources Commission and Governor George Craig approved the Upper Wabash Valley Flood Control Project. We'd advised the Army Corps of Engineers, commission vice chairman Ralph Roessler told the paper, and now it "awaits the approval of Congress."[155] According to Roessler, the article says, Congressman John Beamer had given the project his "full support." The article prompted Edward Keefer of Wabash to query Beamer by mail:

> Why didn't you state these facts when you were in Somerset with the army engineers [Aug. 26, 1955].

> Because of this all our homes will be taken away. They say that the government will pay assessed value for the properties, but some of the homes can't be bought that cheap. It seems we that have homes there don't have much to say about it. Does the leaders in Washington know more about what we want than we the people of Somerset? If you will I would like for you to vote against the dam.[156]

"Can you send me the article in the Marion paper?" Beamer responded. "I never have expressed myself in support of the Upper Wabash River flood control program."[157]

Beamer.

When Beamer responded on March 12 to a letter approving the plan, he wrote W. R. Jones of Lagro that he was "pleased to have your letter in support of the plan,"[158] adding that there was not a lot that could be done as the proposed project worked its way through the bureaucracy.

In April, the congressman privately wrote *Huntington Herald Press* editor and publisher Howard Houghton to quit publishing letters about the project. "Letters don't make a difference," he said on April 9. "They only hurt me."[159]

Also that day, Beamer wrote founding member Carlos Life that his IFCWRC needed to issue a report that countered the "small dam" plan argument.[160] Beamer had had that information already himself since the prior October from Army Corps of Engineers colonel W. D. Milne. I suppose Life would have liked Beamer to forward that information to the public more broadly himself, to forward what Milne had said, that "the three reservoirs recommended in the interim report are preferred over a system of small reservoirs because of lower costs and more positive control of floods than would be obtained by a system of small reservoirs."[161]

Assemble the press, hand out Milne's response, and the "small dams" Funderburg-Kennedy argument would take a big hit. I wonder why Kellum, Life, and Roessler didn't do that, as well. Perhaps they wondered if it might create questions that they did not want to answer about from whom, what, where, when, why, and how that position came.

Cliff Funderburg returned to the fray with an April 22 letter to Beamer that said, "Our only hope is Congress and the Legislature."[162] A three-county group will discuss the matter with candidates for the state legislature, he wrote, and then returned to his flood prevention solutions: "small dams, reforestation, conservation, reclamation. Winter and spring flooding is part of the cycle," he said, that actually improves the soil's condition.

"The few families living in shacks on the river banks move out and back in with no apparent loss of any kind," Cliff Funderburg wrote. "You didn't build or buy your house on the riverbank and I didn't either."

Wabash County historian Ron Woodward told me, "There were always floods that severely damaged property along the riverfronts," and I'd heard about that annual flooding from Tom Snyder, the man who called my great-aunt Vernie "Grams." Aunt Vernie and her husband John Knee owned the Riverside Resort, across the road from Pop's, the man Tom called "Uncle Charley."

"There was flooding every year," Tom said. "Riverside Resort was flooded maybe two or three times in some years. A lot of the cabins were flooded every year. River water ran through the cabins every year. The people would come back. They'd get shovels and shovel the mud out. Every weekend they'd show up again.

"Homes down there at Red Bridge, maybe seven miles from Somerset, flooded all the time. There were farms and homes all along the Mississinewa River, and they would flood. There would be some flooding every spring somewhere along the river. Farmers' fields would flood. People had built homes on the river-bottom side, away from the big hill, and them homes was always getting flooded.

"Dad was smart enough not to build a house in the river bottom," Tom said. "We didn't flood."

Cliff Funderburg concluded his April 22, 1956, letter to Congressman Beamer with a poem. Maybe it was the poem Mark Fisher of Andrews was complaining that Funderburg "got to reciting" at the Huntington County Courthouse meeting the month before.

Cliff, the man who served eighteen years as superintendent of Huntington County schools, wrote the congressman from Roann, "Reread

Goldsmith's Deserted Village. Do you remember?"

> Ill fares the land, to hastening ills a prey,
> Where wealth accumulates and men decay;
> Princes and Lords may flourish or may fade;
> (ours are congressmen)
> A breath can make them as a breath has made:
> (ours get in by vote)
> But a bold peasantry, their country's pride
> When once destroyed, can never be supplied.[163]

When Once Destroyed is a better title, Vern.

Wikipedia says, "Oliver Goldsmith published ['Deserted Village'] in 1770. It is a work of social commentary and condemns rural depopulation and the pursuit of excessive wealth."[164]

Eight days later, Cliff Funderburg sent what he meant to be his last letter to Congressman Beamer. "I don't expect to write you any more regarding the proposed dams," he said. "I'm convinced in your letters that we can look for no help from you. The dams to this wonderful country will be as destructive as war; and someday you'll see it; but now you have your mind filled with other interests; and if you ever knew, have forgotten your duties to us."[165]

Standing apart from the convenient conventional wisdom of his contemporaries, Cliff Funderburg saw what was coming. That reminds me of Dad.

Cliff would write Beamer one more time, almost two years later, a familiar one-page handwritten note dated March 14, 1958, from Rural Route 5, Huntington, Indiana. He told the congressman that his support for "the big dams planned for this region" aligned him with "certain interests downstream desiring a flushing system for city sewage."[166] A "wicked scheme," he called it.

Seven years after that, when the project news was dedication ceremonies, the most prominent opponent of the Upper Wabash Valley Flood Control Project was murdered. Huntington County community leader Cliff Funderburg was shot and killed in his home on August 24, 1965.

Twenty-year-old Carl Sanderson told police he shot Cliff twice after Cliff "said something" as he discovered Sanderson in the Funderburg kitchen.[167] Sanderson was running from a killing in California and reportedly told police he had come to Huntington County to pick tomatoes. The cops captured him with Funderburg's stolen car and found Cliff's body when they went to tell him they'd found his automobile.

Seven years after his last letter to Congressman Beamer, Cliff Funderburg was shot and killed in his own home because he "said something," made himself a target, to an intruder.

30. BIG WHEELS

In 1956, Congressman John Beamer had reason to feel isolated. He was being criticized from both sides of a single issue by people who believed that his voice mattered. He believed that it did not.

Both sides supported flood control. The voices supporting the Upper Wabash Valley Flood Control Project were united and highly organized with a concisely articulated simple argument: no "big dams" means more floods. The voices against weren't well organized, but they made two points: it's wrong to take away people's homes and the small dams plan is better. Both sides wanted their congressman to help them.

It was on April 9, 1956, that Beamer had written privately to Howard Houghton, the *Huntington Herald Press* editor and publisher, pleading with him to quit publishing letters about the project. They "only hurt me. I'm one vote in Congress," he wrote, as if to say, "Only one, that's all," that he had no significant power. All the back-and-forth is theater, much ado about nothing, I believe he understood. "Let me be that I am and seek not to alter me."[168] The play's ending has been written: "Leave me alone."

Up on stage right then, in the spring of 1956, the conflict between Congressman John Beamer and the Indiana Flood Control and Water Resources Commission grew. Along with lacking commission records, I don't have extensive notes and correspondence from Carlos Life, a commission member, or Robert Kellum, its executive secretary. I don't know what kind of letters they were getting. I don't have a record of their phone calls. I don't know what kind of messages were going back and forth between the commission and the Army Corps of Engineers officers like Colonel W. D. Milne. For 1956, I'm working from newspaper articles and the preserved papers of Congressman Beamer and jeweler Ralph Roessler, the Marion, Indiana, Kiwanis Club member who would come to be called the "Father of the Mississinewa Reservoir."

Here's what I can say. Beamer responded to a Carlos Life four-page, single-spaced, scathing, and even threatening denouncement letter of April 19, 1956, with, "I did not tell you over the telephone that I would not endorse the plan. I told you that it was unwise to try to force or pressure the Congress or any of its committees into adoption of this proposal. You have a selling job to do, and I shall continue to help you sell it."[169]

That day, too, Beamer wrote Kellum, telling him to have Life call off the dogs. "Bob, can you prevail on our good friend, Carlos Life, to be patient," he wrote on April 21. "He has had several people write and telephone me with the implication that I was not helping on this case, and this is not true." I'm helping, he said, and still waiting for the Army Corps of Engineers to submit to the Public Works Committee. "I could list many more things that I have done in behalf of this measure during the last six years, but I always prefer to do a good job without fanfare and publicity. In this instance, that procedure is so vital because I do not believe that you want to continue to stir up opposition of any kind."[170]

The congressman's strategy is clear: pay lip service to the opposition while working in the background for the project without stirring up "trouble." If anybody deserved to be mad at Beamer, it was the community members who opposed the flood control project. I suppose they would have been more so if they had seen these letters.

On stage left, Cliff Funderburg could see it. He was finished, by the end of April 1956, with Beamer, but others, like his nephew Ivan, would continue to believe that winning their righteous battle was only a matter of making their case with their representative in Washington, DC.

As I read the letters and I know what's coming, I feel bad for Ivan. And others.

In the last week of April 1956, C. A. Kessler of Wabash wrote the congressman that he hoped Beamer would vote against flooding Somerset, ruining the town and surrounding area. "Homes, churches, schools, lodges, cemeteries, community interests" are at risk, he said, adding that Peru interests are selfish. "There is hardly a family in Waltz Twp. that doesn't have relatives buried in the cemeteries you have to move. Desecration."[171]

The duplicitous nature of Beamer's response, in light of his notes to Life and Kellum, is never clearer. I share your concerns, he told Kessler, but it's not time to vote on it yet. It's "not included in this year's budget."[172]

That's what he told the owner of Somerset Hardware, Gene Smith, May 10. "Gene, I have always felt that it is the job of a representative in Congress to represent everybody instead of taking a definite stand on issues that are not at the stage of requiring a final or definite action."[173]

Smith had called the Upper Wabash Valley Flood Control Project a "pointless program with [the] aim of creating [a] recreational area" that the general population called wasteful and unnecessary. He called Roessler and Peru mayor John Devine "fanatics."[174]

No substantial opposition.

While the sanguine letters from constituents to Beamer persisted, the practical procedural action of bureaucracy continued unabated. Things were moving along, but Kellum, Life, and Roessler remained impatient. Colonel Milne had told an IFCWRC meeting back in January 1956 to move quickly or risk the project, according to a Roessler letter to Beamer later that month.[175] In a May 22 telegram, Life asked Beamer if there was "any money for our project in the public works appropriation bill submitted to Congress yesterday."[176]

"No,"[177] Beamer telegrammed back that day, adding in a later letter to the three of them that the "Upper Wabash Project was not ready for action by Appropriations. Corps of Engineers awaiting report from Budget Bureau and must submit report to Public Works Committee for approval before any action can be taken by the Appropriations Committee."[178]

I'm working on it, he told them, and will keep you informed. "I shall continue to work for this program," Beamer said.

On May 31, it was citizen Roessler who let Congressman Beamer know that the "Bureau of the Budget has passed the proposal to the Public Works Committee of Congress, and we are assured that early action may be expected."[179] He added that approval would be "good for your reelection." In an aside, Roessler said that Beamer should tell those Huntington County people that their water supply is dependent on the project. And, Roessler said, let me know if I can help, but quietly.

While Beamer had been urging patience on the House side, there was quicker action in the Senate. He telegrammed Kellum, Life, and Roessler July 24, 1956, that the "Senate Public Works Committee approved authorization of Upper Wabash Project to be included in omnibus bill. Attempts being made to get it to Senate floor today."[180]

That prompted action in the House, as well, as the *Kokomo Tribune* reported July 28, 1956. Representatives completed congressional action on the $45 million Upper Wabash Valley Flood Control Project after it was added to an omnibus bill by the Senate and the bill had been sent to the president for signing. There was money in the legislation for the Mississinewa, Salamonie, and Huntington dams and reservoirs, the story said.[181] The next day's *South Bend Tribune* called it a $45.5 million project "getting over congressional hurdles before adjournment."[182]

But there was too much wasteful spending in the omnibus bill, according to President Dwight Eisenhower. He vetoed it. The Upper Wabash Valley Flood Control Project was not what the president had objected to, however. According to the August 11, 1956, *Indianapolis Star*, the president sent a telegram to Indiana senator Homer Capehart saying that it should be approved when Congress reconvened in January.[183]

The *Star* article provided a good rundown of approvals the Upper Wabash Valley Flood Control Project had gotten so far: governors of Indiana and Illinois; the Agriculture and Interior Departments; the Department of Health, Education, and Welfare; the Bureau of the Budget; and the Federal Power Commission. And it had won recommendation by the United States Army Corps of Engineers, the guys who created it. For the rest of August, September, and October 1956, there's nothing in the files, Vern. No letters to Beamer, no notes from Roessler, no newspaper articles, and no notices from the army or the IFCWRC. Congress was recessed for election season.

31. SMALL DAMS

While the Upper Wabash Valley Flood Control Project moved forward through the practical bureaucratic procedure of 1956, a theater of negative public opinion continued on two other tracks. One of those tracks was the impact the three big dams and reservoirs would have on the people who lived on the land the project would cover. The other track was the idea that while controlling floods is a good idea, there's a better way to do it. That was the "small dam" plan. That's the plan that was brought to the attention of Congressman Beamer in June of 1955 by Wabash Circuit Court judge Byron Kennedy. Kennedy referred Beamer to the "philosophy of engineers of the Soil Conservation Service, who contend that flooding can and should be controlled in the upper reaches of the drainage areas where the rain falls and before it reaches the rivers and streams."[184] Primarily, that would be with smaller dams, he said.

To his credit, Vern, Beamer pursued answers to the question that Judge Kennedy raised. It was a few days after the initial letter from him, on June 11, 1955, that Beamer wrote to Donald A. Williams of the Department of Agriculture's Soil Conservation Service in Washington, DC.

> Inasmuch as the villages of Dora and Red Bridge and the town of Somerset would have to be relocated on nearby higher ground, numerous questions have been raised in regard to the feasibility and necessity of these three high dams that are proposed by the

> Army Engineers. In fact, one proposal has come to me that the Soil Conservation Service experience in other areas might be of value in the Upper Wabash River area. Am I correctly informed that in numerous instances a series of many small dams would serve the same purpose as the three larger dams at less cost and with less permanent inundation of land?[185]

Williams responded on June 21, 1955, that his agency "has not undertaken detailed surveys in the Upper Wabash River area for the purpose of investigating the need and desirability for flood control work."[186] That means, he said, the Soil Conservation Service has nothing to say about what the army is doing there. He wrote Beamer that in seventy-one places around the country, there were watershed programs underway "for soil and water conservation and the reduction of floodwater and sediment damages on watersheds and tributary streams."

You'd have to have asked for that, though, Williams said.

As a matter of fact, Williams said, here's somebody you can talk to if you should want to check into how to get into a program like that: "Mr. Charles E. Swain, State Conservationist, Soil Conservation Service, 215 E. New York Street, Indianapolis 4, Indiana."

That would have been a forty-minute walk from the offices of Robert Kellum, Indiana Flood Control and Water Resources Commission executive director, on the third floor of the State Board of Health Building, 1330 West Michigan Street, Indianapolis. A forty-minute walk is a lot to ask. Indianapolis can be cold. Indianapolis can be hot. Kellum probably would have been more likely to make the seven-minute drive at some point in the 6,307,200 minutes between 1943 and 1955.

It's important that I mention, Vern, that Williams wrote Beamer that while "the installation of floodwater retarding structures in tributary areas as part of these [Department of Agriculture] programs has demonstrated their effectiveness in reducing floodwater and sediment damages, we do not wish to imply that small floodwater retarding structures are a substitute for large dams on major streams. The small structures are most effective," Williams wrote, "in the small tributary areas of watersheds."

Perhaps there might have been a place for a combination of both the small and big dam plans—that is, if someone from the IFCWRC had checked into it. Perhaps someone did.

Beamer passed the Williams note to Judge Kennedy and two days later wrote constituent Fernie Trigalet, "I certainly agree with you that this entire matter should be resurveyed and reconsidered before any such drastic moves are made as proposed by the Corps of Engineers."[187]

Did Beamer not have the small dams plan in mind when, in the note to Trigalet, he said, "The proposals about which you have read in the newspapers are only those that have been offered by the Corps of Engineers"?

Beamer said it. It's not the only plan; it's the only plan offered by the army. There's another way, one that is not the army way. "I certainly agree with you that this entire matter should be resurveyed and reconsidered before any such drastic moves are made as proposed by the Corps of Engineers." That's what Congressman Beamer said. And, he called the army plan "drastic." Beamer. "An enigma wrapped in a riddle inside a puzzle that smells like an onion on top of a ladder." Is that it, Vern?

Beamer had received the postcard note dated August 29, 1955, from A. G. Allen, the self-described farmer and high school teacher, that said dams on small streams were the answer, at one-tenth the cost.

It was a month later, in September 1955, that Beamer queried Army Corps of Engineers colonel W. D. Milne, why not the small dams "as recommended by [the] soil conservation service in other areas instead of three large dams?"[188]

That's when Milne responded, on October 3, without providing Beamer with evidence or evidence of evidence, that it simply wasn't feasible. The army must have considered it, studied it, but when? And what did they discover? How did they discover it? That information was and is simply not available. The army said it wasn't feasible. It was, therefore, not feasible. My Freedom of Information Act request revealed nothing.

Cliff Funderburg tried to keep the idea alive. The former state legislator and longtime school superintendent from Huntington County had mentioned the "small dams" plan five months after Milne's response to

Beamer in a letter to Beamer dated February 29, 1956. "Dam the small streams coming into the rivers," Cliff said. And after meetings with plan opponents, the elder Funderburg returned to the idea in his next Beamer letter in March. That's the one in which he quoted the conservationist writer Louis Bromfield. Bromfield said, "Floods and erosion aren't stopped at the bottom of rivers but upstream in the forests, fields, and low pastures."

It was after he got another small dams constituent letter on April 2, 1956, that Beamer wrote commission member Carlos Life that the IFCWRC needed to write a report on the small dam idea to "satisfy objectors." There would be no report, though, only the letter from Kellum to Beamer that sounded a lot like Milne's undocumented report to Beamer from back in October 1955.

The next small dams plan mention in the Beamer file appears in a letter dated June 6, 1956. Eight months after Colonel Milne had dismissed the idea, Beamer was still giving it some thought. He'd gotten in touch with Gladwin Young, deputy administrator of the Soil Conservation Service of the Department of Agriculture. The Soil Conservation Service was being touted by small dam proponents as the agency that could make that happen, a sort of lightweight competitor to the United States Army Corps of Engineers. Young wrote,

> This is in further reference to your recent phone call regarding the proposed Corps of Engineers' project on the Upper Wabash River in Indiana.
>
> We have reviewed that proposal and find that the project is designed to protect several cities and towns from major floods. In providing this flood protection, of course, certain valley lands in reservoir sites will be flooded. The Soil Conservation Service administers a program of watershed protection and flood prevention which is directed toward protecting the bottom lands and property on the small tributary streams of the major rivers from

> flood damage. This program is just getting under way under the Watershed Protection and Flood Prevention Act which was passed less than two years ago. It could not be looked upon as a substitute for major dams which the Corps of Engineers is authorized to build.
>
> No watershed surveys have yet been made in the tributaries of the Wabash River under authority of the Watershed Act. We undertake such surveys only at the request of soil conservation districts or other legally organized groups responsible for flood prevention and soil and water conservation.
>
> I am enclosing some publications which explain the program authorized in this new Act and how assistance may be obtained under it.[189]

Young's letter referred to the Watershed Protection and Flood Prevention Act that Congress approved on August 4, 1954. It "authorized the Secretary of Agriculture to cooperate with States and local agencies in the planning and carrying out of works of improvement for soil conservation, and for other purposes."[190] Watershed surveys had been the federal government's responsibility before the new law, which repealed a 1936 act that itself included "conferring authority upon the Department of Agriculture to make preliminary examinations and surveys and to prosecute works of improvement for runoff and waterflow retardation and soil erosion prevention on the watersheds of rivers and other waterways."[191] The new law didn't create the avenue for investigating a small dam plan; it changed by whom it could be done. The opportunity to pursue the idea had been there already. Donald Williams had made that clear in his letter to Beamer a year earlier, when he said watershed programs had been authorized by another law, the Flood Control Act of 1944. Both Williams and Young carefully clarified that someone, though, would have to ask about the programs. The IFCWRC was most certainly entitled to ask.

Young's response to a Congressman Beamer phone call came a year after Beamer's initial inquiry on behalf of Judge Kennedy. It was thirteen years after an initial indication that the small dams plan was out there.

That's clear by virtue of Ralph Roessler's note-keeping. By his own account, the Marion jeweler, Kiwanis Club member, UWVFCP originator, and IFCWRC founding member made it clear in a report for the then-new IFCWRC. Roessler gave that report to a January 1945 Army Corps of Engineers' "public hearing." Roessler told the hearing that in the "spring of 1943 this territory suffered another very disastrous flood." As a result, the Upper Wabash River Association formed and soon joined with a Lower Wabash River Association to create a statewide group to promote flood control. Roessler said,

> Work was immediately started by these men to further interest on the part of the federal Government in the need of a more unified program for the entire valley or the tributaries of the Upper Wabash.
>
> This action was based upon the idea that the problem of flood prevention and control was one of wide ramifications, taking in not only the construction of levees, the widening or deepening of channels, but that it could be made most effective by a general plan of detention and retention, of conservation as well as protection, of the creation of many small reservoirs at head waters, as well as larger ones nearer outlets, and conservation by including soil erosion prevention.[192]

On August 9, 1943, "the creation of many small reservoirs at head waters" was in the mix. But in both Williams's June 21, 1955, letter and Young's June 6, 1956, letter, there's no indication they knew that anyone involved in the Upper Wabash Valley Flood Control Project had ever pursued it.

Like Williams's, Young's language was cautious and hardly arguable. The flood control project, he said, "is designed to protect" localities from "major floods." A watershed protection plan administered by the Soil Conservation Service would not substitute for the "major dams the Corps of Engineers is authorized to build," he wrote. Williams had said the same thing a year before. Fair enough, but would it have made sense, as part of a program of flood control, to include "the creation of many small reservoirs at head waters, as well as larger ones nearer outlets, and conservation by including soil erosion prevention" and levees and channel dredging? That's Roessler's 1943 notion. It turns out that even within the IFCWRC, the Ralph of 1943 was not alone. For a little while, anyway, Vern.

Back in October of 1946, at a meeting between the Army Corps of Engineers and the Indiana Flood Control and Water Resources Commission, IFCWRC chief engineer David H. Harker said that along with sites for reservoirs, "sites had been found which could store inches of rain and provide flood control barriers for many areas. 'If these sites can be utilized to the fullest extent . . . less expensive local protective works will be required.'"[193]

Harker told the Indiana Academy of Sciences in 1947 that "our Commission feels that, for Indiana's sake, we need smaller reservoirs farther upstream."[194] The commission, he told them, "has come to the conclusion" that "remedial measures for floods must fall into four categories." He included soil conservation and reforestation, and flood walls and levees, and dams and reservoirs, and channel improvements. As for the big dam projects, Harker told the meeting of scientists in 1947,

> The U. S. Corps of Engineers has had a comprehensive plan in mind for the midwest for a number of years which was to include many reservoirs, some of them quite large. Two of these reservoirs were recommended by the District Office at Louisville in its Wabash Basin report. In the federal plan they are fine and, personally, I have no doubt that they are needed downstream. However, there was considerable local opposition to these two projects and they

> were finally deleted from the plans by the National Board of Review and the Chief of Engineers. Our Commission feels that, for Indiana's sake, we need smaller reservoirs farther upstream.[195]

"The Father of the Mississinewa Reservoir," Ralph Roessler, does not include any communication or comments about Harker's position in his papers and extensive project diary notes at the Indiana State Library. Harker was gone before John Beamer became a congressman, having resigned as IFCWRC chief engineer in February 1949. According to the February 27, 1949, *Indianapolis Star* article, "David H. Harker Heads Drainage Association," Harker "said he thought the position might become a political football." He became Indiana Drainage Association head that month, "to seek passage of flood control laws by the legislature."

Without leaving a record of why, the IFCWRC had decided by 1950 that instead of finding a balance among its own four strategies as noted by Harker, or the five strategies outlined by Roessler back in 1943, the Upper Wabash Valley Flood Control Project would settle on one. The army had the money. The army was not into small potatoes. It would be big dams and big reservoirs, or it would be floods.

When in 1954, according to Roessler's address to the commission, it came time to sell it, that's how it would be sold.

Vern

32. NORMAL

Dear Vern,

My first memory of Normal is that of Vern carrying me above the overgrown grass in the yard we were about to buy. It must have been the summer of 1957, when I was four.

My brother said, "I remember going out there and them showing it to us." Stan was six. "It was completely overgrown as I remember. It had to be cut down. Dead weeds. It was hot. We had to cut it down. I remember that."

Later, I would discover two cherry trees and a rhubarb bush with grab-and-eats in the yard. All the chipped and peeling buildings needed paint, but they were coming down, so they never got it. Along with the two-story house and the barn were a garage, three outbuildings, an outhouse, and a picket fence. What living there would mean could not have been even remotely clear to me. All I could have wanted would have been that it made my parents happy. My sister, Linda, was ten years old, so she would have understood the ramifications. She had friends in the sixth grade of an elementary school that was close enough to walk to, teachers who liked her, her own room, and a toilet inside the house. Only once, from then, and in all the years after, have I heard her say what that house meant to her. Sixty years later, she said, "I hated that house."

She added, "Living in that house was an adventure. It was so primitive." I never saw Linda take our parents to task, though, for the move.

"From the get-go, Dad told us he was going to build a new one," she said. "They asked me if I wanted to move because I was the oldest. It was moving out of the sixth grade in Marion and going to Green Township school. They explained to me the things I would be giving up but that others would be added to my life, how much my life was going to change. It would be a country school. I wouldn't have to go to junior high. I'd have more space. I remember the downside was I wouldn't be able to get a job. If we stayed in Marion, I could get a job when I was old enough to work. I felt grown up that I was asked. I said, 'Yeah, let's do it.'"

What I thought I heard in the '57 Chevy while she was in school did not register with Linda at all. "They did not tell us we would not have to go to school with African American kids, absolutely not. Just the opposite. I had a birthday party before we moved in sixth grade, and Ronald and Donald, the two Black kids in my class, were there. We were in class together from kindergarten up.

"I knew, too, that there were plans to build a new consolidated high school at Coles Station, which was about three miles from where we were moving," Linda said. "Sims and Franklin and Liberty and Green Townships would have a central high school right there. And a junior high and one grade school, which would have been fabulous. That would have been so much easier than living in that house with the constant chaos of not knowing what school you were going to go to." When the Coles Station school idea collapsed, we were on the outer reaches of three other school districts.

Linda graduated from Fairmount High School in 1964 and in three years graduated from Ball State, the college that Vern had dropped out of in 1935. "Dad wanted me to be a secretary. He wanted me to take business courses. We had a discussion. I was a freshman or sophomore in high school, and I said I wanted to teach, and my mother, for once in her life, agreed with me, and Dad said, 'Yes,' and he started saving money right then for me to go." Linda taught third grade for forty-two years. Dad worked a lot of seven-day weeks and third shift because it paid better.

Flood

33. IN PLAY

Dear Vern,

This is a rather long account of what happened to Huntington County farmer Ivan Funderburg in the course of his appearance before a congressional committee considering the Upper Wabash Flood Control Project. So I've divided it into five segments.

1.

In May 1956, Cliff Funderburg's nemesis, Huntington County prosecutor J. Edward Roush, lost the Democratic Fifth District congressional primary to Anderson attorney William Whitehead by four thousand votes. Republican congressman John Beamer then defeated Whitehead by 13 percentage points in November's general election. A few days before winning his fourth term, Beamer got a copy of a letter that was sent to Ivan Funderburg, Cliff's nephew, from Congressman J. Harry McGregor, a long-serving Ohio Republican. McGregor was a World War I veteran who, like Cliff, had been a local school leader and a state legislator before he entered Congress in 1941. McGregor had written Ivan Funderburg, "If I am re-elected, I assure you that I will do everything in my power, with the cooperation of Congressman Beamer, to arrange a time for a hearing and we will keep in contact with Congressman Beamer so that he can make whatever arrangements that are necessary."[196]

The letter from McGregor said that Ivan had written him "relative to the construction of a dam in your area" at the end of October. While Uncle Cliff had given up the fight, Ivan had moved around his own representative and gotten the attention of a member of the US House of Representatives Public Works Committee.

The motivation behind Beamer's willingness to assist Ivan is clear from back in April 1956. When the Congressman was hearing it from the Indiana Flood Control and Water Resources Commission's Robert Kellum and Carlos Life, he had explained his strategy to them in separate letters: placate the critics while helping move the plan through the bureaucracy and Congress.

After the McGregor letter, the first available correspondence between Ivan and Congressman Beamer is a November 21 letter in which Ivan thanked Beamer for sending Ivan "the list of literature, thereby indicating that you sincerely want us to give a good argument for our cause when the big showdown arrives."[197] That Beamer would do that, contribute sources of information to assist in Ivan's case, confuses me. That's more than placating plan critics. I did not find in the files the letter that Beamer sent Ivan with the material, only Ivan's response.

Ivan had prepared himself for "the big showdown," as he called it, already, he also told Beamer, by attending the Annual Convention of Soil Conservation Supervisors as "guests of the President of the Association." He said he met delegates from Wabash and Miami Counties "who were on our side. It's shaping up into a struggle between the bureaucratic Army Engineers and the common citizen." Sharing with Beamer, it's as if Ivan is writing to an ally.

He got a chance to look at the Upper Wabash Valley Flood Control Project maps, he wrote, and noted the destruction of ten cemeteries and four towns. Also, he said, he learned at the convention that the Soil Conservation Service "now can work over our valleys, giving sufficient flood control" because of a change, he said, in "Public Law 566." That's another name for the Watershed Protection and Flood Prevention Act of 1954 that Soil Conservation Service administrators Donald Williams and Gladwin Young mentioned in their responses to Beamer about the small dams plan.

Finally, Ivan Funderburg asked Congressman Beamer to help him arrange a meeting with Republican Indiana senator Homer Capehart. "Before the next session of Congress," he said, "since none of us know him and I don't know his address." Capehart, a senator since he defeated Governor Henry Schricker for election in 1944, was also on the IFCWRC board. It was Schricker, you remember, who gave official sanction to the commission at its inception. Small world, that Indiana.

Beamer included his home address in a neutral December 4 response to Ivan with the information about how to reach Senator Capehart.[198] Ivan showed no reason to believe the matter was already settled in a letter he wrote to Beamer the same day.

In it, Ivan noted that he and his wife and two other Upper Wabash Valley Flood Control Project opponents had been to an Indiana state legislative planning session since the last letter at the invitation of Huntington Republican state senator Carl Moldenhauer. "Mr. Moldenhauer introduced us to quite a few legislators who were apparently on our side,"[199] he wrote.

IFCWRC executive secretary Robert Kellum was there, he said, along with Joseph Perrey, the IFCWRC chief engineer who replaced David Harker, and Indianapolis commission member B. A. Poole.

We heard their presentation, Ivan Funderburg wrote. "Flood control" was the first reason for supporting the Upper Wabash Valley Flood Control Project.

"Flushing sewage away from downstream cities" was the second, Ivan wrote, "the first anyone admitted it." That way, he added, they won't have to spend their own money to treat it. "You can imagine how we feel about sacrificing our beautiful valleys, fertile fields, and beloved homes to aid downstream cities violate the law."

The third? "Keeping a steady flow of water in the Wabash to provide water to cool the generators of the new power plant below Terre Haute now being built to be the world's largest."

He called that a case of using public money to support a private venture, that of "Michigan Indiana Electric Company." If they needed the water from the project so badly, Ivan wrote Beamer, they would have waited to start construction until they knew they had it.

Ivan assumed they hadn't known they had it. Terre Haute was the hometown of IFCWRC chairman Tony Hulman, the owner of the Indianapolis Motor Speedway. Small world, that Indiana.

"These last two purposes of the dams," he said, "mean filling the reservoirs every spring then gradually releasing them in late summer and fall. This detracts greatly from flood control but since the Army Engineers never used the $9.5 million to build levees to protect Wabash, Peru, and Logansport, we don't really believe flood control has too much to do with the situation."

In June 1943, as noted in Ralph Roessler's diary, Congress passed legislation to provide money for flood control work on the Wabash River. The bill, HR 2957, allocated not more than $10 million to "repair, improvement, and extension of levees on the Wabash River and its tributaries, and in such other flood-control work as the Chief of Engineers may find to be necessary to control the flow of the waters of such river and its tributaries"[200] In August of 1943, the Upper Wabash Valley River Association merged with the Lower Wabash River Association, and together they initiated a statewide water control needs survey. That group led to IFCWRC's formation in 1944. The IFCWRC then partnered with the army, stewards of federal money and champions of big dam projects all over the country. The levees authorized by HR 2957 in 1943 never materialized. The focus shifted to big dams. The Upper Wabash Valley Flood Control Project followed.

Ivan reiterated to Congressman Beamer in his December 4, 1956, letter that he was not against controlling flooding; he was against the "destructive and expensive" big dams. He supported instead, he said, "many small, beneficial, and economical Social Conservation Service Dams and soil treatment."

He also said the meeting with Senator Capehart had been set for "next Friday. I'm sure he cannot ignore the many facts we have unearthed that were intended to remain buried."

And in closing, Ivan wrote Congressman Beamer, "It isn't necessary for you to answer all of my letters although I always appreciate hearing from you."

It's a friendlier letter than Beamer ever got from Roessler, from Life, or from Kellum.

2.

As a Department of Defense press release from January 16, 1957, announced a 9.7 percent increase in their request for 1958 money for the Army Corps of Engineers,[201] Congressman Beamer was helping Ivan. He wrote the House Public Works Committee chairman to request that "certain people involved in the Upper Wabash Valley Flood Control Project be permitted to present their arguments before your committee."[202] He asked Chairman Charles A. Buckley, a Democrat from the Bronx, to let him know when that might happen, and Beamer sent a copy of that letter to Ohio Republican representative J. Harry McGregor and to Ivan Funderburg. McGregor was the Public Works Committee member who'd already helped Ivan. Then Beamer wrote a January 23 memo to himself that said that he'd asked the same of Public Works Committee members in the Senate, even though it "had been felt" that only the Army Corps of Engineers and "agencies involved" would be heard.

After Ivan wrote Beamer on January 21 that, for the hearing, "we would like sufficient notice so we can get our farm work in order,"[203] the congressman from Roann replied on January 24 that he couldn't say when, for sure, in that moment, but that he'd let him know when he found out.[204]

Beamer had a letter in hand from the Indiana Farm Bureau on the matter the next time he heard from Ivan. Hassil Schenck, the IFB president, advised him that the bureau preferred the small dam plan. Schenck, a Lebanon, Indiana, farmer, wrote Beamer, he said, in response to his request for information about a visit from a "Huntington County group" that included Ivan and Cliff Funderburg. "I have talked with Mr. Charles Butler, the Land and Water Use Department Head of the American Farm Bureau Federation and find our national philosophy bears out the contentions of the Funderburgs," Schenck wrote. "However," he said, "the AFBF also has the philosophy that this is not a problem for national determination, but should be handled on a state basis."[205] There's probably a book, Vern, about the use of "state's rights" as a means of retarding progressive American social policy. You should read that, or maybe write one.

Ivan's February 4 letter thanked Beamer for trying to get him into the Public Works Committee hearing. It also said that the Army Corps of Engineers had worked in secrecy for ten years before then, trying to push through their plan. Furthermore, the army land acquisition and reimbursement tactics were corrupt, he claimed, with their own real estate agency and manipulated pricing. "I would appreciate your checking into these matters," he said.[206]

By February 9, 1957, Peru's Carlos Life, the Wabash Valley Trust Company president and IFCWRC founding member, had heard enough about the possible Public Works Committee hearing. He wrote Beamer that the hearing was the only thing left impeding the Upper Wabash Valley Flood Control Project.

> I talked to Bob Kellum this morning. He advised me that the Ominous [*sic*] bill covering the local flood control project has been re-submitted and is now pending in Congress. Our information is that all the projects in this bill have been approved by the White House and all of the other Federal Agencies necessary; and unless someone asks for a hearing that the bill will pass without any further hearing.
>
> As I recall, when I talked to you in your home in Wabash, you indicated that you had promised to secure time for the people from Huntington to file a protest with any committee holding hearings on this bill. If you still feel that you must do this, we sincerely urge that you advise us of the same and secure equal time for the State of Indiana so that we may appear in favor of the project.
>
> We have been advised that if you do not require any time for either side and will let the project

> follow its normal course that it will be passed, and we sincerely urge you to give due considerations to the benefits of this project before you make arrangements for them to appear before the committees in an effort to kill the same.[207]

Life included at the letter's end a note that he'd send a copy of his diversity, equity, and inclusion request to the publishers of the *Peru Tribune* and the *Wabash Plain Dealer*, John and Joe Nixon.

Beamer's secretary responded to Life, noting that the congressman "has returned to the district for Lincoln Birthday meetings." Nancy Brown wrote Life that the Senate was working on the omnibus bill and that House action would follow.[208] At the end of February, Beamer himself wrote to Kellum with a reference to the Indiana Farm Bureau support for the "small dam" plan. He said that he was writing to provide Kellum with some sense of the opposition.[209] Neither letter mentioned the House Public Works Committee hearing that Ivan Funderburg was then planning to attend.

Beamer returned to the subject March 11 in a letter referencing a phone call he'd had with the Public Works Committee flood control subcommittee chairman about setting up the hearing Ivan was planning to attend. He wrote Tennessee Democrat Clifford Davis, "You promised to make it possible for representatives interested in the Upper Wabash River Valley Flood Control project to appear before your Committee. I shall be glad to give you the names of those interested and who have contacted me in this behalf."[210] He let Ivan and Congressman McGregor know, but then Davis wrote back that it was possible there wouldn't be a hearing at all.[211] That was followed by McGregor writing Davis to say Beamer's witnesses should be heard. "The Congressman tells me that all he wants done is to see that the people be given an opportunity to express themselves which will 'take him off the hook.'"[212]

"Take him off the hook," Vern. Maybe representing citizens in Congress wasn't the right job for John Beamer.

There was background noise at this time, too. Leaders in Peru blamed the absence of flood control for a power outage that was actually caused by a missing check valve at the municipal power plant. Peru mayor John Devine went public with his criticism of Beamer, who, he said, wasn't doing anything to move the project along. Life and Devine started a pro-project petition drive. *Peru Tribune* manager John Nixon wrote Beamer March 29 that he wasn't doing enough. "There seems to be growing feeling among those who are working for the flood control project in this area that you are withholding your support. Is this true? Do you plan to initiate favorable action when the bill reaches the House Public Works Committee? I think a full statement on your position on the whole program would clear the air for our people,"[213] he said.

While John ran the *Peru Tribune* at the time, his brother, Joe, was editor and publisher of the *Wabash Plain Dealer.* Their dad, Don, had been the publisher of both newspapers until he was killed in a car wreck in 1934. Their mother, Eugenia, then married Wabash industrialist Mark Honeywell after Mark's first wife died in a 1939 boating accident. Eugenia would be killed in a 1974 house fire. Honeywell, John and Joe Nixon, and both papers publicly and privately supported the Upper Wabash Valley Flood Control Project through its development. Of area publications, only the *Marion Chronicle-Tribune* objected to the plan, and only insofar as it had neglected their city.

3.

For the big-versus-small-dam-plan debate of 1956 and 1957 to have been meaningful, it needed to have happened long before. By the time it did, all the talk made no difference. But people on both sides of the issue thought it did, so it continued.

So, too, did continue procedure, on a different track I could call *reality*. The March 29, 1957, *Logansport Press* reported, "The three reservoir . . . project . . . included in a bill passed by the Senate and sent to the House Thursday [yesterday] . . . [is] . . . almost identical to the one Eisenhower vetoed last August."[214]

Beamer wrote on April 1 to thank for their support Mr. and Mrs. Sam Colby from Peru and to explain,

> The bill now comes to the House Public Work Committee where hearings should be held. It should be further explained if it receives the approval of the House Public Works Committee and the House of Representatives then it must receive the necessary appropriation. This may well require additional hearings and, perhaps, intensive study. I mention all this because sometimes there is a long lapse between the actual authorization of a measure or project and the appropriation of the necessary funds.[215]

On April 2, 1957, Congressman Beamer addressed a letter to the House Public Works Committee member and flood control subcommittee chairman, Clifford Davis. Again, Vern, that's who would decide if Ivan Funderburg would testify. Beamer said,

> When consideration of S. 497, the Omnibus Rivers and Harbors Bill, comes before your committee, I would appreciate it if the following could be given an opportunity to be heard briefly on the Upper Wabash River Flood Control project before your subcommittee:
>
> Ivan Funderburg, RR5, Huntington, Indiana
> Mr. Robert Kellum, Indiana Flood Control & Water Resources Commission, Indianapolis 2, Indiana[216]

Kellum, the IFCWRC executive secretary, followed his notice of that letter from Beamer with his own letter to Davis, urging him not to invite Ivan—or anyone else, for that matter—to a hearing where people could talk about the project. There's no need for a hearing, he wrote, "in view of the fact that the project was endorsed fully and cleared fully in the original Omnibus Bill of the last session. It was definitely not one of the projects to which the President objected in his veto last year. In fact, he voiced complete support of the Upper Wabash plan in a special telegram to Senator Capehart at the time he vetoed the old bill."[217]

However, he added, if he were going to have the hearing, then he should also invite the mayors of Wabash, Peru, and Logansport or other area representatives.

When Davis responded to Kellum, he said he agreed that when it came to the Upper Wabash plan, the new bill would look like the old one and that "I doubt very much that it will be necessary for us to have you come in again."[218]

Kellum then wrote a long, private letter to the cooperative *Wabash Plain Dealer* publisher Joe Nixon, challenging Ivan's argument, what he called "this farm pond thing." Kellum said, "The entire [Upper Wabash Valley Flood Control Project] plan is so good; there's no other way." Moving people was tough, he said, but "when a move is made, the people have better towns, better housing." It hadn't been easy, he said in the April 22, 1957, note, to get "the Army Engineers to give us the attention they give to Kentucky, since their office is in Louisville. One thing for me is certain," he concluded, "the Army Engineers do a complete job, really dig in, as they have on this Upper Wabash report."[219]

Kellum showed no sign of knowing in the letter that the prior Friday, April 19, 1957, Congressman John Beamer had suffered a heart attack while on a visit to his son in North Carolina. The Monday, April 22, *Kokomo Tribune* reported that Beamer was in serious condition, a downgrading after doctors said he had "developed 'unfavorable signs.'"[220] Doctors said, according to the report, that he would be out of his office for several weeks.

The first indication of Beamer's heart attack that appears in his Indiana State Library files papers is in an April 23, 1957, letter from the congressman's executive assistant, Robert Williams. He told Mrs. O. E. Bearse of Peru that Beamer was in Hugh Chatham Memorial Hospital in Elkin, North Carolina, recuperating from a "minor heart attack."

"His condition is satisfactory and we are encouraged by his response to treatments and expect him back in the office, after a little rest," Williams wrote. In the same letter to Bearse, Williams added that IFCWRC member Carlos Life and Peru mayor John Devine were lying about Beamer's poor support for the flood control project. The actions of Life, he said, "have caused John some concern."[221] Do you suppose, Vern, that Williams associated the actions of Life with the heart attack?

Two weeks later, Ivan Funderburg found out that he was wanted in Washington, DC, in a Western Union telegram from Williams saying, "Chairman Davis advised us that you may be heard at 10:00 a.m. on Tuesday May 14. Only one person scheduled. Please advise immediately if this date acceptable to you."[222]

You can't blame Ivan for being excited. He'd worked hard on a matter that was near and dear to everything that meant something to him, and he was going off to the nation's capital to testify in Congress.

Cool. Or whatever the 1957 equivalent might be.

Ivan wrote to Congressman Beamer thanking him for setting the stage for his appearance. A week, he said, would give him time "to plan for our farm work." He added, "We have accumulated more information and believe we have a very good case prepared." It reads like he's talking to a friend. "We were sincere saddened to hear of your illness and we wish you a speedy recovery.

"I'm going to send a telegram immediately to Chairman Davis informing him that we will be there at the appointed date. I say, 'we' because my wife is going along for the trip."[223]

What an exciting time for the Funderburgs.

He concluded, "Again, thank you very much for all you have done for us."

Splendid.

4.

On Tuesday, May 14, 1957, the House of Representatives Committee on Public Works met in the new House office building with the Honorable Clifford Davis, Democrat from Tennessee, presiding. Davis was a strict segregationist and, in addition to his work in Congress, a leader of the Ku Klux Klan.[224] On this day, he was leading a committee meeting to consider the River and Harbor Flood Control Act of 1957.

Davis began with an effusive welcome to the newly appointed chief of engineers for civil works of the Army Corps of Engineers, Brigadier General E. C. Itschner, and a review of the six other chief engineers it had been his privilege to know. "Our relationship has always been so cordial based upon the long and historical integrity of the Corps of Engineers,"[225] he said.

With the general on the stand, most testimony came in conversation from the congressmen themselves, about the projects in the omnibus bill, some that the president had cited as wasteful when he vetoed the measure passed in the previous session.

After several minutes of that discussion, Congressman Davis turned the committee's attention to the Upper Wabash Valley Flood Control Project. He began, "Our colleague, John Beamer of Indiana, it was disclosed yesterday had suffered a heart attack," acknowledging the fact in passive voice, "news to me"—like, twenty-seven days after it occurred. Quickly, back to the business at hand, the measure was in last year's bill, he said, and it was supported by the Army Corps of Engineers and by Congressman Beamer. "However, at his great insistence, we promised to hear briefly, Mr. Ivan Funderburg, of Huntington, Indiana. He may be opposed to it. I do not know."

We're doing this citizen guy a favor, is what I hear, Vern, *by listening to someone who is actually affected by the policy we mindlessly push along. Make it quick.*

Ivan told the committee that the plan was developed in "semi-secrecy." He testified, "There was not a one of us, and we live in the upper valley, that knew we were in danger of losing our homes and farms in all these ten years that the engineers worked on the project."

He told the committee that the project costs were underestimated and the benefits were overestimated. He said that Indiana Flood Control and Water Resources Commission member Carlos Life "has made the public statement the benefits from recreation will figure more highly than flood control." He said that the Soil Conservation Service "small dam" plan was a better alternative, and he gave the committee for evidence a Jerry Durnbaugh *Wabash Plain Dealer* newspaper column opposing the project. It had been published April 13, and in it, Durnbaugh claimed the small dam plan would help preserve the topsoil that modern farm techniques were destroying at a rapid rate. Durnbaugh wrote,

> Seventy-five years ago, the average topsoil depth in Indiana was 16 to 18 inches. Today, the average depth is six to eight inches. Those other 10 inches have washed away and may be found in the vicinity of New Orleans and suburbs. Under the very best conditions, it takes a minimum of 100 years for nature to produce an inch of topsoil. Better soils require longer to build, from three to five centuries per inch. Indiana has washed nearly 5,000 years of nature's work down its rivers. At this rate, Indiana farmers (except some of those along the river bottoms) will be without topsoil in another half-century.[226]

Maybe it's off topic, but I'm compelled to mention, Vern, that Durnbaugh grew up in Wabash County. He left the *Plain Dealer* in 1960 for Maine, where he started a weekly paper with his wife, Gayle. He'd tell a reporter from the *Bangor Daily News* that in Wabash, "there were differences of opinion on news policy. One thing I liked about Maine people," he told the reporter, "they didn't keep talking about my beard. It was mine and they let me wear it in peace."[227]

Along with Durnbaugh's piece, Ivan Funderburg submitted to the committee a sworn statement from Somerset resident Earl J. Lindsey in which Lindsey said that he knew firsthand that sometimes the cost of flood damage is overstated. Ivan told the committee that while money was authorized for flood protection levees, it was not requested by the cities whose leaders now wanted big dams to protect their towns from flooding. He said an army engineer told project opponents at a meeting in Bluffton,

Indiana, that city leaders wanted downstream reservoirs instead, but he did not name that engineer.

After he was interrupted by committee chairman Davis with, "How much more time do you require, Mr. Funderburg?" Ivan told the committee he had learned that a hidden motivation for the reservoir was that of flushing "raw, untreated sewage" away from the cities of Wabash, Logansport, West Lafayette, Terre Haute, and Vincennes. "They are polluting the Wabash River and do not have sewage disposal systems," he said.

When Congressman Frank Becker, a Republican from Long Island, New York, asked Ivan to substantiate with evidence a claim Ivan made about cost overruns on the project, he could not. "I may have overstepped my bounds" with that assertion, Ivan admitted. He was also not immediately able to tell Congressman McGregor what percentage of the entire area impacted by the project would be represented by 1,063 signatures on a petition he had brought to the committee.

Davis then closed the session by telling Ivan to contribute anything else he had to say in writing.

5.

"I don't doubt that I failed," Ivan wrote to Robert Williams a month later. "I don't know what the committee decided." He'd written a letter to the congressman, he said, but had gotten no reply. "We can't find out what is happening. There is nothing in the newspaper about it.

"I would appreciate any information you can send us and I would like a copy of the Congressional Record for that day."

A souvenir, at least.

And Ivan wrote, "We hope Mr. Beamer is feeling much better. I wrote to him that his staff couldn't have treated us with any more courtesy."[228]

As to what the committee decided, on July 19, 1957, another month to the day after Ivan wrote Beamer's office, the *Logansport Pharos-Tribune* reported, "A flood control project which is expected to save Logansport, Peru, and other cities along the Wabash river from perennial flood threats is included in the public works authorization bill sent to the House of Representatives for action Thursday by the Public Works Committee."[229]

No substantial opposition.

With the US House of Representatives Public Works Committee support in July of 1957, it was clear that there was bipartisan support for the Upper Wabash Valley Flood Control Project. If Congressman John Beamer's intention had been to show everyone that Ivan Funderburg's testimony in May was the best the opposition had to offer, he was clearly quite astute. While cloaking himself in the guise of neutrality, he cleared the ground like the coming bulldozers. In the process, though, he sacrificed himself, I think, both his health and his political career.

In July of 1957, if there was one person involved in all of this who was not upset with Congressman Beamer, it could well have been Ivan Funderburg, the person who most should have been. Nearly two weeks after the Public Works Committee gave the Upper Wabash Valley Flood Control Project its approval, Ivan again wrote a kindly note to Beamer, who was back in Wabash, recovering from the heart attack he had in April. "You and your people were considerate," he wrote. "I realize more than ever how difficult it must have been for you to arrange our hearing and we shall be forever grateful to you. The Engineers have methods of suppressing opposition that are difficult to overcome. I hope they didn't give you a rough time because you arranged my hearing."[230]

Still fighting an enemy that was not close enough to see, Ivan included in his letter a scathing Army Corps of Engineers critique written by Harold Ickes, the US Interior Department Secretary from 1933 to 1946.

In his reply, Beamer updated Ivan Funderburg on his health and the project and thanked him for the maple syrup he had left for him in his Washington, DC, office. "Mrs. Beamer and I are both very fond of maple syrup," he wrote.[231]

There are five more Ivan-to-Beamer letters in the next eight months, containing mostly challenges to Army Corps of Engineers' integrity. Beamer responded with accounts of ongoing project approval procedure. In the last, March 27, 1958, Beamer asked Ivan for some more maple syrup.

It's easy to fault Ivan Funderburg for a lack of preparation for his appearance before the Public Works Committee. Making assertions to professional debaters without evidence to support them makes one's argument weak. That doesn't mean there wasn't an argument to be made.

The small dams plan should have been heard in a fair and open forum going back to at least 1943, when Congress passed legislation to provide for flood control work on the Wabash River and its tributaries. But it wasn't. Instead, the IFCWRC was created to promote the Ralph Roessler reservoir idea. With help from the US Army Corps of Engineers, that became the big dam plan.

By the time Wabash Circuit Court judge Byron Kennedy first made mention to Congressman Beamer of a small dam alternative in June of 1955, planning for the Upper Wabash Valley Flood Control Project was essentially complete. After years of survey, study, and planning, which started no later than 1945, the army had requested the IFCWRC to authorize the big dam plan in 1952. There was no alternative. Because the records are not accessible, we don't know what considerations might have been made for the strategies Ralph Roessler himself proposed in 1943.

By 1952, "the construction of levees, the widening or deepening of channels, conservation as well as protection, the creation of many small reservoirs at head waters, as well as larger ones nearer outlets, and conservation by including soil erosion prevention"[232] had become only the big dam plan.

When Ivan entered the House Public Works Committee hearing on May 14, 1957, one might say he should have been better prepared. One might also say he never had a chance. The small dam plan didn't get seven years of study. The small dam plan was barely being promoted by the Soil Conservation Service of the Agriculture Department. The Indiana Farm Bureau said it was a good idea but not their business. Ivan Funderburg entered the halls of Congress alone, with a pipsqueak small dam proposal of some malcontent Huntington County farmers. The big dam plan? That was the full-throated United States Army proposal before a sympathetic Congress in a 1950s political atmosphere of patriotic anti-communist compliance and conformity.

In 1957, the only serious alternative to the Upper Wabash Valley Flood Control Project, the Mississinewa, Salamonie, and Huntington dams and reservoirs, was more flooding. And in 1957, every time somebody's basement flooded, it was because "we" didn't have the Upper Wabash Valley Flood Control Project already.

34. FLOODS

Although residents of a flooded town usually consider the river a trespasser, nature would look at it the other way round.

—Stanley Meisler, "U.S. Rivers Spill Over Levees Despite Flood Control Program," *Lafayette Journal and Courier*, March 27, 1963

Somerset never flooded. It was built on the top of a limestone ridge that overlooked the Mississinewa River. The European settlers who took the land were fortunate that their Indigenous predecessors were wise to the ways of water. It wouldn't make sense to stay in a place that floods, would it?

Somerset didn't flood, but places downstream did. Pretty often. High water a mile east of Peru, where the Mississinewa joins the Wabash River, is still common. The Upper Wabash Valley Flood Control Project was designed to put a stop to the worst of that, so if you lived in Peru or in the other places along the Wabash and its tributaries that were flood-prone, the project made a lot of sense. In the end, according to Wabash County historian Ron Woodward, it's been "successful, but not completely. We still have flooding," Ron said. "Part of the downtown [Wabash] area was flooded for a time in 2005, but it was nowhere to the extent of what it was beforehand." Wabash is not shielded by the dam that flooded Somerset but rather the other two reservoirs in the system.

The 1913 flood that Ralph Roessler used repeatedly to kick off his pro-project presentations drowned eleven people and destroyed or damaged two-thirds of Peru. There was serious flooding, also, along the Wabash and its tributaries in 1943 and 1950. Low-lying areas along the rivers, places like the Riverside Resort that my great-aunt Vernie helped run, flooded on an almost annual basis. For some of these areas, including farmland, it was more often than that. People either moved away or figured out how to accommodate it.

Flooding elsewhere made the national news in 1951 and 1952. The Kansas and Missouri Rivers swelled to seventy times their normal size in July 1951, killing seventeen people and putting more than half a million out of their homes. The April 1952 flooding in the upper Mississippi River area prompted President Truman to call for a flood control program "from Denver to Pittsburgh and from Minnesota to the Gulf of Mexico."[233] It was later that year that the Army Corps of Engineers called on the Indiana Flood Control and Water Resources Commission to authorize the big dams plan for the upper Wabash Valley in north-central Indiana.

In January of 1957, four months before Ivan's congressional testimony, Peru suffered a power outage related to high water and the absence of a shutoff valve at the municipal power plant. Jack Ellis, the Peru Chamber of Commerce head, wrote Congressman Beamer, "Please realize that as long as our city and other cities in this area must continue to be harassed by the ever present hazard of high water, we are severely hampered in our quest for industrial and civic expansion."[234]

Before word got out about the shutoff valve, Peru's mayor John Devine wrote that if the "project" were done, the flooding would have been prevented. Carl Schini, a city council member who was also plant manager of Square D Electrical Equipment Company of Peru, wrote Congressman Beamer, "If the flood control facilities had been in existence it is probable that run-off water from fast melting snow would have been impounded."[235]

When Beamer wrote back about the missing shutoff valve, Schini replied, "It also would not have happened if the river had not risen nine feet."[236]

While that controversy petered out, Beamer continued to defend himself against critics from both sides. The April 1, 1957, front page of

John Nixon's *Peru Tribune* most prominently displayed a "forty-four years ago this week" article. Above pictures of flooded streets and homes from 1913, the headline read, COULD THIS HAPPEN AGAIN? NOT WITH ADEQUATE FLOOD CONTROL.[237]

Then high water returned to the area a week later in a spring storm containing sixty-mile-per-hour winds, sleet, and heavy rain. Water spilling over the Wabash River banks across four city streets in Wabash prompted a large front page headline RISING RIVER CHASES RESIDENTS OF WABASH and a Marion newspaper story that said, "More than 40 families left their homes" as the "Red Cross set up a precautionary shelter."[238]

Two letters to Beamer from different Peru furniture makers said high Wabash River water was threatening their operations and forcing them to consider moving. What are you doing about it? they both asked.

An April 10 *Peru Tribune* editorial supporting the project urged readers to show their support by writing to Congressman Beamer.

That same week, the *Wabash Plain Dealer* ran a report on Ralph Roessler's pro-project address to the Wabash League of Women Voters, and it ran verbatim IFCWRC member and Peru banker Carlos Life's pro-project address to the League of Women Voters of Peru.

Flooding returned in the late spring of 1958. The *Indianapolis Star* reported that Bluffton, Huntington, Wabash, and Lafayette were being threatened by the Wabash River; Marion by the Mississinewa; and Anderson by the White, adding, though, that "the weather bureau expected little trouble at Peru, the hardest hit city along the river."[239] In their official capacities, flood control commission engineers and Carlos Life inspected dikes at Peru, the *Star* reported, and said they would hold the surging river.

Two days later, June 16, it reported that the Wabash River was fourteen feet over the flood stage in Terre Haute and that there was flooding throughout the state. The *Star* added that IFCWRC chief engineer Joseph I. Perrey said that "the three-reservoir plan to control Upper Wabash River flooding would have prevented the floods at Wabash, Peru, Logansport, Lafayette and in adjacent Wabash farm bottomlands. The plan is now before Congress for authorization."[240]

June 17 and 18, 1958, Maude Clasmas, Mrs. Fayette Phillips, and Mrs. Russell Keith of Peru, and Mrs. James Faust of Wabash, wrote Beamer separately, urging him to support the legislation that would enact the big dam project. On a postcard, Mrs. Keith wrote, "If you could see what my beautiful garden looks like, you would know why I hope Congress passes a bill [that] contains flood control for the Wabash and Mississinewa Rivers."[241]

Joe Nixon, the *Wabash Plain Dealer* publisher and sometime correspondent, had written the congressman, June 14.

> Dear John:
>
> This flood certainly emphasizes the need for permanent flood protection. Farmers [sic] fields are covered with water. People live in a state of fear, anxiety and apprehension. Many homes and basements are affected. There is always the possibility of disease and water problems. The only sensible answer is permanent flood control. Factories were preparing to close and this would have made the situation worse. Many of their employees worked long hours to move motors, machinery and equipment up.
>
> Cordially,
> Joe
> J.H. Nixon
> President
>
> P.S. It has been estimated that more than $1,000,000 in damages have been suffered by farmers.[242]

The inevitability hatched in 1939 that found form in 1944 climaxed on July 3, 1958. A Rivers and Harbors Act that contained the Upper Wabash Valley Flood Control Project passed and, with the changes he deemed acceptable, was signed into law by President Eisenhower. That seems like a formality to me, but 1958 would be the year that Florence Roby, Ron Woodward, and the Wabash County Museum designated as the time when residents of Somerset learned they'd have to move.

Most of the last citizen letters Beamer would get on the matter supported the plan. One is a thumbs-up postcard with twelve signatures. The last two, though, were both negative. David Hicks of Montpelier wrote on July 14 that the flood control plan "don't make sense to me. Blow the hell out of all the dams in the rivers," he wrote, "and dredge them so this water can get away. Furthermore, I think they ought to quit playing with bombs and rockets all the time or one of these times they are not going to have any place to play."[243]

Mrs. Florence Sanin of Huntington wrote on July 18, "Our first major flood in 45 years does not rate a destruction of thousands of acres of farmland: lands, homes, cemeteries, churches . . . heart attacks, nervous mental ailments, sleepless nights," lives lived "in dread and fear caused by irresponsible interests in our government; our homes are dear to our hearts and for you or Capehart to be a positive part of those who would destroy us in the name of a cruel ruthless flood control should have no part of our votes. You should do every thing in your power to protect us."[244]

The "every thing" was nothing, and the "power," by Beamer's own admission, was an illusion. The protection would be for people and businesses downriver.

Vern

35. DISPLACED

Dear Vern,

I began to let a few people know my letter to you was becoming something more a few months after it started. My friend Mel Brown told me, "You need to talk to people." Among the first were two cousins.

"It was devastating to all of us," Kay Peas said when I visited with her and her sister, Janet Schenkel, at Kay's home in Wabash in September 2021. Kay and Janet are Shroyers, the daughters of my dad's second cousin Bob, and they grew up in Somerset in the final generation there.

"The spirit of Somerset left when it was flooded," Janet said.

"The loss of the school and the new gym was especially hard," Tom Snyder said. Tom's dad, Fred, was the adopted son of my great-aunt Vernie. Fred Snyder owned a meat locker plant and a grocery store in Somerset. He would become the most active individual in the community resettlement.

Fred Snyder's mother died in giving birth to her tenth child when Fred was three years old. According to Tom, Fred's dad, Henry Shambaugh, was distraught. When neighbor Verna Snyder came over to offer her assistance, Henry looked at her and said, "That boy sitting there on the floor crying, you pick him up and take him home with you." And she did. Vernie picked him up and walked out of the house saying, "I'll get back with ya'; we may wanna adopt him."

Six months later, she and Tom Snyder adopted Fred. "She took him home, and Dad's life changed completely," the son named for Fred's father told me. The first Tom Snyder died in 1931.

Fred Snyder joined the navy after high school in 1940. He was a survivor of the attack on Pearl Harbor. After that, Tom told me, Fred nearly starved to death on an abandoned ship that for eighteen months had a problem procuring food. Then he was interred in a Hot Springs, Colorado, mental hospital for rehabilitation, where, because of his traumatic experiences, he was thought to be permanently disabled.

About what was happening to Somerset, Tom said, "Dad would tell me after all he'd been through with the Navy, Pearl Harbor, being controlled for six years: 'Just like when I was in the navy.'

"Dad was going to all these meetings. He'd come home. He'd be all bent out of shape. 'They're gonna come in here and they're gonna take it, and there's nothing you can do about it,' he'd say."

After July of 1958, Congressman Beamer was no longer getting letters about stopping or supporting the project. And while published newspaper accounts that Somerset would disappear began in 1955, local histories mark the local awareness of it as 1958. Both the Ron Woodward and the Florence Roby accounts of Somerset history mark 1958 as the year when, as Roby wrote, "the little village learned that one day it would be under water in the 45-million-dollar Upper River Flood Control Project."[245]

Under glass in the display on the first floor at the Wabash County Museum, the account reads, "In 1958 residents of Somerset learned their hometown would be under water by 1968 as part of the Upper River Flood Control project."

"In 1958 residents learned that the town would become part of the Upper River Flood Control Project of the Corps of Engineers,"[246] Woodward had written. While my research prompts me to make 1955 the year Somerset learned its fate, Ron told me, "I think that it was more like '58 when they began to present the information to the public, more than just an article or two in the newspaper, that this is being considered, that it might happen."

Might is not a word I would use, either.

We don't dispute the effect.

Woodward wrote next that "most residents were unwilling to move."

Roby said, "Some became ill and it is thought were hastened to their death by this terrible experience."

Tom Snyder told me,

> There were two old brothers, last name Slagel. They had two beautiful old homes in Somerset, built back in the 1800s. The Slagel brothers had a business.
>
> You know the metal roof. They invented the raised rib on the outside edge so it wouldn't leak when you connected it to the next piece. They had a patent. They started the Slagel Brothers, a metal shop in Somerset. Noah and Carl Slagel. I remember very much because of my father. These guys were old when I was a kid. They were so upset. One of 'em died before the reservoir even got done. Stress. They lost a whole bunch of the old people in old Somerset because of the stress. They were gonna make people move. They were gonna buy them out.
>
> I think it was tough on Charley. Charley didn't have a good time with it either.

"Charley," or "Uncle Charley," is what Tom called my grandfather, the man my dad called "Pop."

"It wasn't something that caused Evie, your grandma, any problems, I think," Tom added. "Of course, she died in '58."

Grandma Shroyer died on April 30, 1958. Eva Arrick Shroyer died from an apparent heart attack at her home, the family farm, two miles north of Somerset. She had celebrated her sixty-seventh birthday on April 9. Dad's cousin Larry Knee remembers that Grandma was sick on the couch and "Charlie was on the back porch with the radio," listening, I assume, that night to the Cardinals play the Redlegs at Cincinnati's Crosley Field. "They called him in, and she was gone."

My only memory of her death, and it's a strong one, is when my Uncle Wendell said to me, "You want to look?" at the funeral home viewing in

Converse. Then he lifted me up and I saw a plastic version of Grandma, my first glimpse at the odd ceremonial presentation of a loved one's death.

I was four, Vern, and it's possible my memory is bad. My sister, Linda, remembers that the "viewing" was not at a funeral home at all but rather at Grandma and Grandpa's home. Grandma's *Kokomo Tribune* obituary says, "The body was taken to the Zook and Larrison Funeral Home at Converse, and will be returned to the residence this afternoon, where friends may call until time for the funeral.

"Funeral services will be held at 2 p.m. Saturday at Pleasant Grove Wesleyan Methodist Church, with burial in Pleasant Grove Cemetery."

A "viewing" at the house is how my cousin Greg Hoback remembers it, too. "I remember seeing her when she wasn't in a casket yet. She was lying in bed," Greg said. "I was just a little fart, eleven or so. Maybe it was just a day thing for the family to come in."

Linda says we were paraded through the house past Grandma, "in the front door, through the living room, the kitchen, a bathroom, and then into the bedroom. She was in her bed." Maybe that's where Wendell lifted me up. In my mind, it's a Civil War–era house that we paraded through behind ropes on a 1962 family vacation to places like Gettysburg, Appomattox, and Shiloh. Linda says it was her first experience with the death of a loved one, made even more difficult because we'd only recently moved from a more comfortable home in Marion to Normal. Linda was eleven years old.

It was additionally tough for Dad, too, Linda told me. Because we were apparently in some financial distress, "Grandma had told Dad, 'Don't get me a Christmas present'" at the end of 1957. "He didn't," Linda said, "and he never forgot it."

She continued, "That regret was something that he wanted my kids to know about. Because he wasn't able to get her a Christmas present at the last time he could have, he always felt bad, and he wanted to warn them that there are some chances that don't come back around." Every once in a while, she said, it "popped out. He'd tell the story."

It doesn't sound like a story written by someone who thinks he's going to see his mother in heaven. I got that message about mortality without him ever telling me the story, but still, I wish he had. People that

I should have treated better are dead, too.

Uncle Wayne was away at sea when his mother died. "I was aboard the USS *Midway*," he said, which was stationed for an overhaul at Bremerton, Washington. "She had a heart that would fibrillate, and she had medicine, but at that time, there wasn't anything they could do for it. Your dad had the same heart problems as your grandmother had. When Vern came down with it, there were operating procedures to try to correct the problem. Valves from pigs. That's what he lived with until he passed away." We lived in such secrecy that I was surprised when Wayne told me he knew that about Dad.

Dad died when he was seventy. He'd had a bad heart attack at work my senior year of high school, when he was fifty-four, followed by one major bypass surgery, a second operation when he was sixty-four, and a third when he was sixty-nine, the year before he died. I didn't worry. I thought he was immortal. Until he wasn't.

Tom Snyder remembers when Grandma died.

"We were living a few miles south of them, and Mom and Dad loaded us kids, everybody, up. We went over there because Mom was gonna try and work in the kitchen, help, you know, whatever she could. Mom cooked her whole life. Like Aunt Evie. Aunt Evie always had an apron on. I remember Aunt Evie and Vernie talking, laughing, I don't remember seeing Aunt Evie in bad health. I remember going over to the house. She died on the couch in the living room. Some of the boys were there.

"When we got there, Uncle Charley said, 'I want you guys to take that couch, take it out the front door of the house, take it down the steps, and take it across the road and throw it in the creek.'

"I still remember—I was ten years old—I remember standing there on the steps and looking over there in Goose Creek, on the other side of that road, out there in front of the mailbox. I remember looking over there and seeing that couch lying in the creek. It was probably soiled and wet there when she died on the couch. Charley didn't want to have to deal with it. He didn't want to look at it anymore. 'Get it out of the house.'

"I think maybe later he put some brush on it and they burned it," Tom Snyder said. "It was vivid in my mind as a ten-year-old. She had just died, you know, the day before or hours before. I don't remember the timeline. I don't know if she had died that night and we went over the next morning sometime. Charley I'm sure called Dad and told him or one of the boys, or somebody did. Maybe Grams did. They probably called Grams–Vernie–and she called Dad. I think Grams was there in the house. She was there with Charley, trying to figure out how she was gonna feed some of that group, as they was showing up. She was always thinking about feeding.

"She was widowed twice and now her brother lost his wife."

That was that.

I have no memory of being at Grandad's farm after Grandma died. "When she was alive, your dad and his brothers were there a lot," Larry Knee told me. "I don't remember too much going on at Uncle Charley's after Evie died," he said. "It had been the place to be. I lost track of things when the gatherings were at the kids' homes. When she died, it changed a lot."

Uncle Charley, Pop, Aunt Vernie's brother, Evie's husband, Vern's dad, my grandfather: Charles Devere Shroyer would move into a trailer in my aunt Mary's backyard in Windfall. Sixty-five years later, I learned that Vern lived with the regret of not buying his mom a Christmas present. I don't remember anyone ever talking about Grandma Shroyer again. I remember Wendell lifting me up to have a look. Maybe my vague memory was a vivid dream.

The coming summer of 1958 was our first summer in Normal. I suppose by that time it must have felt to my five-year-old self that we'd been there forever. I remember things, but the six years in the old house seem like one year to me. Stan and I slept together in a bed at the attic's east end. Linda slept on the other end, next to the window down on the west end that faced State Road 13. There's nothing solid about the image I have of her down there, getting ready for class at the Point Isabel grade school and then Fairmount High School. It was an open attic. I suppose she made it a point to get ready for school before we woke up, for the sake of modesty. I wasn't paying attention to what she had to do, how she felt when she woke up in a winter cold, with the outhouse down the narrow, winding stairway and past the room between the living room and the kitchen and out the back door, thirty yards away. She was my big sister.

I never thought, either, about how Dad felt that first summer in Normal after his mom died.

The first tractor Vern got when we moved was by today's standards little more than a garden tractor. Five acres to farm is little more than a garden. It was a farm to me. It was a refuge for Vern.

The tractor was a red Farmall model B. To the left of the driver's seat, the axle housing was a good place for me to sit. I hung on to the fender as Dad pulled first a one-bottom plow through the spring soil, and then the tractor-width disc, and then a two-row planter for corn or soybeans. He never bought a corn picker. Neither of us said a word while up the rows we rode, circling around and back when we got to the creek that bordered our land. Most likely, he motioned with a finger, "Come with me," but I do not remember how I happened to be there. I could have fallen off, I suppose, when we hit a limb or a rock, or if I had fallen asleep before a change in direction, but I didn't, and at the time, it never occurred to me that I could.

Stan remembers, "Me and Sid running behind the plow, a one-bottom plow, sticking our legs in the trench that was created as the dirt moved back over it, and we'd pull and pull to get our legs out of there. We thought it was the funniest thing ever. Mom and Dad didn't think it was funny. We thought it was funny.

"He taught me how to drive that tractor," Stan said. "He would run that tractor all the way to that ditch. He knew how to make it turn on a dime. I was always worried we were going into that ditch. *We're going in*, I'd think.

"He tried to teach me how to do it. You have to step on the brake, there was a separate brake pedal for each wheel, left and right, to get it to do it, and he put a rotating knob on the steering wheel to help. I can remember one time I was driving and I couldn't get it to turn. The wheels wouldn't hold. They were pushing the dirt instead of turning through it. I wasn't stepping on the brake hard enough, and we were going right for that ditch. He stepped in. Stopped the tractor and got it to turn. I just remember the ditch. Worried about going in. He never said a word. Didn't yell at me to stop the tractor. Just took care of it and moved on."

I learned to drive the Farmall model H he got later, when we were shucking corn instead of watching the World Series. We took the corn off the stalks ourselves and threw it into the back of a red wagon he'd made from the abandoned bed of a pickup truck. I'd move the tractor forward when the time came. That was a lot easier than trying to miss the ditch like Stan had to do. I had it easier than Stan in every way except that I had to deal with Stan, and Stan didn't. He had to deal with Dad. Dad didn't have to hit me, because I'd watched him hit Stan.

There was a vacated chicken coop that Stan and I would light but fail to burn down. There was a paint-chipped red barn with a roof that sloped from its peak to a level low enough for Stan and me to climb onto and then up. Once, we nailed two boards together in the shape of a cross and called it an airplane. We then dragged it up to the rooftop; I suppose that's thirty feet high. My memory is as clear as the moment just before my three-year-old self stuck a finger into a moving lawn mower blade and thought, *I'm going to stop that blade.*

This time I thought, *I will hop aboard and fly.*

Stan said, "We'd better not."

Sometimes a big brother tries to kill you. Sometimes he saves your life.

The barn was the last original building to go. Into high school, long after all the other landmarks we lived alongside after the move from Marion had disappeared, it still served as a backstop for one-on-one tennis-ball baseball.

My grandparents' farm was the place where I put my hand into the spinning blade of a push mower, my first memory. By the summer of 1958, their land's fate had been decided. Did they know? How could they not? But it's been clear to me for a long time that what people know and what they admit to themselves they know are two different things.

Flood

36. GRATITUDE

Dear Vern,

John Edward Roush was making his second run for a seat in Congress in 1958 when he visited the home of Indiana Flood Control and Water Resources Commission vice chairman Ralph Roessler in Marion. We know about the meeting because of a letter Roessler wrote to Roush ten years later that remains in his Indiana State Library files.[247] After Roush introduced himself, Roessler noted that the candidate said, "His mission was to obtain such information as could be made available to him regarding a controversial project under way by the Army Corps of Engineers and the Indiana Commission on Flood Control and Water Resources." It's odd that in a letter to Roush Ralph refers to him in the third person. "His mission."

According to Roessler, Roush told him he'd gotten a lot of letters about the flood control plans.

Roush had been referred to Roessler by IFCWRC executive secretary Robert Kellum. Roush had written to Kellum on July 26, 1958. I'm running, he said, and I'd like information on the flood control project, to speak to commission members. "I have informed the various people who have spoken to me that I would take a definite stand on this matter after I was thoroughly informed," he wrote.[248]

Being "thoroughly informed" would come to mean relying on information from the people who designed the plan in their own interests. Whatever controversy existed about it was only the remnants of what had concluded when Congress authorized it three weeks before in the Flood Control Act of 1958. Clearly, by the time Roush began that campaign, all that remained was to get the money for it from the feds.

There were some obstacles with that, but none of them challenged Roush politically. The only alternative to the Upper Wabash Valley Flood Control Project was more flooding for Wabash, Peru, and Logansport. Roush's self-righteous "taking a stand" meant aligning himself with Kellum, Roessler, and Peru's Carlos Life in support of a matter that had already been settled. What it provided was a means of separating himself from the incumbent, Congressman John Beamer.

"My opponent in my first election had not been particularly against the flood control projects, but he hadn't been for it either," Roush told Kathleen McKinzie in a June 20, 1969, oral history project interview.[249] John Beamer had been a supporter, but he'd been vilified, especially by Life, for not campaigning for the project. Roush being "for it" really meant being willing to carry their water, pardon the pun, Vern. He signaled that to Roessler when they met in Marion. For his part, Roessler signaled Republican support for a Democratic candidate in a traditionally Republican district.

The Roessler letter to Roush ten years after the fact said, "After a full afternoon of discussion on proposed flood protection, conservation of water resources and great benefits in economic and social resources, augmented by maps, exhibits, progress in studies, a program of one hundred years of future growth in contemplation, carefully listening and appraising, he made this decision, 'You have cleared all doubts in my mind. I will adopt this as a major plank in my campaign platform,' [Roush said] or words to that effect."

A few days later, Roush let the newspapers, and Ivan Funderburg, know. "I could not conscientiously, after careful study and deliberation, take a stand other than the one which I have expressed in this statement," Roush wrote to Ivan on August 13, 1958.[250] One can infer that Ivan represented the "very vocal and very demanding" opposition Roush said he was up against in his interview with McKinzie because that's the only such letter I found in his Indiana University archive papers. The candidate included in that letter the statement of principle he'd sent to newspapers supporting the project. The statement mimics Roessler's position.

My opponent, Congressman Beamer, did not take a firm stand on the project, Roush wrote. "We are informed by responsible people that our Congressman refused to take the initiative in the matter of flood control and conservation of water resources, that he was inactive and neutral in his position and that it was not until the 1958 flood had caused millions of dollars' worth of damage and inundated thousands of acres of farm land that he decided flood control through the expenditure of federal funds was necessary in the State of Indiana."

I've met with both sides, he told the Nixon brothers and all the other Fifth District newspaper publishers. "We must accept the conclusion that a system of reservoirs and dams as proposed is the most effective and practical approach in solving our flood problem."

"We now pledge ourselves," Roush wrote, "to the task of not only encouraging action now by those in positions of authority but also to a program of action on our part if we should be given this responsibility in the Congress of the United States."

Ralph Roessler, the man who started the ball rolling as a Kiwanis Club project in 1939, would remember in 1968 that Roush became "one of the most enthusiastic and important factors in Congress in support of the three-reservoir project in the drainage area of the upper Wabash River basin. His first address from the floor of the House was an appeal for approval of Congress and needed appropriations to carry on the project."

He said in the letter to Roush that that afternoon and Roush's subsequent election victory over incumbent Republican John Beamer led to a "deep and abiding friendship and admiration" between the two. "I do not recognize him as a Democrat nor myself as a Republican," he recounted.

That's an odd thing to say in a personal letter addressing someone directly.

While the letter begins with a personable "Dear Ed," Roessler throughout only addresses his friend in the third person, as "his" and "him," not "your" and "you." It's a letter to J. Edward Roush, but it was written like an account for the historical record for someone else to read. It's got all the warmth of a recommendation letter.

It's good information to know, though, Vern. We're lucky Ralph cared about writing recommendations and the historical record.

Roessler wrote that Roush had been "dedicated and efficient" and that he cared about the people of the district "where control and protection of our water supply is a vital necessity for the preservation of life and property and the future of our community."

The letter was timed to acknowledge Roush's five terms of service to Roessler, as redistricting in 1968 had shifted the congressman's representation away from the Marion area. Roush would not be working for him anymore, and Ralph wanted to say thanks.

Roush was from Huntington County, and when it shifted into a congressional district dominated by Fort Wayne, he had to face an incumbent Republican named E. Ross Adair. He lost to Adair in 1968 but defeated him in 1970 and served in the Fourth District for another three terms. Roush would lose that seat to another Huntington resident, the future vice president Dan Quayle, in 1976.

A friend of Roush's named Joe Mettler would serve as Indiana Fifth District Democratic Party chairman from 1958 to 1968. By the time Mettler talked to Kathleen McKinzie for her oral history project in 1968, he was hyperbolically asserting that Roush "introduced the whole idea of flood control and reservoirs"[251] in the Fifth District. He told McKinzie that he had been Roush's insurance agent since "about 1941." They were a couple of young Democrats in a place where that was rare. My best friend, the late Lotis Freeman, and I were like that when we met at a lab table in a 1968 classroom. I wonder if Roush and Mettler were Cardinal fans, too.

Anyway, two weeks after Roush had made his flood control position clear to the newspapers and Ivan Funderburg, Mettler got a letter from a colleague in Peru suggesting that candidate Roush seek out Carlos Life, the Peru banker who'd been on the Indiana Flood Control and Water Resources Commission since its inception in 1945.

Bob Tillet wrote, "I should like to suggest that when he is in Peru to make a special effort to see Mr. Carlos Life, President of the Wabash Valley Trust Co., who is a member of the State Flood Commission. He is also a Republican, but very bitter against Beamer, outspoken about it because of Beamer's attempted block of the flood aid. I should like to see Roush take advantage of this in this area."[252] By Tillett's account, we can see that "Beamer's attempted block of the flood aid" had become an incontestable assertion; that is, in fact, an erroneous evidence-poor conclusion expressed as a premise that then supports another argument. Learning about logical fallacies will serve you well, Vern.

Thanks to Tillet and Mettler, Roush made the connection with Beamer's "bitter" opponent, Life. Life created a Roush appearance before the Peru Kiwanis Club in September, and Roush wrote the club on September 12 that he'd like to talk about flood control. "I have been informed that Mr. Beamer has completely misled . . . people . . . with his stand on flood control. I would, of course, keep personalities out of my talk and be factual and correct in my approach."[253] And, with a straight face, Vern, allow me to mention.

In October, Roush let the Peru Chamber of Commerce know that he'd be an "active," strong flood control plan supporter, even though, "frankly, this stand has lost me a few votes."[254]

Even though a lot of people who communicated with Beamer and Roush said that it would make a difference, the Upper Wabash Valley Flood Control Project did not affect the election. Beamer lost. Roush won. Accounts of the election show it mattered little.

Beamer did complain about what Roush was saying about it and him in a telegram that he sent to the *Kokomo Tribune* on August 15, 1958. The paper was seeking comment on the press release from Roush charging Beamer with failing to back flood control projects in the Fifth District. That's the one Roush stuck in the envelope with the letter to Ivan Funderburg about his flood control position. Beamer called the release a "gross misrepresentation of true facts" and a "failure to check the records before making irresponsible statements."[255] As evidence of that, Beamer cited remarks from Congressman J. Harry McGregor of the Public Works Committee in the *Congressional Record*, commending his efforts supporting the project. And he referred the Kokomo paper to a bill he introduced "to increase amounts paid for land acquired for public works projects in order to protect interests of those who may suffer damages."

I couldn't find that the *Tribune* ran either the Roush release or the Beamer rebuttal. I'm guessing the paper figured they canceled each other out.

Beamer forwarded the McGregor praise to Roessler and Life to elicit a helpful response, I think, a "say something nice about me, guys" response. It never came. He did get a later lift from Indiana Republican governor Harold Handley in October, during his own campaign for the US Senate against Evansville mayor Vance Hartke. Handley said in remarks he delivered in Marion that Roush was making "irresponsible statements" about Beamer's work on the project. "It is time," Handley said, "for the Fifth District voters to expose Mr. Beamer's opponent for his technique of misrepresentation and distortion of the truth."[256] Roessler was not inclined to describe Roush that way. He could have. I guess he was doing for the election what Beamer had been doing for the Upper Wabash Valley Flood Control Project, not campaigning, letting things run their course.

The flood control controversy was, in fact, pretty minor stuff compared to the other "issues" in the campaign.

Roush attacked Republican "foreign policy" while Beamer said he would provide "leadership to restore faith at home and abroad." Beamer called Roush "ultra-liberal, even radical," according to an October 7, 1958, *Indianapolis News* article.[257] But that article also included mention of an unidentified "Republican friend" saying Roush is "a man of unimpeachable integrity," the kind of thing you might hear in a recommendation letter. In the *Tipton Daily Tribune* on November 1, Beamer said he opposed socialism and supported individual rights.[258] Roush's newspaper ads mentioned experience, his familiarity with "farm problems," and a "favorable labor record."

A Democratic Central Committee ad for Roush that appeared in the Tipton paper the Friday before the election called out Beamer for not supporting an "Education-Defense Bill," a "Community Facilities Bill," a "Food Stamp Plan," and a "Labor Reform Bill, a bill designed to correct abuses in labor unions and to rid our unions of racketeers."

Neither of them was saying much about floods.

If people in Wabash County were upset with Beamer for supporting the big dams and reservoirs that were coming, it didn't show. Wabash was one of only two of the district's ten counties that gave Beamer the most votes. If there were people in Peru and Miami County who were upset that Beamer didn't do enough to promote the project, their numbers were not significant. Only fifty-six votes separated Beamer and Roush there, and Roush won the Fifth District total by over thirteen thousand. The disgruntlement with Roush in Huntington County like that expressed by Cliff and Ivan Funderburg was more than offset by his familiarity there as county prosecutor. Roush, at the time of his election, was the only Democrat to hold a county-wide office. Folks there seemed to like him; he won the majority of Huntington County's sixteen thousand voters by nearly three thousand.

It was an off-year election with an incumbent president in his second term, a sure sign of bad news for "the party in power." A sour economy combined with the increasingly industrialized, and unionized, workforce in the district's three biggest counties were significant factors that year. You can see that in the results.

Madison County, home to Anderson's General Motors Delco-Remy plant, gave the Democrat Roush eight thousand more votes than Beamer. Howard County, home to Kokomo's GM Delco Radio and Chrysler's transmission plants, favored Roush by 2,200. Grant County, with the GM Fisher Body factory in Marion, where Vern worked, favored Roush by a mere 125 votes, but up until then, it was a county that Beamer had never lost.

It was a bad year for Republicans all over the state. They lost a Senate seat and six seats in the House. From nine Republicans and two Democrats, the congressional delegation became eight Democrats and three Republicans. Mayor Hartke's win over Governor Handley for the US Senate made Hartke one of thirteen Democrats nationwide to take over what had been Republican seats. That's huge; 1958 marked the start of an eight-year era that would see the passage of progressive legislation that for the twentieth century was second, perhaps, only to the New Deal. There was a wave in 1958, but it wasn't connected to floods.

On the Fridays after an election, my memory says, the Marion paper would print the precinct-by-precinct, township-by-township, candidate-by-candidate results, and my memory tells me that we could find

Vern's vote, along with Mom's, because they were the only two people in our Green Township in Grant County who voted for Roush or John Fitzgerald Kennedy or Vance Hartke or Birch Bayh or any other Democrat who was on the ballot, unless maybe it was somebody's friend or relative or an old teacher or something, I guess. That's my memory.

Mom voted for whom Vern told her to vote, and without him, she would have voted differently.

Vern

37. DEVOTION

Dear Vern,

I can see Dad at the kitchen table in the new house. It's late. A filterless Camel cigarette burns in his hand next to a clear glass ashtray. A cigar box is open. The only other light is the lamp from another room. Vern is rolling coins into sleeves by denomination: pennies, nickels, dimes, and quarters. The dollar coins and the fifty-cent pieces he sets aside because there aren't enough to make a roll. Vern inhales smoke from the cigarette and puts it on the ashtray. The rolls go back into the cigar box above the bills that he's also sorted into piles by denomination. It's Wednesday night. On Saturday morning, he'll drive with me and the cigar box to the bank in Swayzee and deposit last Sunday's collection plate money from the Methodist church in Point Isabel.

Vern was the church treasurer.

We went to church every Sunday. Church at 9:00, Sunday school at 10:00. Afterward, except for the six or seven times a year when there was a family occasion, we drove mostly to the Mangas Cafeteria in Elwood for what we called dinner right after services. Once or twice a year, we'd go someplace else to eat, but mostly it was Elwood. There was a restaurant on State Road 37, or maybe it was 9, near Fairmount, called the Country Kitchen, which we considered "special," and that I remember mostly because a waitress there told us that Lee Harvey Oswald had just been killed. I started to cheer because we liked President Kennedy, but Vern gave me a dirty look. Lots of people I went to school with, and so I have to assume that also includes their parents, too, were glad that Kennedy was dead. That wasn't us, but Vern gave me the sign: a man dead, any man dead, is no cause for celebration. Maybe we had chicken and dumplings that day.

In Elwood, at the Mangas Cafeteria next to the railroad tracks, I alternated between "Swiss Steak" and fried chicken, with mashed potatoes, a little bowl of corn, and chocolate pudding. I filled a plastic glass with ice and Coke. That was a treat, too. I got a bottle of Coke or RC from the water-filled cooler next to the bench inside White's Grocery in Normal from time to time, but Mom didn't bring pop home from the store.

"Going to Elwood to eat after church, that was a ritual," Stan remembers. "Sometimes you had to wait outside the line was so long. Dad would feed the whole family for five bucks. I loved that fried chicken and coconut cream pie."

The Swiss Steak, I learned many years later by eating the delicious Greek stifado your Grandma Shroyer made, was a dish derived from Greek recipes, but calling it *Swiss Steak* made more sense in a town where I learned as a kid that Negroes (the Sunday word, Vern) were not allowed. Not just not after sundown. Not at any time.

"The guy would always say something to Dad about his family as we went through the line," Stan recalled. The Mangas brothers, who said hello to us on Sundays with a smile and who owned and ran the cafeteria, were dark complected and spoke with accents that make me think they were immigrants, treading carefully in Elwood, Indiana, in 1964. It feels now like we were part of their secret underground. Our only permissible hate was for Texas. Vern hated Texas, even before Kennedy got shot; he'd spent some time there during the war.

Church didn't change a whole lot from Sunday to Sunday.

We went to church in "Point." We called Point Isabel "Point." I went to 4-H meetings in Point. I went to school in Point. I played toy soldiers with Jerry Hannah and smoked a ten-year-old's cigarette with Kenny Bethay in Point. Point was three miles south of Normal on State Road 13. Ninety-one people live in Point now. It was bigger than that then, maybe like the two hundred who once lived in Somerset.

We had to get dressed up to go to church. A white shirt, a clip-on tie, a jacket that was red for a while, and our uncomfortable, best, never-broken-in shoes. I didn't care for that, but that didn't make any difference. I don't think any of us but Mom wanted to go, least of all Vern, but he considered it a community obligation is how I look at it now. I thought about the things we heard while we were there, but I never considered going a choice. I was the youngest, the last in line to the crown. We just had to go. We went.

Dad's cousin Larry Knee told me a story he'd heard from his mom several times about Dad going to church when Vern was a kid. Dad's folks, "Aunt Evie and Uncle Charley, would take the kids to the revival," Larry said, a week of every-night churchgoing that happened once or twice a year. It was at their own Pleasant Grove Methodist. "Your dad was getting tired of going to church every night. It was getting dark when they got there in the horse and buggy." Looking around at the churchyard cemetery on his march up the steps, Larry said that according to Aunt Vernie, Dad said, "If I wasn't so scared of those dang ghost-es, I wouldn't go in." Ghost-es.

"Mom told that story so often," Larry said, and I think it was because of what she perceived to be Dad's comical little-boy way of speaking. I, myself, think Dad understood Christianity at a pretty young age. The fear factor, like I did. "If I wasn't so scared of those dang ghost-es, I wouldn't go in."

Nevertheless, he marched his own crew forty years later into the Point Isabel Methodist church every Sunday. We sat in the back, but not all the way in back, of course, in the next-to-last row because the last row would be too conspicuous. It was fifteen cement steps up into the lobby and then through the doors into the sanctuary. We always sat in exactly the same place. The five of us, and then four when Linda went to college. When Stan went to college, I was sixteen, and Mom said to me, "You don't have to go anymore if you don't want to," and I never went again.

Vern never said a word about church. We simply went.

He never said a word at church, either. He didn't sing. He didn't respond to responsive reading responsively. He stood up when we were supposed to stand, and he sat down when we were supposed to sit, and sometimes an impish smile appeared from out of nowhere that no one knew the name of. His thoughts were his own. I've heard his voice in dreams once or twice in the last thirty-six years, so it's there, in my memory, but I can't call it forth. God, how I wish I could hear the power of a voice that is rarely heard, saying things like, "Let's get out of here," "It's our flag, too," and "Watch number six."

"I was always so confused," Stan told me when I asked him to remember going to church. "Am I supposed to sing or am I not supposed to sing. Dad's not singing. I would just sort of do it halfway and mutter."

Once or twice a year, the congregation was called to the altar. To be saved. From damnation. People lined up to enter the Kingdom of Heaven. For such an occasion, it was an orderly procession, one row from one right, center, or left section at a time. Reverend Hall or whoever would preach in a more agitated fashion than usual, the music would send a signal, and people would rise from their seats and follow the person ahead of them to the front, at the altar below the pulpit, and stand there while Reverend Hall or whoever touched them or sprinkled something on them and asked a question or made a statement to which each individual would nod and move away with a glance that said, "Is this what I am supposed to do now?" and then awkwardly file back to a hard wooden pew seat, newly guaranteed of that spot in heaven. Getting saved.

I'm uncertain of what exactly happened up there, because we never went. The Shroyers, Vern's brood, ignored all the signals, the heightened agitation in the voice of Reverend Hall or whomever, the music, God, and, my God, the peer pressure.

"Nope," said Vern. Turned it down. Like the insufficient recognition handed out by the GM rewards program.

Everybody else followed the procedural clues into heaven, and there we sat.

Nobody had to tell me what "all right then, I'll go to hell" meant, when I read *Huckleberry Finn.*

Vern never said to us, "You know those people are fools," on the way to Swiss Steak, mashed potatoes, corn, chocolate pudding, and a Coke in Elwood or at any time else, either, but I remember thinking in the car on those days that being Vern's kid put me among the absolute luckiest and best people on the planet. And although I have to admit our planet was pretty small then, I'm pretty sure there was something to that. We were the free ones. He read Zane Grey and Mark Twain during down times at the factory. Not the Bible.

There was a stretch of State Road 13, about a half a mile, that curved from the north-south to the east-west and then back again, where Vern used to see if he could make the Chevys and then the Pontiacs go one hundred miles per hour. He just did it, and we loved it. On the way to Elwood after church. No words before, no words after, from Dad. An agitated and thrilled "Vern!" from Mom.

Flood

38. MONEY

Dear Vern,

There was more flooding in the upper Wabash River valley in the winter of 1959, but with the Upper Wabash Valley Flood Control Project having been approved in July of 1958, the problem linked to a different solution. The 1959 flooding proved that getting the money for the project was the imperative.

The *Indianapolis Star* reported on February 13, 1959, that "disastrous floods [were] now raging down the Wabash Valley from Huntington to below West Terre Haute" and that new congressman Roush, "from flood-menaced Huntington, said he will attempt to increase the funds for the Corps of Engineers to make final designs for the Upper Wabash three-reservoir project in the budget before Congress.

"Ralph Roessler of Marion asserted the reservoir system, if completed, would have prevented" the flooding, the article continued.[259]

Along with the *Kokomo Tribune* reporting that day that Congressman Roush had announced the availability of loans for flood victims, the paper also editorialized that recent flooding in Peru, Wabash, and Logansport showed that Congress needed to appropriate money for dams on the Wabash, Mississinewa, and Salamonie Rivers.

The *Star* reported the next day that Indiana governor Harold Handley, back in the statehouse after losing his bid for the US Senate, was urging the state legislature to pass multimillion-dollar flood control bills. Indiana's new Democratic senator distributed an *In Washington with*

Senator Vance Hartke newsletter that was mostly about the flooding issue, on February 16, 1959. President Eisenhower was delaying money for a project that would have prevented flooding, it read. "Senator Hartke's office will be the scene of a meeting of Hoosier congressmen and senators at which a united front for flood control will be formed," he reported.[260]

Hartke, Senator Homer Capehart, and Congressman Roush responded agreeably to letters from *Wabash Plain Dealer* publisher Joe Nixon that same week, letters advising them that recent flooding was a problem that proved the Upper Wabash Valley Flood Control Project was a necessity. Roush's response said, "I have decided, in an attempt to prevent such future disasters to introduce a bill to appropriate $302,000.00 for the Mississinewa Dam and Reservoir, $202,000.00 for the Salamonie Dam and Reservoir, and $202,000.00 for the Huntington Dam and Reservoir. These sums shall be expended by the Corps of Engineers for advancement of engineering and design for these dams and reservoirs."[261] It would take more than five years to complete the dams once they were started, but as was often the case, proponents spoke of them as if they would have been more immediately useful.

On February 18, 1959, Democrat J. Edward Roush's "first address from the floor of the House was an appeal for approval of Congress and needed appropriations to carry on the project."[262]

Roessler and the Indiana Flood Control and Water Resources Commission had a congressman, now, who would campaign. Roush had gotten right at getting busy. Six weeks after being sworn in, he summarized his work at that point in a letter to a rural Huntington County constituent named Herman Elett.

> I have contacted the Corps of Engineers and consulted with them as to what must be done and how much money is needed. I have discussed this matter with the Speaker and the influential leaders in Congress and have asked their support. I might add that they were very sympathetic. I have met with the entire Indiana delegation including our

> Republican colleagues and the two United States Senators and we have developed what we believe to be a coordinated program. I have introduced legislation calling for the appropriation of funds in order that these projects might be started immediately. Yesterday, I gave my first speech from the floor of the House of Representatives and felt that I was very well received. I am enclosing a copy of this speech. These have been the highlights of the activities of the past few days.[263]

Life and Roessler both noted how nice it was to have a congressman better than the last guy. Life passed along to Roush that he'd had a "confidential telephone conversation with the Corps of Engineers"[264] about how to get money from Congress for flood project planning and construction more quickly in order to speed up the process. "I suggested we ask for ten million, as a start for both planning and as a start of construction, but I was told we could not get it, but we possibly could get the $250,000, and we will have their backing on it. You should immediately take whatever steps are necessary to secure the amount requested, with authority for the Corps. of Engineers to use it for planning on both of the two dams suggested."

The IFCWRC was never an agency of Indiana regulation; it was an advocacy group for the US Army Corps of Engineers. So, too, were the strongest voices in the Indiana press.

The *Indianapolis News* added its editorial support on February 14, the *Indianapolis Star* on February 16. The traditionally conservative *Star* said it was worth the money. And in order to remind people of what this was all about, Joe Nixon's *Wabash Plain Dealer* gave Roessler, in its February 18 edition, space for his standard project rationale and history, starting with the 1913 Peru flood.

Everyone, it seemed, was on board, and the new congressman was swimming with the flood control project tide.

John Beamer, the former congressman, still had something to say about all this hullabaloo. He wrote a "what about me?" letter to Senator Capehart on February 20, 1959, on House stationery that he almost never used while he was in office. From his home on Miami Street in Wabash, he wrote, it's wrong for the "new senator from Indiana" to "cash in" on the flood control project. I made a lot of calls, wrote a lot of letters to the Army Corps of Engineers, Beamer said. "Don't let a newcomer take away the credit we deserve. You and some of us are entitled for credit."[265]

In March, he gave a more detailed account of the project and his work on it to the League of Women Voters in Wabash. He kept the speech.

> Senator Capehart and I worked continuously on this project and we did it without any publicity. It was felt that in this manner the minimum of opposition would be created. Sometimes the zealousness of some members or promoters almost killed bills of this nature. In fact, one of the Indiana Flood Control and Water Resources Commission members almost injured the project by extreme pressure on the [public works] committee. The chairman of the subcommittee, knowing of my work for this measure asked me to urge this man to do more "selling and less demanding."
>
> It also must be remembered that some people will be damaged in order that many others may be benefitted. Some 25,000 acres, or more, will be permanently submerged. Three towns and many farm homes, cemeteries and landmarks will be moved. It seems only fair that these people should be well reimbursed for this relocation that is required of them. I introduced legislation that was designed to help these people.
>
> It was felt by the Public Works committee that both proponents and opponents should be heard

> and I helped each group to secure hearings before the committees.[266]

Congressman Beamer concluded the prepared remarks he saved with his congressional papers by talking about the process of appropriating money for the project and potential problems.

That's the last we hear from him. An anticipated appearance before a House Appropriations Committee hearing on legislation for funding the project and a concern in the Roush camp that he would run again in 1960 never materialized.

Roush maintained: bills and hearings and press releases and reports and interviews and lots of letters and speeches and community meetings and radio addresses all the way through. Whatever it took, he was on it, for another two years. While the ten-year-old memory of his friend and party's Fifth District chairman that Roush "introduced the whole idea of flood control and reservoirs" was patently false, we can read Joe Mettler's thought as an indication of how hard Roush worked.

The Indiana General Assembly passed and the governor signed a $1.25 million flood control bill on March 7, 1959, that included $250,000 for the Upper Wabash Valley Flood Control Project. Action on the matter, along with Roush's own appropriation bill that would pass the House in June, included an announcement from Indiana Republican senator Homer Capehart in March that "the Administration has found a way to give Indiana an additional $350,000 for the three Upper Wabash Reservoirs."[267]

That, though, was followed by an Eisenhower veto of money for the project in August, and so Roush's fight for funding for the project, for both planning and construction, would continue into a new presidential administration. Finally, at the end of September 1961, Congress approved, and President Kennedy signed a $3.9 billion public works funding bill that included $700,000 to start work on the Salamonie Reservoir in November, $500,000 to start work on the Mississinewa in the following spring, and $53,000 for a final study on the Huntington project. Work began.

In December 1961, the IFCWRC reported to Indiana Democratic governor Matthew Welsh that

> on Nov. 28, the ground-breaking ceremonies were held for start of construction on Salamonie Reservoir, the first of three units in the Upper Wabash flood control system. Federal money is at hand to start on Mississinewa Reservoir in the spring of 1962. The third unit, Huntington Reservoir, will follow, with a construction start contemplated for fiscal year 1963. This three-unit project is the largest in the history of water resources activities in Indiana. The Corps of Engineers has charge of the work. Planning was done jointly by the Corps and this commission.[268]

Roessler kept a Salamonie ground-breaking picture of himself with Senators Capehart and Hartke, and Congressman Roush setting off the dynamite.

Vern

39. THE OLD HOUSE

Dear Vern,

Your great-grandpa didn't watch a lot of television, the CBS news when he could find the time, but mostly Dad was too busy for anything except a Sunday afternoon World Series game and the Indiana state high school basketball final. The exception was Saturday nights, *Have Gun–Will Travel* and then *Gunsmoke*. I'm on Vern's lap, and when I fall asleep, he carries me up into my attic bed.

When I was ten, I stole one of Vern's Camel cigarettes, took the matches we used to burn the trash, and made an attempt to smoke in the outhouse.

The old house.

Vern and Patty, my mom, had a bedroom downstairs sideways from the living room at the front of the house. Every room was on a slightly different level, maybe that was a quarter inch up or down.

I remember the porch mostly as the place where I collected a nickel from Stan because I won my first bet—the Pirates beat the Yankees in the 1960 World Series against the odds he thought would prove once again that he could take advantage of me. That's why I remember it so well. I showed that he might not.

We had dogs, always outside dogs that slept under that porch and the one in back. I remember a dog that went for a ride in the car with Dad that we never saw again. I remember dogs that were killed by cars and trucks that would not stop afterward on State Road 13 a few feet away.

That gave me a chill that maybe never went away.

A living room furnace burned oil that a truck brought to pour into a tank on the side of the house. What radiated from it was our only heat. In the winter, we'd cover the oil furnace with our blankets to warm and then, inside them already, trudge up the attic stairs to where we'd fall asleep before the blankets were cold.

We called it the *old house* after we moved into the new house. Vern built the new house in the old house's backyard. It took him six years, and he did it almost entirely by himself.

"South of Swayzee," Uncle Wayne said, "he built that house himself. He had some help from Burnell. He built it himself, a beautiful home. That's where you guys was raised. He was dedicated to work. Even then, after he built the house and everything, I can remember coming down with Dad and shucking corn just to fill in to help out. He was quite the guy."

"I remember him," said Wayne. "He was a very, very nice man, but he had a streak. He said he wanted to go somewhere at 5:00 or 6:00, you better be ready. 'Cause he'd go off and leave ya. That's just the way he was. The other boys, of course, Burnell, they had a little bit more patience. But Vern was very much that way."

Moving into the new house that Vern built was among the happiest times of my life. It had a bathroom instead of a bucket in the kitchen corner, and every electrically heated room had its own thermostat. I was so glad that we could live like other people and that in the winter I wouldn't be so cold. Up until then, pretending that living in that old house wasn't so bad was how we coped.

One morning, I woke up in our attic bed to a pile of snow over my feet. Everything was okay, though. We didn't complain, and nobody complained for us.

There were comic books strewn all over the floor around our bed up there. Downstairs, there were bookcases full of books. The supermarket put out a series of picture book encyclopedias that we seemed always to be in the process of collecting. *Life*, *Look*, and the *Saturday Evening Post*, *Reader's Digest*, and *TV Guide* were strewn around the living room along with the Marion paper, the *Chronicle-Tribune*. I had a library card to check out books I wanted from the Swayzee library three miles away. I liked history and current events. My favorite book was about the fighter planes from World War II. I liked the P-38, and Abe Lincoln, and I knew Dean Rusk was secretary of state, that Robert McNamara was secretary of defense, and that the president's brother was attorney general when I was eight years old.

I collected astronaut trading cards with the twenty-five-cents-a-week allowance money Mom gave me. You might find them in the baseball card stacks I'm keeping for your dad in my attic. Gus Grissom. Mercury 7. I had a savings account at the bank.

I could tell you some stuff that would make you say, "That was terrible," but honestly, it didn't seem so bad then, and so I don't know why it should seem bad now, to you or anyone else. I mean, look at us. Pretty well off, aren't we? Your folks, me, your grandma, and you. You grew up in that old house, too. There's no Vern II without a Vern I. Being Vern's kid put me among the absolute luckiest and best people on the planet. I believe that still.

Flood

40. MARION

Dear Vern,

I was born in Marion, Indiana, the county seat of Grant County, in 1953. Marion is known for state-championship-level high school basketball and the 1930 courthouse lawn lynching of two men that produced the iconic photograph that inspired "Strange Fruit," the Abel Meeropol song that Billie Holiday recorded in 1939.

There were rumblings in Grant County early in 1959 because the Upper Wabash Valley Flood Control Plan that had been authorized by Congress in 1958 didn't do anything to help Marion. Some people even maintained that it would make flooding there worse. That's ironic, of course, because the initial idea came from a Marion jewelry store owner who wanted to do something beneficial for his town. The Kiwanis Club project Ralph Roessler envisioned in 1939 became something people in his town criticized. That had to hurt, twenty years later, but at least Ralph had a congressman's ear.

Roessler let that newly elected congressman, J. Edward Roush, know by mail in March 1959 that while the army maintained it was not true, the *Marion Chronicle-Tribune* was reporting that Mississinewa Dam backwaters would cause flooding in Marion. Was it possible that water backed up behind the dam could extend to the city's north side? Congressman Roush used a letter to Colonel C. C. Noble at the US Army Engineer Louisville District to set up meetings with people in Marion to explain why the new dam would not hurt the city and to tell them that flood prevention there was also a priority.

The new congressman had already received a letter expressing a general dissatisfaction with the Upper Wabash Valley Flood Control Project that mentioned potential Marion problems from a rural Wabash County constituent on February 25, 1959. Charles Courtney wrote sarcastically that "it sounds like a great idea when Marion is the first to flood to back more water in on their city then to tell them to look after their own flood programs."[269]

Marion-area state representative Wayne Townsend had written to Roush the next week that "several people have expressed to me their reservations about the project," that it "may harm rather than help flood control in Grant County."[270]

It was a conflict that put the *Marion Chronicle-Tribune* into a dispute with the army and the flood control commission as Roush navigated concerns he did not see as mutually exclusive. It's possible, as he saw it, that the project was worthwhile and that more attention should have been paid to flood control issues in his new friend Ralph Roessler's hometown.

Before the meetings with the army that Roush set for April, the mayors of Marion and nearby Gas City told the Marion paper that measures they had suggested to the Indiana Flood Control and Water Resources Commission had been ignored. Gas City mayor Robert Ray said, "We sent the recommendations five years ago to Indianapolis and that's the last we heard of them."[271] Ray and Marion mayor Willard Blackman said in a March 27, 1959, *Chronicle-Tribune* article that those recommendations were for channel deepening, soil conservation, and watershed protection of the Mississinewa River. That would have been consistent with the small dam plan championed by Upper Wabash Valley Flood Control Project critics. They also suggested surveys for possible upstream measures to alleviate flooding in Marion's direction, the area east of what would be the Mississinewa Reservoir. The paper reported that Roessler, the IFCWRC vice chairman, and its chief engineer, Joe Perrey, admitted in Marion on March 6 that "no survey has been made for Marion area flood prevention above the dam site, that no soil conservation practices have been considered, and that Marion and other upstream communities would have to solve their own high-water problems." Both mayors "question the advisability of [the] final project," the paper reported. They agreed that the project's economic and recreational benefits would not accrue to them. "Being excluded from state flood control plans and projects," the paper reported, "city and county officials were at a loss yesterday as to how Marion, Jonesboro and Gas City were to benefit in 'the master plan.'"

That final project was for "downstate flood relief," S. M. Bailey, the chief engineer of the district Army Corps of Engineers in Louisville, had told the paper in the March story. "No plans," he added, "were contemplated in present projects for flood control measures above proposed dam sites." Marion, Jonesboro, and Gas City are above the dam sites.

For those towns, all that Roessler and Perrey said the IFCWRC did contemplate were "plans to make plans."

But then, after an April 14, 1959, survey request letter from Roush, the army changed its tune and decided that a survey of the river around Marion would be a good idea after all. Roush let the Marion newspaper know on April 20, 1959. "I have received a reply," he wrote,

> from the District Engineer telling me that they have sufficient congressional authority for investigation and study of the localities mentioned. The Engineer also informs me that field surveys of the flood damage in the communities of Marion, Gas City and Jonesboro are now scheduled for the near future and that the necessary investigations and studies will be prosecuted as rapidly as funds and the availability of personnel will permit.[272]

Fewer than four months in office, Roush had made himself a force to be reckoned with.

The army and the *Tribune* continued to dispute for a year if a survey was or would be done. And they debated through Roush whether or not the water held in the reservoir would back up far enough to flood Marion.

"Would you please," Roush wrote Bailey on July 21, 1959, "prepare a statement using laymen's language explaining specifically how this project could not possibly adversely affect the Marion community and why it could not possibly increase flood danger in this community above the dam? I believe their contention is that because the water will be held back at the Mississinewa Dam it will not only back up into the Marion area but will prevent water in that area from getting away as rapidly as it normally would."[273]

The army replied that a flood in Marion would recede by the time the reservoir was full enough to have an effect on the city. *Marion Chronicle-Tribune* publisher Gardner Thomas cited the 1913 flood in a letter to Roush the next year disputing that idea and added for good measure that "it was very evident that the Indiana Flood Control and Water Resources Commission was quite interested in creating a recreational reservoir and that the flood condition was merely an excuse."[274]

Both the paper and the army would agree that more study was needed on the matter of flooding by the Mississinewa River in Marion and the surrounding area. There's no doubt that the Upper Wabash Valley Flood Control Project did not incorporate the flood control needs of Marion in its original planning or implementation. All this back-and-forth about Marion in 1959, through 1960, and into 1961 was an afterthought, at least in part generated seventeen years too late by people in the Fifth District who had not been served, saying, "Hey, what about me?"

The *Marion Chronicle-Tribune*'s ongoing project criticism led to a November 1961 inquiry from Ken Francis, a reporter for Joe Nixon's *Peru Tribune*, about the *Chronicle-Tribune*'s editorial stance, suggesting it objected to the Upper Wabash Valley Flood Control Project and asking the Marion paper to publish an alternative.

Jim Mitchell, the *Chronicle-Tribune*'s executive editor, bypassed Francis and wrote publisher Nixon directly, and "not for publication," that his paper did not oppose flood control. "But we are opposed to leaving Marion and other communities up along the Mississinewa River to flounder in flood waters while the government uses our tax dollars to protect communities along the Wabash River." In a postscript, Mitchell said, "Enclosed are some recent editorials and a Sunday feature."[275] One was an editorial titled "Recreation or Flood Control?" and one was an article by John Chambers with the headline DAM MEANS MOVE TO PEOPLE OF VALLEY, BUT WHERE TO GO. In part, it read:

> In Peoria, white-haired and grizzled Milo Behney looked over the cottage in which he and Mrs. Behney set up housekeeping 53 years ago. He could picture the Mississinewa spillway crossing his property and pushing up the cliff to the old cemetery next to the Methodist Church.
>
> "We don't have any plans . . . no money. We love to live here. It's beautiful. The water has run us out a few times, and we've lost a little work in cleaning up afterwards, but I knew the river and was ready.
>
> "There's a great deal of resentment here. That church is a landmark. People have been buried in that cemetery 150 years, I expect."[276]

The *Tribune* returned to the dispute over the project's usefulness with a January 17, 1963, editorial decrying an increase in the amount of land being seized for the project, again by saying the federal government was more interested in recreation than flood control. A glance back at 1939 suggests that was an interest then shared by Marion's own Roessler when he started the whole thing but not shared by the federal government's Army Corps of Engineers. The army was all about big dam flood control. The emphasis on recreation came from Ralph initially and percolated among other local and state officials and business interests.

There's one more thing worth noting back in the March 27, 1959, *Chronicle-Tribune* article. According to Marion's Mayor Blackman, "City officials were informed by federal agencies that all funds were depleted when requests were made for government aid to repair and rebuild city levees."[277]

This is where I remember, Vern, that in June of 1943, Congress created a law that allocated as much as $10 million "to be expended in the repair, improvement, and extension of levees on the Wabash River and its tributaries, and in such other flood-control work as the Chief of Engineers may find to be necessary to control the flow of the waters of such river and its tributaries."[278] That was HR 2957. The work never happened. I suppose it could be that the money was spent in a way for which it was not originally intended. The levees along the Wabash River and its tributaries were not fixed. The Army Corps of Engineers and the IFCWRC had other ideas.

Somerset

41. TOWNSMAN

Dear Vern,

Two weeks before its articles began criticizing the Upper Wabash Valley Flood Control Project for ignoring Marion, a singular Somerset-perspective article appeared in the Marion newspaper. The March 12, 1959, *Marion Chronicle-Tribune* page 14 feature story, "Residents of Somerset Must Move If Dam Is Built,"[279] is about one-third page, with a long-view picture looking west from the middle of Somerset's Main Street and three portrait shots of men the author, James S. Ward, interviewed. In it, grocery store owner Robert Drook pitched the small dam plan alternative while service station owner Robert King said the coming big dam and reservoir were a done deal.

Somerset resident Melvin Harrison said, "The town better get together and decide on what we want to do. We can't sell property, values are hurt. Some people won't put a price on things 'cause they don't know which way to jump."

The *Chronicle-Tribune* article revealed residents' uncertainty about moving the town, and it's apparent that four years after their fate was revealed, some people would have simply rather not talked, or thought, about it. "Where else would I relocate?" an unidentified resident said.

"To some, such as Russell Dubois of Hammond, Indiana, there is an additional problem," Ward wrote. "His parents and other relatives are all buried in Somerset Cemetery and he made a special trip here to find out what effect the proposed dam would have on grave re-location."

Waltz Township trustee Earl Kern talked like he thought the flooding still might not happen. "'You know,' he observed, 'I remember seeing similar plans for this project and these dams 27 years ago. And with the national budget the way it is, how do you know what will happen in Congress?'"

Nine months later, a classified ad in the *Elwood Call-Leader* that ran for several days said, "New oil heaters. Used coal, oil and gas heaters. Kern at Somerset, Indiana."[280]

It's hard to imagine what Somerset would be like today if the Upper Wabash Valley Flood Control Project had never happened. Could it have maintained its identity through the second half of the twentieth century and into the twenty-first?

When Janet (Shroyer) Schenkel said wistfully to me, "We can't go back to share the things that we liked when we were growing up. We can't take our kids there," I wondered how long that the visible aspects of that idealized community condition would have lasted, anyway, without the dam. For how many years would an abandoned Somerset High School have stood? Would Dollar General have sprouted on the edge of a town abandoned by the Gruener Grocery when area residents found the Walmart that found nearby Wabash? While Somerset remains idyllic in my own memory and imagination, how different would it have been, really, from the rest of our world if the dam had not come? Did the project only serve to accelerate the inevitable?

I'm reminded of "To an Athlete Dying Young" by A. E. Housman and the lines, "Smart lad, to slip betimes away / From fields where glory does not stay,"[281]

Smart, town.

By modernity obliterating the town in what amounted to a preemptive strike, modernity never got a chance to gradually change it in the manner it did the rest of us. Maybe, Vern, from my modern perspective, that's why "Somerset" looks so good.

42. GRAVE SIGHTS

Somerset was never incorporated, so there were never any municipal services or lawmen. People there "took care of things" themselves.

Dave Compton, the local businessman I met during my visit to the Somerset Lions Club when I first started to talk to people about the dams, told me about an early-twentieth-century Wabash County sheriff when I visited him at his home in Huntington County. "He was a rough old boy," Dave said.

"The sheriff from 1910 to 1912 was John Niccum, a veteran of the Civil War, Company F of the 153rd Indiana Volunteer Infantry," Compton said. "Niccum was deemed the only one qualified to be sheriff of Wabash County." He said Niccum was the sheriff only a short time because of a family of some influence that did not want him in the role.

For a long time, the jail in Somerset, Compton told me, was also a storage shed for fresh vegetables, so there was ice beneath the floor. The only law officers in town were volunteers, "vigilantes, a bartender, who knows?" Dave said. When someone caused trouble, usually after drinking too much, "they'd take 'em and throw 'em in there and lock the door. It didn't matter if it was summertime or wintertime." Dave chuckled. "They were froze by morning."

The next day, he said, the sheriff would come down and pick him up. "No shivering-overnight prisoner wanted to come back to that jail."

One story, Dave said, is that Niccum "was taking a guy from the jail over to the county courthouse" in Wabash. "He didn't put any handcuffs or anything on the guy, and the prisoner said, 'Well, what if I decide to take off?'

"Niccum said, 'You won't get far.'

"The guy never took off."

John Niccum died in 1934 as one of the last remaining Civil War soldier survivors. His grave, near Somerset, was among those moved at the Army Corps of Engineers' direction to make way for the reservoir flood.

The grave of another former Wabash County sheriff, Asa Ross, was also among those moved north to the consolidated Mississinewa Memorial Cemetery along State Road 13. Ross also served in Company F, but unlike Niccum, in the 138th Infantry Regiment Indiana. Ruth Rudicel mentioned him in her handwritten note on First Christian Church stationery dated June 2, 1955, that was in response to the news that Somerset would be lost. She wrote to Congressman John Beamer from her home in the unincorporated town of Nineveh, Indiana, the day after the "New Dam May Force Out State Town of Somerset" article appeared in the *Indianapolis News* (1955). Ruth wrote, "I feel constrained to ask you if the cemetery there will be affected by the move. My maternal grandparents and an aunt are buried there," she said. "My grandfather was Asa S. Ross, a veteran of the Civil War, [who] served two terms as sheriff of Wabash County. He then bought a home on West Maple Street in Wabash where he lived until his death, which occurred in about 1897."[282]

Ruth concluded in the note that her two sisters, one in Logansport and the other in Temple City, California, would like to know what was going to happen to the remains of her relatives, too.

In the letter Beamer got from C. A. Kessler of Wabash in April of 1956, Kessler had said, "There is hardly a family in Waltz Township that doesn't have relatives buried in the cemeteries you have to move."[283] That had to be true. There were more than three thousand graves to move in the Mississinewa Dam area alone. The population of Waltz Township in 1960 was half that. "It's desecration," Kessler wrote.

Is any place more sacred than a cemetery? It would be hard, I expect, Vern, to find a culture anywhere at any time in the world that doesn't value the preservation of its forebears' remains. At the same time, it would be not hard to find lots of examples of grave desecration in the relationship between a conquering culture and those being conquered. Conscious or unconscious, the disrespect is simply sanctioned, certainly not prohibitive.

The Upper Wabash Valley Flood Control Project precipitated the moving of more than seven thousand graves from the areas in and around the three-reservoir project in Wabash and Huntington Counties. Congressman J. Edward Roush announced the removal plan on August 10, 1961, after meeting, he said, with the Army Corps of Engineers. Roush told the Associated Press that day that he had sympathy for persons upset about the idea, because his own father's grave would be moved from within the Salamonie Reservoir area in Huntington County. The grave of Roush's father, Herman Amos Roush, was moved along with around three thousand others in the Mount Etna Cemetery to an adjacent township. According to the AP story that ran in the August 11, 1961, *Kokomo Tribune*, the dams for all three reservoirs in the system would "produce water up to 30 feet deep on more than a dozen cemeteries in the three areas."[284]

Roush promptly began to get letters about the moving of graves. Some were from people looking for business and employment opportunities. Most were from people concerned about their relatives' remains.

Wabash County sheriff Asa Ross's grave was among the five hundred in the Somerset Cemetery, which was on the west end of town, between Water Street and the Mississinewa River. It would indeed be well under the new water. The other Mississinewa system cemeteries' immersion level would vary, depending upon their location. Some graveyards would only be touched by water on rare occasions of excessive rainfall. Some, it's hard to tell, because they were very remote.

When the Army Corps of Engineers Louisville District office issued its *Final Report, Cemetery Relocation Plan No. 2 for Ten Cemeteries, Wabash County, June 1968*, it included ten Mississinewa Dam area cemetery pictures, as they had been before moving, all taken on September 26, 1963. With the dam by then well under construction and property in the area already condemned for confiscation, it's clear in the photos that cemetery upkeep had already declined. The Somerset grounds appear to have had a summer without mowing. The bushes at Mount Vernon, just south of the river and just east of State Road 13, needed trimming. The Ogan Cemetery on the other side of the river from there, and the Pleasant Grove grounds, about five miles west of Somerset, both look pretty good.

My grandmother Eva Arrick Shroyer was among 450 people buried at Pleasant Grove at that time. Eva Shroyer was your great-great-grandma, Vern's mom. John Niccum had been buried with many members of his family and one thousand others at Ogan. My parents would both be buried in what later became the Pleasant Grove section in the consolidated Mississinewa Cemetery. When I visit their graves now, I see more tombstone names I know than I did before I started writing this letter to you.

The Sugar Grove Cemetery picture shows what looks like an overgrown, weed-infested field on the edge of a woods with no grave markers clearly visible. That plot, which was on the west side of Hoover Road, where it bordered my grandparent's farm on the east, contained forty-one graves. For eight of them, the identity is "unknown." All but two people there were buried in the nineteenth century, the oldest grave being that of Mary Shackleford, who was interred in 1853. When the excavators hired by the army from the Irwin-Jones Company of Honesdale, Pennsylvania, dug her up, I wonder what they found.

The Captain Dixon Cemetery contained three graves, "Capt. Dixon," "Capt. Dixon's Daughter," and "Baby of Capt. Dixon." The captain died in 1839. There's no date of death listed for the children. The edge of a barn that had been built over the young ones' graves is visible in the photo. No word on Mrs. Dixon. The army report says it was an "Indian Cemetery."

The Bank Cemetery had four graves and is called a "family cemetery," but there's no one named Bank. The picture confirms the "fenced, but untended" report remark. D. C. Shannon was buried there in 1815; Sarah Shannon followed in 1819. An "infant of M & L Eltzroth" and "Matilda Stewart" followed in 1845 and 1849. D. C. died before Indiana was a state, when the territorial name that meant "land of the Indians" implied it would be a place for Indigenous people to live safely. These are some old graves.

Graves and old people you never heard of. I know this gets hard to follow, and I wonder if you haven't given up on what I have to say a ways back. Maybe your grandchild will come across this account.

When you were born, my perspective changed, and I suppose that's a big part of why I'm writing all this. When you were born, I saw myself suddenly in the middle of a thread of five generations that stretched from my grandfather to you. It's a line of sons. In my mind's eye, I could see "Pop" and I could see you. I've heard it said that our lives extend across the span of time that exists in the memory of the people who knew us. My memory keeps my born-in-1888 grandfather alive. By that measure, when you die in 2098, I'll be 210 years old.

My parents both came from big families, and both experienced the death of infant children siblings. People were born at home, especially in rural areas back then, and some children didn't make it. Sometimes the mothers didn't make it. My grandfather Shroyer's mother died when he was eleven. He stayed with his father, Asberry, but his sister, my great-aunt Vernie, was brought up in the home of Asberry's sister, Mary, and her husband, Milo Stitts. When Vernie was grown up, she and her first husband, Tom Snyder, adopted a baby boy named Fred, who would become a leader in guiding the Somerset resettlement. Fred Snyder was also the father to the best Somerset information source I had for this letter to you. His name is also Tom Snyder.

Taking care of needy children meant adopting them sometimes and sometimes not. I suppose a long trip into town to deal with the legalities might not have always made sense in a household that didn't need to be told what it already knew. That child is one of us, period. People of Somerset "took care of things" themselves.

Adoption is not unusual for your grandma Shroyer's family, either. Your second cousin Sophie was adopted by your great-uncle Peter and your great-aunt Sheree. Your second cousin Eleanor was adopted by your great-aunt Janice. Eleanor was named for your grandma Shroyer's mom, just as you were named for your grandpa Shroyer's dad.

The grandparent I remember best is my mom's mother, Grandma Fuller. Agnes Fuller. Her maiden name was Cartwright. Agnes Fuller lived to be ninety. She lived with my grandfather John Fuller on a farm where my mom grew up only three miles from our house in Normal. I spent a lot of time there when I was a kid. She was a nice lady. They sold apples and vegetables and eggs and chickens and noodles and pies, I remember, from a farm stand.

My mom told me that she remembered when she was a little girl, "a family of colored people" stopped to buy, and her mother refused to sell to them. Could she be a nice lady and do something like that? That lesson about the nature of prejudice is somehow more frightening than if she had been mean. I made myself believe it was my grandfather's fault because I didn't like him. When I was a little older, he proudly showed his family a souvenir picture of the 1930 lynching in Marion, Indiana, and said, "That's how we handled it in my day." There's a chilling side to the notion that the people of Somerset "took care of things," too, because the notion of "justice" is subject to a bigotry filter that even nice people like my grandma Fuller can hold.

43. WITNESS

I knew all four grandparents. My grandmother Shroyer is the one I remember the least. She died when I was four years old. Eight years later, her grave was moved.

My brother, your great-uncle Stan, was there when that happened. "It was a summer day," he told me. "I remember going to the cemetery with Grandpa and Dad. I remember driving up there." The Pleasant Grove Cemetery is a place in my memory going back as far as memory goes. A picture of its archway entrance that Dave Compton showed me startled me like a vision from a forgotten dream. Pleasant Grove was the cemetery in the Pleasant Grove Methodist churchyard where Dad worried about the ghost-es. Some gravestones there I remember were like sand, gray sand, and so old it was hard to read the names and numbers. In my mind, it's a sunny day and already summertime hot.

Vern took us there every Memorial Day weekend. Soldiers marched with flags and shot a twenty-one-gun salute. My sister, Linda, remembered that on the Sunday before Memorial Day, we went to church services inside before the gravesite ceremony. "Church there was scary," Linda said, "because the minister yelled about what would happen to you if you were not a Christian.

"After church, we went to the cemetery, right out the door. The kids roamed the cemetery looking at the monuments. We looked at names and dates trying to find the oldest and newest." After the twenty-one-gun salute, Linda told me, "We went to the farm for lunch. I am pretty sure we changed out of our church clothes."

On the day Grandma's grave was moved, Stan remembers, "There was a black plastic tarp stretched across the whole front of the cemetery. To me, that seemed kind of evil."

In the late spring of 1966, the Army Corps of Engineers had begun moving the seven thousand graves from the area on the verge of flooding to make way for the three Upper Wabash Valley Flood Control Project man-made lakes. They'd hired a company from northeast Pennsylvania to do the work. In turn, the Irwin-Jones Company of Honesdale "hired some local guys to do some of the excavation," Tom Snyder told me. It began at the Pleasant Grove Cemetery in the churchyard where my grandparents worshipped on May 31, 1966, according to the "Grave Index" log released by the army in their final report from 1968. That it was the day after Memorial Day is altogether fitting and proper.

"I remember there was an entrance to the front of the cemetery, and we walked through," Stan said, "and there were two guys with shovels digging in the ground. The thing that struck me was they had no front teeth and was smiling as they dug. On the way home in the car, Grandpa told Dad they were convicts."

"I don't remember going and watching anybody, because Mom and Dad were still living," Bonnie Truss told me. "My grandparents were still living."

I'd spent a cold and gray November 2022 day with Bonnie and Duane Truss in the farmhouse where they've lived since 1957, two miles north of my grandparents' former farmland. I was there because Dave Compton had told me that Duane was a cemetery board member during the moving of graves.

Bonnie told me, "What I always heard was how respectful they were and how they were so respectful of what they were dealing with and so maybe you came away with the feeling, 'Well, they cared.' I don't know. That's what I've heard from many people."

My cousin Greg Hoback had earlier told me the same thing. "Moving the graves was done in a dignified manner," he said.

That's how Ralph Roessler, the guiding force behind the Upper Wabash Valley Flood Control Project, had described it. In prepared remarks he saved, Roessler told the Fort Wayne Exchange Club on March 10, 1964, that "in the Mississinewa flood pool 3,500 graves will be moved to new locations. The moving of graves is done under special contract with experienced movers. No digging machinery is used, graves are dug manually, remains carefully placed in required receptacles, moved to new locations selected by next of kin. Whatever markers now exist will be placed properly at the new location. No cost to next of kin."[285]

There was a cost to people who wanted graves moved to locations other than the single designated site, the one not so much selected by next of kin as agreed to by the next of kin. There is a difference. "Experienced movers" were hired guys without teeth, according to Stan, "convicts," according to Pop. My brother saw that there were digging machines. When Bonnie and Greg, who weren't there, tell me it was all done in a dignified manner, I wonder how they separately got the same idea. It didn't seem so dignified to my brother, and he was there. What Tom Snyder's dad told him about it doesn't seem real dignified to me, Vern, and Tom's dad was there.

Duane Truss said, "Whoever they found first of the family, that was how people were notified to come be witnesses. That person could've contacted somebody else and said, 'Here's what's gonna happen. Do you want to go with me, or do you want to go?'"

I suppose they called my grandpa–Pop–at his new home in Windfall, and he called my dad, Vern, and Vern asked my brother, Stan, if he'd go. He said yes. I wasn't there. If they asked me, I said no. I don't remember. It was a couple of months before my thirteenth birthday, which I remember most for the sticker from *Mad* magazine that said, "Leave me alone, I'm a teenager," which I put on the door of my room.

"The government didn't spend too many hours making sure someone would be a witness after their initial contact," Duane said.

"The Army Corps of Engineers had to locate a close relative by phone," Tom Snyder said, "for purpose of witnessing. They had to contact one person. I don't think they had to contact anybody else. They mailed stuff, too. A lot of people were in the process of moving. They didn't have the same phone anymore, and it became hard to contact some people," Tom said. "Seventy to 75 percent of the families of the people's graves being moved never responded."

Stan said that when he arrived, "They were digging in the front of the cemetery in the oldest graves where Dad had two infant sisters. Dad said that in those graves, nothing was usually found, and dirt was placed in a coffee can and that was what was reburied."

The "coffee can" was actually a burial box.[286] A diagram in the 1968 army report shows that it was made from an inch-thick "gray color lumber," three feet long, a foot and a half wide, and one foot high. Snyder, who worked for the Army Corps of Engineers, told me, "The burial boxes were used for real old graves. They would dig down, and if they found a handle from a coffin, or if they found soil that was a different color, they would put that in that box."

Tom wasn't a witness to the process, but his dad, Fred, was. "The boxes were backup for what they found," Tom said. "Dad told me that in one case they got down to a casket that did not have a vault. They tried to get under it with straps so they could lift it. He said they got it up aboveground, and the casket broke in half. All there was, he said, was some long red hair that fell from the casket. It was a windy day. That team of guys who were in charge, they were running across the cemetery gathering all that up, trying to keep it so they could move it."

The smiling guys with no teeth.

"A dignified manner."

"Grandma's grave was dug up with a backhoe," Stan said. "The burial vault was brought up with chains. I don't remember the coffin. I think the whole thing was loaded on a truck and transported to the new cemetery. We all just stood around and watched, not much to say. Then we took Grandpa back to Windfall, and we went home, on a summer day.

"What I was told, beyond what I saw, I heard in the car, from Grandpa. He was telling Dad. Convicts. It was just one of those things that sticks with you from when you were young."

44. LOVE US

Starting in 1955, when he began addressing complaints about what was happening to the Somerset area, Congressman John Beamer often emphasized the fair settlement that would come for the people losing their property. That idea came to him directly from Army Corps of Engineers colonel W. D. Milne, the man who would soon reveal the loss of Somerset. Milne, the lead man on the Upper Wabash Valley Flood Control Project in Louisville, said in a March 3, 1955, letter that "landowners will be adequately compensated for all real estate rights acquired."[287] "Adequately compensated" would be determined by the army.

At an Indiana Flood Control and Water Resources Commission *Marion Chronicle-Tribune* press briefing in June 1955 to shore up Congressman John Beamer's perceived weak public support for the project, commission member Carlos Life said that displaced residents would be reimbursed. As also reported June 3, commission executive vice president Robert Kellum told the *Wabash Plain Dealer* that the $700,000 set aside for Somerset was more than the town was worth. They could build an "ideal, model town," Kellum said.[288]

They should be happy about the destruction of their community, Vern; they should like the idea.

Commission vice chairman and Marion jeweler Ralph Roessler had made the strategy clear in his June 5, 1955, letter to Beamer. "Many of the buildings are very old and there is considerable sentiment involved, but once the residents understand they will be well taken care of, they will be paid for any damage incurred, and will end up by a replaced village on high ground and in an admirable location to become a revived lakeside resort village, then they will see the benefits against the disturbance incurred. It would seem to me," Roessler wrote, "you will have little trouble convincing your constituents that relocation means a great improvement to Somerset and of great value to each individual involved."[289] Sell it. Make them love us. That's how in 1955 Roessler, Kellum, and Life saw the congressman's job. They didn't think Beamer did it very well.

However, the congressman had passed the sentiment along several times. Remember, Vern, it was back in July 1955 that Beamer wrote concerned Wabash County farmer and World War II veteran Lawrence Scheffer, "You may be assured that I shall do everything to protect your interests and the interest of all of the people in the district."[290]

And that early in 1956, he wrote Huntington County farmer and former state legislator Cliff Funderburg that people losing property would be "well paid."[291]

At the end of 1956, Beamer replied to Hueston Schaaf of Amboy, "Any property that is to be relocated or vacated because of a flood control program is appraised at current market values and under the present law an additional sum can be paid for relocation purposes. Consequently, the chances are that every person who must be relocated would be reasonably well paid for their property."[292]

In an April 10, 1957, editorial supporting the project and denouncing its opponents, John Nixon's *Peru Tribune* said, "Mr. Beamer wants to protect those who will be hurt, those who will be forced to move off their land. He wants to see people adequately repaid for their land as well as for the cost of relocating. This is only proper. But those against the measure could easily throw the picture out of focus with their many arguments."[293] That sounds like a veiled threat to me, Vern.

In his final reported statement on the matter, five months after he was voted out of office, Beamer told the March 1959 Wabash League of Women Voters meeting that for damage to people, farmland, and three towns, "people should be reimbursed. I worked for that."[294] Inarguable consensus, but by how much, the specifics would be a matter of dispute.

"The story as I got older," said Somerset native Tom Snyder, "was 'The government is going to compensate you for your farm. They're not gonna take your property. They're gonna negotiate with you. You're gonna get paid.'"

After the settlement for his 120-acre farm, my grandfather lived in a little trailer in his daughter's backyard in Windfall, Indiana. That's what I know.

45. WINDFALL

When Grandpa was ten, his mother died. It was one of those things that stuck with him from when he was young. I remember that Pop would travel back to a Miami County, Kansas, cemetery once a year, to visit.

By the time his wife's body was moved from Pleasant Grove Cemetery, Pop had moved into the larger of two trailers, where he lived until he died in 1974, after leaving the farm near Somerset across Hoover Road from the Sugar Grove Cemetery. That new spot was in Windfall, Tipton County, in my aunt Mary's backyard. Aunt Mary Hoback was Vern's sister. I'd travel fifteen minutes in the silent car with Vern alone on Saturday morning to visit Pop. I remember the tiny first trailer best, unkempt and with the odor of bacon fat. That rounded green trailer is one of those things that stuck with me from when I was young. I told your grandma Shroyer once that I'd be moving into a tiny place like that after she died. She didn't find that funny.

Pop's little place had lots of a weekly newspaper called *Grit* scattered around, seeming to cover every surface inside that wasn't covered already and some that were. The *Grit* was made for country people like Pop who needed some relief from the trouble that living can bring.

German immigrant Dietrick Lamade owned and ran the paper. According to a biography of Lamade by Damon M. Laabs, Lamade told his employees:

> Always keep *Grit* from being pessimistic. Avoid printing those things which distort the minds of readers or make them feel at odds with the world. Avoid showing the wrong side of things, or making people feel discontented. Do nothing that will encourage fear, worry, or temptation. Wherever possible, suggest peace and good will toward men. Give our readers courage and strength for their daily tasks. Put happy thoughts, cheer, and contentment into their hearts.[295]

After Lamade died in 1938, his son George became publisher. George, all out of strength and courage, got tired of being sick and killed himself, on a day I could have been visiting Pop, in 1965.

My cousin Greg Hoback, Aunt Mary's son, told me that Pop was happy in Windfall. "In all the times I was around him . . . I never remember him expressing any bitterness." Leaving the Waltz Township farm near Somerset was not the worst thing for our grandfather, Greg said. "Maybe he was getting a little lonely out there, all the boys are gone. Uncle Wayne is in the navy. Mom's in Windfall.

"He seemed so happy. He'd sit out there. He had an old neighbor, Chester Mitchell. They would just solve the world's problems in a couple of lawn chairs. He had someone to visit with. He had his radio to listen to baseball games."

I can remember one cold, snow-covered night going with Dad to watch Greg play basketball for Windfall High School. He was a senior the same year as my sister, Linda: 1964. Greg was modestly surprised when I told him recently that I was there, but he remembers Pop.

"I remember my senior year of high school, we lived close enough to the gym that he would walk to the basketball games," Greg said. "I'd always find him at one corner. He didn't sit on the home team side; he'd sit on the other, munching on his popcorn. He took himself down there. You know the old schools and the rickety old bleachers. I thought, *Oh, man, Granddad, don't fall.*

"I never heard him complain. When the family left, he was ready to get around some people, so we got him set up. He pretty well took care of himself back there. He'd come up for Sunday dinner. Mom would say, 'You want to come up to eat with us Sunday?' And he'd say, 'Well, if I don't get a better offer.'"

Uncle Wayne told me that Pop had intended to leave the farm after Grandma died but that the news right then about the reservoir complicated things. "Dad was gonna give up the farm, I think. He was gonna sell it, move to Windfall. That was where Mary was at. He had sort of planned it, but he didn't have a buyer. And then they came along with the reservoir." There was no better offer than that provided by the Army Corps of Engineers real estate agents.

"I don't think it was near the going rate for a farm in Wabash County at the time," Tom Snyder told me. His uncle Charley's farm "wasn't the best. It wasn't all tillable, wasn't flat like some property north a mile, where if you had a woods you could bulldoze it down. You could farm it if you wanted to. Charley's farm had a lot of woods on it. He had a big creek running right through it, lots of crawdads in that creek."

The Army Corps of Engineers real estate agents ran the property sales from an office in Wabash, Snyder said. "The building is still there. It was an office building for a factory. That was their main office for buying all the real estate for all three reservoirs. They bought all the property and did all the negotiation, and a lot of old people went to them offices to get everything finalized." That property, for "a bunch of the older folks, some of them, it was the home they grew up in," he said. "Second generation, maybe third."

Pop moved into a trailer that you could just about pull behind a car in the backyard of his daughter's house. Thanks to FDR and the Democrats, Dad told me in the car, Pop had Social Security. Social Security made a big difference in the lives of a lot of people. "Republicans want to get rid of that," Dad said. That's one of the things I remember him saying from when I was young.

46. RESETTLEMENT

After new congressman Ed Roush informed the people of Somerset in late 1959 that the purchase of their property would begin after July of 1961, he began to get letters about the specifics. His answers showed sympathy and a genuine desire to help but at the same time asserted his position on flood control. He wrote Somerset High School teacher Robert Dawes, "I weighed the consequences of building the dams to a hundred people against the financial loss to thousands, the hardship of being homeless to many others, the economic disaster of continued floods and the loss of human life, for which there is no monetary compensation, and decided if I was to fairly and responsibly represent the Fifth District, I must fight for flood control."[296]

I discussed your concerns with the army, Roush responded later to the Reverend LeRoy J. DeLong of Somerset, and "I feel confident that, in the very near future, you will receive a letter from the Louisville office answering the inquiries you propose."[297]

Told there was no town government to relay his message to the citizens of Somerset, Roush instructed the postmaster to put the congressman's ideas about federal aid programs that would help in the relocation on his office bulletin board.

Roush suggested that the town form a committee to study possible federal help, and he sought questions from the residents of Somerset that he could take to the army for a December 14, 1961, meeting.

Wabash County attorney Don Mote urged, then, that for residents of Somerset, an "association" would be better than incorporation. According to the *Wabash Plain Dealer* story, December 21, Mote told a county commissioners' meeting attended by three Somerset representatives that it wouldn't cost as much and could be just as effective as an organizing structure for legal negotiations with the federal government.

Four hundred people came to a January 4, 1962, Somerset meeting with army representatives to address the list of twenty-two questions and concerns that Roush had solicited. Along with Roush, that meeting in the high school gym included Army Corps of Engineers Louisville District engineer Colonel James Lewis, and corps district office chief of real estate operations Fred Morgan. Four Indiana Flood Control and Water Resources Commission associates were present: member Carlos Life, executive secretary Robert Kellum, chief engineer Joseph Perrey, and engineer Robert Jackson. Seven members of a newly formed Somerset Citizens Committee were there along with Wabash attorney Robert McCallen, who had been retained as their counsel. McCallen ran the meeting, according to the memo that Kellum wrote for the IFCWRC the next day.[298]

Roush began by telling everyone again that Somerset would have to be sacrificed for the Mississinewa Reservoir. No going back. It's best to accept it, he told the crowd, and move forward. Morgan told the assembled that the purchase and easement payments would start in the summer of '62 for land below the elevation of 785 feet. Morgan said there would be no mechanical equipment used in the moving of graves. He said, "All hand work is required in grave moving," according to Kellum's memo. And as for a new town, Morgan said, already "66 families in Somerset had voted to move as a community to a new site."

Things, of course, did not proceed from that night as smoothly as Kellum's memo might have suggested. McCallen wrote Roush in July that people were getting conflicting accounts from the army on resettlement. Also, he said, "I would appreciate it if you would put me in contact with the proper agency which could lend the contemplated non-profit Somerset development corporation the money for sewers and sewage disposal system. This is essential if we are to succeed in our endeavor."[299] Roush followed up with a letter to the Farmers Home Administration, which told him, money for water: yes; money for sewage: no. For sewage funding, the FHA responded, try the Communities Facilities Administration.

In July 1962, Roush wrote Missouri congressman Clarence Cannon, the chairman of the House Appropriations Committee, requesting another $800,000 in the budget to specifically aid in the relocation of Somerset. "If the appropriation could be increased to $2,500,000, the Corps would be able to move very quickly in the real estate acquisition," Roush wrote. "A year delay in the relocation would be a severe handicap to these people. They are already working under serious limitations and are undergoing much financial hardship because of the move."[300] Roush's emphasis was not his own political benefit but rather a personal concern for the welfare of a small, distressed community within his district.

In October of 1962, McCallen and Somerset Citizens Committee members appealed at the IFCWRC monthly meeting for help in setting up the legal entity for unincorporated Somerset that would help its residents get water and sewer service in their expected new location. Commissioners were supportive; one member suggested that with an estimated sewage plant cost of $200,000, they should qualify for federal aid. "Certainly this is a distressed area," the unidentified member said, as reported in the *Wabash Plain Dealer* on October 27.[301]

Back in 1955, officials with the IFCWRC had begun suggesting that a transplanted Somerset would become, as its executive director Robert Kellum had said, "an ideal town."[302] That's when founding commissioner Ralph Roessler said it would be "a replaced village on high ground and in an admirable location to become a revived lakeside resort village."[303] After that, though, the IFCWRC didn't do much to help make that happen. The army, constrained by the rules governing Somerset's status as an unincorporated settlement, created impediments. When the people of Somerset figured out that they were more or less on their own, they set out to establish that new town themselves. The efforts paid off at the beginning of 1963.

"The newly organized Somerset Development Corp. Monday afternoon bought the site for the new town,"[304] the *Plain Dealer* reported on

Tuesday, January 8, 1963. The purchase of almost ninety-four acres at the corner of Indiana State Road 13 and the Frances Slocum Trail from Mr. and Mrs. Lorrin D. White was completed in attorney McCallen's office in Wabash. Next, McCallen told the paper, would be the "platting of the area for a subdivision of around 140 lots, a business area," two churches, and the Masonic lodge. With sixty-six families in Somerset having voted to move as a community to the new site, deposits for thirty lots, by then, had already been made. A lot of bureaucratic hurdles would have to be cleared, but with a physical location now a reality, a new Somerset was coming into being, almost eight years after Congressman John Beamer heard from the army about their relocation plans. Making that happen fell to the people of Somerset itself, and especially those sixty-six families who had agreed to move as an entity a year earlier.

Neither the army nor the IFCWRC led the way for the people who owned the property confiscated for the Upper Wabash Valley Flood Control Project. Leadership came from the Somerset Citizens Committee: Fred Snyder, Chairman Myron Darby, Vice Chairman Gerald Myers, Mrs. Rex Snyder, Floyd Bowman, Aubrey Jacobs, and Earl Kern; and the Somerset Development Corporation, its president, Fred Snyder, and the other directors, Robert Hahn, Floyd Bowman, Bill Frank, Guy Garst, Aubrey Jacobs, and Mrs. Rex (Mabel) Snyder. Losing Somerset wasn't their idea or something they wanted. Some of the same names show up on the petition against the project that Congressman John Beamer turned over to IFCWRC commissioner Carlos Life back in March of 1956. But they loved their town and one another enough to put their rightful anger aside enough to make their situation better than it might have turned out to be. It wasn't easy.

"It was a time I wouldn't wish for people to go through at my age now," Fred Snyder's son, Tom, told me. "It was quite an education just to see what was happening. My dad was all the time going to meetings, dealing with army real estate guys, meetings at the grocery store, announcements in the paper, announcements of coming meetings."

Of course, a lot of town and area residents did leave for good, like your great-grandfather Pop, for instance. Left to only the army, the town could have easily dissolved into nothing, with its residents scattered totally to the winds. But it didn't. There is still a place called "Somerset," and from talking to people there, I can tell there's a lot of pride taken in the fact that they were able to keep a form of it going.

Flood

47. ROUSH

Dear Vern,

Somerset was not the only place with relocation and reimbursement issues. Democratic congressman J. Edward Roush dealt with a complaint from the Millington Truck Body Company in his hometown of Huntington in August and September of 1963. Sales manager Frank Campbell said they needed information about whether or not they'd have to move. Roush got an answer.

Yes.

"In two weeks you got us an answer we had tried to get for two years. Your usefulness and kindness is exceeded only by your good looks and extreme virility," Campbell wrote Roush. "Thank you very much."[305]

Another controversy arose when the people of Red Bridge began to believe that the people of Somerset were getting a better deal than they were. Red Bridge was a village of around forty people along the Mississinewa River about five miles downstream from Somerset. Dr. Rose Wenrich, whose grandmother Omma Sweet worked with Aunt Vernie on the Somerset schools' cafeteria staff, remembered a gas station there and a restaurant. "It was a little gathering place," she told me. Along with weekend street movies, Vern's cousin Larry Knee remembered that Red Bridge was the place where he first watched TV. One store there, along the river, Larry told me, set up the "first TV I ever seen, a little black-and-white," for the Indiana high school state tourney finals in 1954. In Red Bridge, Larry watched small school Milan's famous win over big school Muncie Central.

Red Bridge was a place that, unlike Somerset, experienced flooding, and it was a place the army decided early on would have to go. There were no plans to relocate. When removal became imminent, the people of Red Bridge formed a group they called the Red Bridge Group shepherded by a man who'd complained before about the army settlements with Congressman Roush, a man named L. Ferol Bussert. Roush had intervened on Bussert's behalf in 1962.

"Before this project was started," Bussert wrote Roush again on November 26, 1963, "properties in Red Bridge sold higher than similar properties in Somerset. Now the situation is reversed."[306]

That's the dispute in a nutshell. It had come up when the Red Bridge Group met on November 7, 1963, at the Conservation Club building in Red Bridge. After Charles Hudson complained about the offer for his property that he was getting from the army, a general discussion ensued, and according to the meeting minutes that Bussert submitted, "Many comparisons were made of prices paid in Somerset and prices offered or paid here so far, for homes of comparable age, condition, or accommodations. Finding little favorable comparison,"[307] that's when the group agreed to write Roush.

I haven't been the most favorably disposed person toward Roush, Vern, going back to his get-together with Ralph Roessler in the run-up to the 1958 election and what Cliff Funderburg had to say about him in 1955. But, we should both recognize the congressman's work that is happening pretty privately here. There's no political advantage in this. It speaks to the congressman's character that he'd gained the credibility required to make the Red Bridge people believe he would help them. And he did. It speaks to my own memory's sense of the time's Kennedy-esque idealism, I think, that doing right is the right thing to do. It wasn't a political calculation.

According to the minutes at the Red Bridge Group meeting, "Mr. Charles Hudson handed the chairman a letter of condemnation he had received after three sessions with his negotiator." That would be the Army Corps of Engineers Real Estate Office negotiator headquartered at their office in Wabash.

The minutes continue, "Several asked questions. He disclosed that he had gotten the letter of condemnation ten days after first meeting with his negotiator. That first offer was $3,800. Final offer was $4,300. He contends the price offered is too low. Also, he admitted swearing some about it."

In a postscript added to the minutes that he created after the Red Bridge Group adjourned at 9:45 that night, Bussert noted that the Wabash office "agreed to reopen negotiations with Mr. Charles Hudson, if he so desires." Speaking for the group, Bussert added that upon his return to the negotiations, they would suggest to Mr. Hudson that he "swear less and talk more turkey." In addition, "we have consulted two local carpenters about his house and compared his final offer quoted in this report with prices paid for comparable properties in Somerset."

Roush followed up with a note to Colonel W. Roper, district engineer in the Army Corps of Engineers Louisville office, who replied that the Red Bridge Group investigation "fails to reveal any discrepancies in price for similar properties."[308] He added that the army was willing to keep talking, though, to Mr. Hudson.

That was followed by Roush agreeing to attend a Red Bridge Group meeting on the Sunday after Christmas at the Conservation Club building and telling Roper to send an army representative. Roush wrote Bussert, for future reference, "If you have any specific instances where unfair pressure or other malpractice was indicated, please let me know and the matter will be investigated."[309]

"Time and time again I caused the [Army Corps of] engineers to hold meetings in our area and explain what was happening," Roush told Kathleen McKinzie in her 1969 interview. "They have a tendency not to have too much compassion," he said, "nor do they display too much concern for people who might be adversely affected by such projects, for individual or small groups. They're overly objective . . . calculating; they are engineers; they live by the slide rule. When the slide rule says something should be done or not done, that is what is either done or not done."[310]

48. REAL ESTATE

Tom Snyder said his dad, Fred, would come home from meetings with army officials "all bent out of shape." Fred Snyder was a Somerset Citizens Committee member, and he was Somerset Development Corporation president. In addition to taking care of town business, Fred had property in Somerset, and he had a farm, 160 acres, near Somerset. Also, Tom said, "he was dealing with Vernie's property, 220 acres that included the Riverside Resort and all that, negotiating for settlements, plus the old Ogan grocery store that he owned by default.

"Dad said there was no stopping it. He'd say, 'They're gonna come in here and they're gonna take it and there's nothing you can do about it.'"

From the perspective of Congressman J. Edward Roush, the relationship with the army was fairer, however. He told Kathleen McKinzie in the 1969 Indiana University oral history interview, "You had to push them, but my relationship with them, I thought, was fair. They were always honest. They never tried to circumvent an issue; they faced right up to it. I rather enjoyed working with them over the years."[311]

To Somerset businessman Dave Compton, whose family owned farmland that was sold to the government, trying to get more money or not to have to sell it at all "didn't make any headway, didn't go over at all." In most cases, the Army Corps of Engineers real estate agents paid what they wanted to pay.

Compton said, "Once in a while, they paid more than the people thought they could get out of it. The Army Corps of Engineers had a purchaser that went in and made the offer. Roush would be contacted if the seller did not want to sell, and he would try to help them out, and that is when they would go to Ohio and meet with government officials. Usually, that didn't do any good at all, so they would go ahead and come back with the money and say, 'You take this or leave it. It'll be condemned and you won't get anything.' Then, usually the second offer was the same as the first, but sometimes they would give a little bit. It was always questionable as to how that worked. Even the people that sold their homes, they felt that other people were treated more fairly later. 'Caught the government on a different day' was how they saw it."

Looking back at those conflicts, Kay (Shroyer) Peas told me, "Some of the cruelty was the government would pay you what your place was worth, but you couldn't take that money and go buy something comparable any place close around."

The government didn't compensate people for the money that their property would generate, like a farm, say, or a store. They didn't compensate people, either, for the spiritual value they might have maintained by living in the place where their lives and the lives of their grandparents and the lives of their children had been lived. That's the life-living connection like the one that exists between you and me and Pop and your dad and the other guy named Vern.

Many times over. That wasn't worth anything. A December 4, 1977, *Marion Chronicle-Tribune* magazine Somerset retrospective feature said,

> The townspeople were warned (in 1962) that their property would have to be sold for what was called a fair price and that they would have to seek residence elsewhere. At first panic rocked Somerset. Indignant residents vowed they would never leave their peaceful homes. The older members of the community were especially outraged. Many had spent their entire lives in the community.[312]

Snyder said, "There was some very bitter people, the older people, I mean, very bitter. They fought 'em. They went and hired lawyers." But, he said, "the lawyers run into a roadblock. There was a point where it become eminent domain. The government had a lot of lawyers hired when this was going on here, for the people they were prepared for who would take them to court."

The December 4, 1977, *Chronicle-Tribune* article continued,

> Faced with an unconquerable foe, the town's residents began to give in, one by one, until Somerset was deserted—a virtual ghost town.
>
> "First, they started spray-painting numbers on the houses, in the order they were bought," Ed Vossler, Rt. 1, LaFontaine, remembers. "It really looked spooky at night. After the government first bought the property, the homeowners had the option to buy back their house and move it elsewhere.
>
> "If the owner decided not to buy back the house, it was put up for sale to the general public with the stipulation—it had to be moved. Finally the houses that weren't sold were burned."
>
> Many of the residents were able to watch the incineration of the remaining homes and buildings of old Somerset from new homes built on higher ground.
>
> "The thing that was really hard for the oldtimers who couldn't afford to move their houses was to watch them be burned," says Mrs. Berniece Ringbaugh, Rt. 1, LaFontaine. "My husband and I watched our old house burn from a window in our new house."

The town dissolved.

"I know there was a lot of complaining about it," Bonnie Truss told me, "because, especially, I knew about some of the little people that were in Somerset. You know, they offered them practically nothing for those houses, but they had to move. They had to go somewhere else," Bonnie said. "They had to find another house. It didn't matter if it's only worth five hundred bucks, you couldn't take that five hundred and go anywhere else."

They did not take into consideration the inconvenience, she said. "Like Bessie Deeter who lived across from the school where we always had an election. Yeah, bless her heart, she was the sweetest thing." Like Omma Sweet, Bessie Deeter was a cook at Somerset High School, among the first hired by my great-aunt Vernie when she started the school lunch program there in 1944, according to her grandson Tom Snyder.

"We went over to Bessie's house for all kinds of things," Bonnie said. "I remember, she was just heartbroken. She didn't know what to do, and I don't remember for sure, she may have died before they actually got her moved, because a lot of them just gave up." According to the consolidated Mississinewa Memorial Cemetery records, Bessie May Deeter stayed at relocated "new" Somerset until her death in 1973 at the age of eighty-five.

Nearby Mount Vernon resident Helen Adkins, who lived in Somerset when it drowned, said, "A lot of the old people, it killed a lot of them off, I think. They prayed about it."

"The government had done this before, and they knew," Tom Snyder said. "They had percentages. A percentage of elderly people are not gonna survive it. They lost a whole bunch of the old people in old Somerset because of the stress. They didn't survive it."

Tom went to work for the Army Corps of Engineers a few years after he came home from his army service in Vietnam after high school. He started at the C. J. Brown Dam and Reservoir in Springfield, Ohio, in 1976, transferred to a reservoir north of Cincinnati in 1979, and worked at the Mississinewa Reservoir from 1982 to 1984. Tom was then chief of operations at the Salamonie element in the Upper Wabash Valley Flood Control Project, he told me, for twenty-one years.

The destruction of Somerset "wouldn't work that way now," Tom told me. "You wouldn't get past the politics of it today. Too many rich people that own property would fight the government on it. The mindset has changed." There are now, he said, "too many people whose parents went through losing property to the federal government through eminent domain."

The December 4, 1977, *Chronicle-Tribune* magazine account continued,

> The school served as a part-time home for Somerset's last resident. John Huddleston, a native Somerset-area resident, was employed as a night watchman to protect the school from vandalism.
>
> "At night, the stray dogs that swarmed through the wreckage of the town and I were the only live creatures in Somerset, with the exceptions of pillagers who often drove up in cars and snuck around in the shadows," he recalls. After the school was finally closed, like so many buildings before it, it was burned. The town's mammoth trees, some of them up to 3½ feet in diameter, were toppled by chain saws. Somerset lay barren. Only tree stumps, bushes, and pieces of foundations remained."

When the water is low now, it isn't hard to get down to the old town's ghost. Head west from State Road 13 on the old Slocum Trail past the community building and the houses that were moved and newly built, for half a mile. Exit the car by the gate at the bottom of the hill and follow the path that was the road, abandoned, beyond the trees and bushes into the clearing. Your grandma and I could see the town's remnants, stretches of crumbling street pavement and the foundations of lost homes, when we walked around down there in the late winter of 2023.

"I can still remember when the water started to rise," Mrs. Ringbaugh told the *Chronicle-Tribune*. "We couldn't believe it, but it finally happened. One hundred fifty years of building and three years of destruction were covered up by the water. You could hardly believe that a town had ever existed there."[313]

Somerset

49. PACKING

Dear Vern,

After President Kennedy signed the bill on October 1, 1961, that provided funding for the Upper Wabash Valley Food Control Project, construction on two dams, Salamonie and Mississinewa, got underway quickly. An editorial in the next day's *Indianapolis Star* praising the project said that Salamonie and Mississinewa ground-breaking would soon follow, beginning that November. "Indiana can be grateful," it said, "for the foresight of those public officials who persisted" in creating "a new era in flood control throughout most of the length of the Wabash. Thousands of lives will be protected. Millions of dollars in property damage should be averted."[314]

An official Salamonie ground-breaking photo on November 28, 1961, included Congressman Roush, Senators Hartke and Capehart, and Ralph Roessler. In Ralph's Indiana State Library files, there are similar photos for the Mississinewa project ground-breaking: April 27, 1962, with Roush, Roessler, and Indiana Flood Control and Water Resource Commission member Carlos Life; and then, finally, for the Huntington reservoir project, June 26, 1965. In that ceremonial picture, the day after the IFCWRC held its final meeting, Roush and Roessler are pictured with Indiana senator Birch Bayh, Indiana governor Roger Branigin, and US Army Corps of Engineers brigadier general Walter P. Leber. Construction at Huntington had already been underway for two years by then. Roush and Roessler stood side by side again in the Mississinewa Reservoir dedication photo the Kiwanian kept from June 14, 1969. Dignitaries cycled through the standard ceremonial photos, but Congressman Roush and his project mentor, "Ralph Roessler, 'The Father of the Mississinewa Reservoir,'"[315] were constants.

The Mississinewa dam ground-breaking story had an interesting twist. According to the *Indianapolis Star* of April 28, 1962, the Indiana State Conservation Department had closed state forests for weeks already by then because of a fire hazard. When officials arrived with their ceremonial dynamite on the appointed day, Frances Slocum State Park superintendent Sherman Emrick wouldn't let them inside. The *Star* reported that he had to "check with headquarters"—that is, make a call down to Indianapolis for special approval to violate the no-burning fire hazard rule. Rules are made to be broken, Vern, by the people who make the rules. What's a little dynamite in an officially designated tinderbox, anyway?

With the special approval conveyed, "Representative J. Edward Roush waved a red warning flag to signal the blast" that "a contractor's engineer touched off with a storage battery," which was followed by "applause from a gathering of high state and Federal officials and about 400 area residents."[316] The conquering heroes did not include our relatives, who would be called later to witness the disposition of Grandma's body.

It doesn't seem like the press had a whole lot to say about what the Upper Wabash Valley Flood Control Project meant to people like your great-great-grandparents who were being displaced until it was well past time to stop it. The newspaper editors and publishers were not visibly interested in generating any concern for the folks whose lives were being upended until after the upending was certain. From 1955 through 1961, the papers had pretty much copied and pasted the official Army Corps of Engineers and IFCWRC line on what a great thing it would be.

But with the battle won and the Mississinewa ground-breaking set for April 27, 1962, the *Anderson Herald* ran an Associated Press story on page 10, Sunday, April 22, 1962, headlined SOMERSET, OLD INDIANA TOWN, TO DISAPPEAR, that said, "Nobody seems to care about the dying old towns, except for the people who live in them."[317] The *Terre Haute Tribune* published the same story that day under the headline MISSISSINEWA RESERVOIR TO KILL TOWN OF SOMERSET, with a picture of kids playing in a

Somerset street near the Texaco station that was captioned "Playing in Doomed Town."[318]

"The Mississinewa is to be chained and Somerset will die," Dale Burgess wrote.

The *Indianapolis Star* previewed the ground-breaking that Sunday with a more expansive piece that considered Somerset's history from before the mid-nineteenth century when, enough said, it was "an Indian settlement." White pines and big maple trees will have to go, it says, but "there is no factory or mine to make it important" in a town that "nobody loves but the people who live there." That a factory or mine is what it takes to make a place important is worth pausing to reflect upon, Vern, as we consider the effects of what has passed for progress in the last eighty years.

MISSISSINEWA TO FLOOD TOWN, DAM PROJECT TO START was the *Star*'s page 6 headline: "The important people are saying, what a wonderful thing the new lake will be for the city folk to play around. There will be fishing and boating and all kinds of recreational opportunities."[319]

To commemorate the days ahead, Congressman Roush sent "the Father of the Mississinewa Reservoir" a copy of a report called *Outdoor Recreation for America*, which Roush signed.

That notion of a big lake for fun times was twenty-three years old by then. It was the original idea, after all, that Ralph Roessler brought to the Kiwanis Club of Marion, Indiana, after visiting the man-made Lake Shafer in May of 1939.

"Dinner at Fishermans' Paradise, Monticello, Indiana, and a trip around the reservoir suggesting the possibilities of a similar development on the Mississinewa River," reads Ralph's May 21, 1939, diary transcription in his Indiana State Library file. It was to "Fishermans' Paradise" for fine dining, after all, and not to where I instead picture the locals on a Friday after work, a place maybe called "Frank's Flood Control Tap."

With recreation in mind, the discussions that would lead to the Upper Wabash Valley Flood Control Project started on May 22, 1939. In 1962, the state's leading newspaper reports, "The important people are saying, what a wonderful thing the new lake will be for the city folk to play around." What went around came around.

The idea that the area would become a prosperous north-central Indiana center for fun like Indiana Beach at Lake Shafer coalesced with the notion that a modern "New Somerset" should make "old" Somerset residents happy. That, as Ralph Roessler had written to Congressman John Beamer in 1955, "a revived lakeside resort village" should soothe people like, say, a Mrs. Berniece Ringbaugh, as she and her husband "watch our old house burn from a window in our new house."[320]

From the ruins, Indiana Flood Control and Water Resources Commission executive vice president Robert Kellum had projected in 1955, "they could build an ideal, model town."

"I remember them saying that," that the new Somerset was supposed to be better for everyone, a site of great growth, Janet Schenkel told me early on in my search for the story of what happened to the community where your great-grandfather was a boy.

The old town was behind the times, according to a United Press International article that ran in the *Elwood Call-Leader* on April 27, 1962. While "old-timers" stuck in their old-timey ways think more about the past than the future, the article said, the new town up the hill promised a shopping center, wider streets, a sewage system, new houses, and maybe some new industry, according to Somerset Development Corporation director Floyd Bowman, "business representative for the new relocation committee." Bowman, the UPI reported, said that a "majority want to move."[321]

"There's a lot of people who were better off for the move," longtime resident Larry Stouffer said at the Somerset Lions Club meeting in 2021. I heard resignation in his voice, the matter-of-fact rationalization of one wounded. "A lot of people," fair enough, but Larry didn't say "everybody." That would not be true. He was there when it happened.

Fred Morgan, real estate chief for the Army Corps of Engineers from Louisville, told the UPI in the April 27, 1962, story that "300 cabins, 90 homes, 10 churches, schools and lodges" would be flooded. But it was a chance to make a "dream town."

"After the land where new Somerset was purchased, the government would offer to sell... the home that the government has just bought to clear the land for the flood back to the original owner so that they could move it to the new town," Dave Compton said when we spoke at his home. "Not the land," he said, "they would sell the dwellings, the homes. They held on to the land.

"Some of the old homes in Somerset, a couple of them got more than they thought they would get. But you're only talking about a total purchase of maybe $5,000."

Most people were not happy to move but understood the reason for it, Dave said in 2021. "After they got moved into the new town, everybody that moved up there really liked it, but there are only two people there left that ever lived in the old town, and one of those is in hospice.

"The first house that was moved up there was Marvin Harrison and his wife. At that time, there were no streets, no sewage, nothing. They pulled the old house in there in the mud and set it on a foundation, and they were the first ones there. Then several others followed after that."

"There might have been six or eight houses that were moved. I bet no more than that," Janet Schenkel said.

Financial constraints prevented more people from making the move up the hill. It wasn't a protest. "They made it so expensive, something about the water, that 90 percent of the people couldn't afford to have gone," said Janet's sister, Kay.

"A few of them did buy their homes back for a dollar, and they had to pay to have them moved," said Janet.

"But you couldn't go buy with the neighbors that you had, the people you had relationships with," said Kay. That was hard, she said, "the thought of not seeing them as you went out every morning with your coffee to see them."

"It was a physical separation, but also an emotional one," said Janet. "For many years after that, when anyone from old Somerset died, everybody wanted to go to the funeral home. You could see the people you had been with all your life.

"That's still the case," said Kay. "When anyone from our school dies, you go there and you will see everybody who is still living who could drive the distance."

"Somerset had a really family culture," said Janet. "It was a very bonded, family-oriented group. And then all at once, it was not there.

Now, you go back when you can and see others, and you kind of feel that bond that was there."

"The local Christian church moved their building," said Janet.

"The Minnick house was moved," Kay said.

"Mr. Harrison died right after they moved his house up there," said Dave. "He never lived in it there."

50. HELEN ADKINS

Helen Adkins, who lived near what is now called Mississinewa Lake when I spoke to her in December of 2021, said, "We lived in the old town, and then we moved out in the country for four or five years." That, she says, was 1963 or '64, "whenever the reservoir went in." That's when her family moved to the country. "We had to move, yeah."

Their home in Somerset before the flood? "You know, you went down over the hill, there, from State Road 13 into the town, when you come down the hill, we were right there, before you get to the bridge."

She and her husband, Aden, didn't want to move, she said, but "it didn't make any difference. You're gonna move, anyway. We found a place to move to and moved to it. The town relocated up there, but since we didn't own our own ground, they wouldn't even talk to us about it. The ones that owned their own ground down there got first pick. We didn't own anything. That's the way it was.

"Like I say, we rented, so we didn't get anything," Helen said.

"It's okay that it happened. It saved a lot of people."

Aden was an independent trucker. He died, Helen told me, in 2015. "He'd had a stroke nine years before that. I took care of him." She paused. "It'll be seven years in January." The couple had lived in Somerset since they were married in 1956, when Aden was eighteen. "I started going with Aden when he was fifteen."

Aden quit school when he was sixteen. "He and I were in the same class," Larry Knee said. Larry called Aden "the hardest-working man I ever knew. He moved everything that could be moved."

"People tell me, 'Aden moved the church,'" Helen said. "He didn't, he didn't, he didn't. He didn't do that, no." When the flood came, Helen said, Aden moved "small buildings, like garages and chicken houses, not the houses; he moved everything else but. He was involved in all of that. He moved a lot of buildings around, side buildings. Somebody else would buy them and move them to their house. I always helped him. He didn't move no church" like people said.

"Yeah, I'd heard that before, like I've heard I drove a semi everywhere. Well, I never drove a semi anywhere." Helen laughed. "There's a lot of stories out around, you know, just like the church."

Helen and I talked while we were sitting at the Bob Evans restaurant in Wabash, a meeting I had arranged because I'd heard from more than one person one of those "stories" about Helen that I needed to confirm:

The story that Helen had been an armed resister.

The story was that Aden and Helen's property bordered the very edge of where the reservoir water was to stop. When "the feds" showed up to seize their land, Helen told them to go away, "held 'em off with a shotgun," I'd heard, more than once, and they did go away. Helen and Aden had to sign a waiver, I'd also heard, that gave themselves full responsibility for damages if and when the water should get to their property.

"If you want to find her," I was told, "she's at the senior center in Wabash playing euchre, and on Monday nights she's in Peru."

I got her on the phone.

"Well, I'm playing cards at the senior center," she told me when I suggested Friday, thinking that I could come down to her house, since I'd heard, again, that she was a final flood survivor, living there in the new town, still, and that since I'd been to the Lions Club meeting and I'd had a look around, I knew she wouldn't be hard to find. Like the old town, the new town isn't very big.

"I don't live in Somerset," she told me. "Our place is on the other side of the highway. Turn left at the first road and then follow along to the right when it splits and keep going till you get to the water. I'm right there."

I was hoping for a street address that I could Google map, and she was giving me landmark directions. "Can you give me that again?"

"Why don't we meet at a restaurant, after I'm done with cards, there in Wabash?"

Between 2:30 and 3:00, she said, "I can't give you a better time than that," at Bob Evans "on 24."

"Twenty-four and 15," I said.

"Yeah. I don't really think I've got anything to tell you."

I made it to the Bob Evans right at 2:30, after I'd had a quick look down the road to where the water laps the land where Vern grew up. Helen came in at 3:00, right after I'd decided to order something to eat.

It took me a little while to get to the reason I came, but with my phone recording—"Why would I mind?"—and my notes on the Bob Evans placemat picture of a chicken breast they don't actually serve, I said—more or less—"What's this I hear about a shotgun?"

"Me and a shotgun?!" She laughed, a sort of cackling laugh. "Shotgun?! That is funny. I did tell 'em to go away, but I didn't have no shotgun." And she laughed some more.

"They come along and put their number on your house. You have so long to get out after that. I said, 'Why are you puttin' a number on my house?'"

"You were in old Somerset?"

"Old Somerset. But I didn't have no shotgun or anything." And she laughed some more.

Resistance was basically futile.

"That church that they moved up the road," Helen said. "They got in front of this one guy's house, and he was gonna have to move his mailbox, and he told them, 'You're not movin' my mailbox.'"

It was a Friday afternoon, she said, and so they left the church there in his path for later. "So they just said, 'Well, we'll go on Monday.' So when Monday come, he said, 'You can move my mailbox anytime.' So they moved his mailbox. That was kinda funny."

Helen was an interesting woman—kind and willing to share things with you through me. "I want to tell my grandson about my dad" was all the explanation I ever needed down there.

"A few years ago, they was working on the dam, so it was dry all summer," Helen said to me at Bob Evans. "This was before Aden died.

We went down there, me and my daughter and another guy, and walked the streets of old Somerset. He'd say, 'So-and-so lives here and so-and-so lives here,' and I'd say, 'Well, no, they didn't live here, because that's where this person lived.' It was interesting.

"They all cared," Helen said. "They didn't like that moving at all."

"It was pretty much a done deal when people found out about it?" I said.

"Yeah, I'm sure. You know, I'm not original from there."

Helen continued, with pauses while I ate in between.

"It just happened.

"I've always liked Somerset.

"I've always liked it.

"It just happened."

51. GOTTA WEAR SHADES

As the old town dissolved and the new one came to life, there was official optimism about the future. On the eve of the Mississinewa Dam ground-breaking ceremony, Congressman Roush told a radio audience in one of his regular five-minute presentations on April 26, 1962, that it appeared certain that the three-reservoir project would develop into one of the major recreation areas of the state.

In the July 5, 1963, radio address, he said that while the dams were primarily for flood control, "at the same time they will be creating an economic potential for the area upstream and surrounding the projects, which holds great promise for the immediate future as well as for the generations which will follow us."[322]

At an October 8, 1963, Wabash meeting of area business and civic leaders, the *Kokomo Tribune* reported, state officials "stressed" that the three Upper Wabash Valley Flood Control Project reservoirs would bring "much revenue into the five-county area when they are developed for recreational use." That would be after all three reservoirs are finished by 1969, they heard. "Joe H. Nixon, publisher of the *Wabash Dealer* [*sic*]" and now himself "a member of the Indiana Flood Control and Water Resources Commission served as master of ceremonies for the reservoir discussion."[323]

"New" and "improved"[324] was how the *Columbia City Commercial Mail* pictured Somerset in a November 1, 1963, photo essay about the new town. "The first business to open in the new shopping center was Floyd Bowman's Garage and Marina in 1964," according to Wabash historian Ron Woodward. "It was followed by Dain Nealis' barber shop (open evenings and all-day Saturdays), Robert King's grocery/service station and the Frontier Restaurant run by Hal Lunsford. The Frontier was known for its turkey dinners every Sunday and the horseshoe shaped counter in the center. The post office with postmaster Inez Drook was the last business to leave the old town. She had been the postmaster since about 1933."[325]

Two hundred and seventy-five people got an optimistic message again in 1964 at the Honeywell Center in downtown Wabash from a Purdue University academic. Extension economist H. A. Wadsworth said the Upper Wabash Flood Control Project "will improve area income by $13.5 million"[326] according to the headline in Joe Nixon's *Wabash Plain Dealer* on November 18, 1964.

Wadsworth had it figured: population growth, industrial growth, business growth, four hundred new jobs every year, half a million visitors to each reservoir every year spending $5 million at each reservoir every year; $6 million for recreation, $1.5 million on new homes. All in all, it's $9 million a year, he said, times a factor of 1.5, he said, because I say so, he more or less said, which comes out to the headline's "$13.5."

I wasn't there, Vern, but I can imagine the cheers: gasoline (yay!), food (yay!), souvenirs (yay!), supplies (yay!), and houses (big yay!) at the Honeywell Center in Wabash meeting with 275 people. Joe Nixon, the stepson of Mark Honeywell and now the "Chairman of the Governor's Upper Wabash Reservoirs Coordinating Committee," while still the publisher and sometime writer for the *Plain Dealer*, told the group that the biggest development at that time was "new Somerset." Nixon said seventy-five out of 140 available lots there were "already sold," that "21 new houses have been built," and that twenty homes had been moved from the old town. That's about three times what old Somerset's Janet Schenkel remembered being moved when we talked in 2021.

Wadsworth also told the Honeywell Center gathering that "young people" would stay in the area because they would have jobs.

The "new Somerset" optimism continued as a Fort Wayne company bought the "center section" of the "Somerset shopping center" for an unspecified amount in July of 1965. The *Kokomo Morning Times* reported that the Dynastry Industries Inc. purchase "includes [the] community's only restaurant, equipped with modern equipment, and four adjacent stores."[327]

Dynastry president Albert E. Toschlog Sr. said, "Somerset is likely to become a popular resort area," and population would "skyrocket."

"Most of the homes now located in Somerset are new, though some residents were able to relocate their former homes from the old sites," the *Morning Times* reported, and then stated as fact that "rather than breakup [sic] a 'way of life' and 'family roots' residents picked up their town and moved it a mile east with the help of the U.S. Army Corps of Engineers."

Like a Hallmark special, Vern.

I see people waving goodbye as the big trucks roll out of town.

Thank you, Engineers!

"You'll be amazed at the bonanza that rolls in," Purdue economist H. A. Wadsworth told a crowd of only eight people at the newly consolidated Southwood High School when he returned fifteen months after the big Honeywell Center pep session. Joe Nixon's headline this time in the February 6, 1966, *Plain Dealer* said EXPECT LOCAL RESERVOIRS TO ATTRACT 2,000,000 ANNUALLY.[328] Two million.

In an undated report that was kept in a Congressman Roush file folder labeled "1968" at the Indiana University Archives, Roush had reduced the expected influx to "600,000 persons per year taking advantage of the reservoirs' recreation facilities," and he'd lowered Wadsworth's $13.5 million annual economic boost to "$5.6 million."[329]

So how did all the optimistic projections pan out? Well, the Somerset "shopping center" strip mall is vacant, and even the convenience market gas station was closed the last time I checked in February 2023. The community center and the little park still operate, and a couple of churches remain in business, but "new" Somerset looks less like a town and more like a subdivision. It's a quiet village of commuters.

It never became what Wadsworth and Nixon and Toschlog foresaw; the economic impact hasn't met expectations. A 2022 report from the

US Army Corps of Engineers Chicago District[330] said that visitors spent a total of 1,478,687 days/nights at the three Upper Wabash Valley Flood Control Project parks combined in 2021. If visitors averaged a two-day stay, that would approximate Roush's estimate of six hundred thousand visitors per year. Wadsworth's 1966 two-million-visitor estimate remains overblown even if each visit was only one day.

According to the same army report, the facilities led to more than $31 million in visitor spending "within 30 miles" of Mississinewa, more than $18 million "within 30 miles" of Salamonie, and over $9 million "within 30 miles" of Roush Lake in 2021. That's an overall figure that's harder to estimate because one must take into account that it's twenty-four miles from Mississinewa to Salamonie, thirty-five miles from Mississinewa to Roush, and fourteen miles from Salamonie to Roush. There's a lot of overlap in the "within 30 miles."

Wadsworth told his 1964 Wabash audience that each reservoir would collect $5 million from visitors every year. According to the Federal Reserve Bank of Minneapolis inflation calculator, that total of $15 million was worth $131 million in 2021. Even without allowing for the park visitor "within 30 miles" overlap, Wadsworth's hopeful projection for visitor spending was more than twice what it turned out to be. Anything is better than nothing, of course, but as far as I know, I'm the first person to suggest some accountability for the cheerleading numbers that went without any sort of critical verification when they were presented as fact in the *Wabash Plain Dealer*.

In 1966, Somerset strip mall owner Maury Toschlog told the *Indianapolis Star* that "Somerset will become a water wonderland, second to none in the nation. Both population and industry will skyrocket."[331]

The new Somerset King's Market owner, Robert King, told the Dayton, Ohio, *Daily News* that September that "the village will become, 'a pretty good-sized town, maybe in 10 years.'"[332]

Community leader Floyd Bowman, who owned the DX gas station that had moved from the old downtown to near the new strip mall, told the *Star*, "It is highly possible for the 200-plus present population to swell to more than 5,000. Higher during the vacation season. We had a good quiet life in the old town, but the future, if everyone here pulls together, promises to be even better."

"Pulls together" sounds like "thoughts and prayers" to me, Vern. Maybe people didn't "pull together" hard enough.

Like Wadsworth's economic forecast, the projected increase in population was way overblown, only more so. Somerset's census data history is incomplete because it has been unincorporated. Ron Woodward's town account says the population was 250 in 1959. Most recent records show its population at 401 in 2010 and at 385 in 2020. Waltz Township, in which Somerset lies, has declined from 1,422 people in 1950 to 1,199 in 2020. Between 1960 and 1980, the population of Waltz Township fell from 1,554 to 1,366. Wadsworth told the slim crowd at Southwood High School in February 1966 that with the Upper Wabash Valley Flood Control Project, the area population would increase by 23 percent between 1964 and 1974. The most current population numbers for all of Waltz Township are less than a quarter of Bowman's five-thousand-people prediction for Somerset alone.

Between 1960 and 1980, the population of Wabash, Miami, Huntington, and Grant Counties increased by 7.1 percent according to US Census Bureau data. In the sixty years from 1960 to 2020, it fell by 5.5 percent. There are a lot of factors involved in the widespread decline of rural communities all over the country. The declarations of a coming prosperity for the Somerset area, however, made no such distinctions.

Along with considering the project's positive economic effects, one must also consider its effects on preventing flood damage. The report prepared for Roush's 1968 file said that "average annual damages" due to flooding in the Mississinewa Reservoir area "amount to about $6,300,000, and it is estimated that the Mississinewa Reservoir will reduce these damages by $955,000. The benefit-to-cost ratio is 1.2 to 1.0."[333] That's the first benefit-to-cost ratio analysis I've seen connected to the Upper Wabash Valley Flood Control Project. Was it worth it?

The lives and livelihoods of many people have been protected by the big dams. Wabash, Peru, Logansport, and other cities along the upper Wabash River and its tributaries have experienced some heavy rainfall and snowmelt flooding since project construction in the 1960s, but nothing like the devastating Peru flood of 1913. Tom Snyder, who was among the last people to attend school in Somerset and later worked for the Army Corps of Engineers, said, "It saved a lot of lives in towns where people were drowning during floods. You cannot argue against life, and that was the key," he said. "If you can, stop flooding in Peru that's running through all of the downtown streets. If you look at some of the flood stories, there's families that were just completely lost. They were gone."

After a 2020 study showed that 81 percent of Peru, Indiana, property remains at risk of flooding, Jim Tidd, the Miami County Economic Development Authority executive director, told the *Kokomo Tribune* on August 28, 2020, that the city hadn't experienced any serious flooding since the Mississinewa Dam construction in 1967. Tidd challenged the findings of First Street, a nonprofit research and technology group, which released its flood risk findings in June of 2020. Tidd said then that the county would ask "for a proposal from a civil engineering firm,[334] with expertise in floodplains, to evaluate the study to determine if it is accurate and valid."

A spokesman for his office in December 2023 told me the study review did not happen.

The Chicago District Office Army Corps of Engineers website said in 2025 that together the three reservoirs in the Upper Wabash Valley Flood Control Project "have saved $1.6 billion dollars in flood damages since their construction in the 1960s."[335] That's an annual savings of less than $30 million, and adjusted for inflation, that's less than the savings Roush had estimated in 1968. That includes but is not limited to the area around Somerset, if not Somerset itself, which, again, did not flood. Major arguments throughout and since the reservoirs' construction have been that the project saves more money than it costs and improves more lives than it harms. Somerset was sacrificed for somebody else's hard-to-quantify greater good. The people most adversely affected were ignored in the process.

An answer to the subjective "Was is worth it?" question depends upon one's perspective. For me, there are values to consider, Vern, that are not prefaced with a dollar sign. For me, Vern, that's a whole lot of what this letter to you is about. For both Dad and his community.

Over two consecutive days in May of 1967, Congressman J. Edward Roush gave statements to the House and Senate Public Works Committees that were considering how best to spend the money that might be coming their way. With the Upper Wabash Valley Flood Control Project man-made lakes already preventing flooding, the time has come to consider man-made rivers, Roush said. Running through the Fifth Congressional District, that, he said, would connect the Saint Lawrence Seaway and the Great Lakes to the Mississippi River. The idea went nowhere. There were three more reservoirs, too, planned for the Wabash River in Indiana. They never happened, either.

The planning stages were the last stages for the Lafayette Reservoir, on Wildcat Creek, the Big Pine Reservoir, on Big Pine Creek near Attica, and the Williamsburg Turkey Run Reservoir, Sugar Creek. The Indiana Flood Control and Water Resources Commission statement for a hearing on the matter on February 15, 1963, had not offered unequivocal support for the new plans. Naturalists and forestry officials rejected the Turkey Run proposal for environmental reasons, and the IFCWRC suggested efforts in that area might best be focused on "Tributary and Small Watershed projects along Sugar Creek valley" that "should be studied extensively to seek flood control benefits."[336]

Wow, Vern, I'm going to put out another cigarette; the commission concluded that the small dam plan would be better.

The emphasis had shifted already, well before the Upper Wabash Valley Flood Control Project was completed, toward the small Soil Conservation Service watershed projects. There were fifty-three "small watershed projects" in a list the army itself had prepared on a Wabash River valley map that included the states of Ohio and Illinois for the February 15 hearing. The last one was for the "Upper Mississinewa River," upstream from Marion.

Former Army Corps of Engineers manager Tom Snyder, Aunt Vernie's grandson, told me that before any more big dams could be built, the political will to do so had expired.

In 1996, the Huntington Reservoir was renamed Roush Lake when Congress supported a resolution authored by Republican Mark Souder to honor the Huntington County Democrat. Souder had followed Roush into the congressional seat serving the Fort Wayne area. Souder was in Congress from 1995 until his resignation in 2010, when he admitted to an affair with a staffer. He died of pancreatic cancer in 2022. After Dan Quayle beat him for reelection in 1976, Roush was an administrator in the Environmental Protection Agency for two years and then was briefly president of Huntington College. He died in 2004.

Mississinewa Reservoir use has been growing. Assistant property manager Jordan Epp told the *Kokomo Tribune* in 2021 that "entrance revenue at the park" was "up at least 15% compared to 2020, when day entrances also hit a then-record by increasing 20% from 2019."[337]

52. RIPPLE

I never appreciated what I had thought was Dad's irrational attachment to draught horses until a year and a half before you were born, Vern. That's thirty-four years after he died. Right there in the city where you were born, I found Dad's spirit in Birchbark Books & Native Arts on an impulse buy during an impulse visit to the Louise Erdrich bookstore with your mom and dad and Grandma Shroyer.

Writers and readers are partners. The best books are the ones we read when we are perfectly present for what the writer has to say. I found myself in *Catch-22* when I was sixteen. I found Vern in a collection of essays by Wendell Berry called *The World-Ending Fire* when I was sixty-five. I hope someone saved that book for you. You may be too young now to get much out of it. Something changes when we're old enough to see the practical applications of essays and themes that seem vague and theoretical when we are young. I had that experience when I reread *Zen and the Art of Motorcycle Maintenance* by Minnesota's Robert Pirsig in my forties.

In any case, when you are ready, read Wendell Berry and reread this to find out about the man who had your name. I'm a little embarrassed to admit that on that day in the bookstore when I was sixty-five years old, I had no inkling of Wendell Berry. Somebody should have told me about him. I should have come to him on my own. But there you have it—in the town where you were born a year and a half later, I found Vern. Better late than never. Maybe the time was right.

If you only read one essay in the Berry anthology, read the one called

"Horse-Drawn Tools and the Doctrine of Labor Saving." I think I'll read it again right now:

> Suppose, then, that in 1945 we had valued the human life of farms and farm communities 1 percent more than we valued economic growth and technological progress. And suppose we had espoused the health of homes, farms, towns, and cities with anything like the resolve and energy with which we built the "military-industrial complex." Suppose, in other words, that we had really meant what, all that time, most of us and most of our leaders were saying, and that we had really tried to live by the traditional values to which we gave lip service.[338]

Vern wanted those draught horses to pull his plow because he wanted to live in the world where draught horses pull a plow. I stood in the way. Now I'm sorry that I wasn't ready to read what he had to say until after he was gone. This letter to you is an expression of that sorrow. When you are ready to read it, a man you never met will wrap his arms around you.

The twenty-five miles of gently rolling hills along the Mississinewa River between Marion and Peru were not that far away, and they were there when we moved to Normal from Marion. We could have moved there, but we moved in the other direction, south instead of north. Sometimes, when the windows were open and I was trying to sleep, I could hear the vague sound of a freight train rolling through Swayzee three miles away. My solitude has never quit being that train.

One April Sunday there, the loss of our electricity alerted my family and me. With no TV to watch, we walked apart outside, as the daylight in a day of sun, spring rain, and thunderstorms came to an end. An odd yellowish sky faded into something darker and more ominous. Something darker than the darkness. The faint familiar sound of the train grew louder. Slowly, uncertainly, we began to see more than the clouds of a thunderstorm.

"No."

"I think it is."

"No, it isn't."

"It is."

We watched a half-mile-wide tornado that on Palm Sunday 1965 appeared to be headed straight at us.

Ten miles west, Aunt Vernie's friend Omma Sweet pulled her car off State Road 22/US Highway 35 on the east side of Greentown because she could no longer see. Omma was driving with her eight-year-old granddaughter, Rose Sweet, in the passenger seat. "She was behind us," Linda Haines Martin told me. Linda was also Omma's granddaughter, Rose's cousin. Linda was in another car, with her family, returning to their home in Greentown.

"'My grandmother pulled into a driveway to ride out the storm at a friend's house,'" Linda said in Janis Thornton's book, *The 1965 Palm Sunday Tornadoes in Indiana.*[339]

"She pulled into the driveway of one of the ladies she worked with," Linda would tell me.

"Omie," as the folks in Somerset knew her, had been on the Somerset school lunch crew, along with Bessie Deeter and Hazel Garst, that my great-aunt Vernie ran in a program she had started in 1944. Before the army came to Somerset, Omma Sweet had been most often on Sundays at the Pleasant Grove Wesleyan Methodist Church along with Vernie, my grandparents, and Dad sometimes, before the war. On this Sunday evening, she was driving with her granddaughter back to Greentown from a family gathering in Wabash.

It had been a beautiful day, Linda said. "All the kids were outside, having fun, at my Aunt Jeanie Maple's house in Wabash."

Rose told me, "I was going to go spend a week with her at the new house in Greentown for spring break. My baby brother had been dedicated at church on that Palm Sunday, and the whole family had gathered at this old cafeteria that used to be in downtown Wabash, and so it was like this happy family gathering, and then I took off with Grandma to go to Greentown for spring break."

Omma Sweet, whose husband, Jesse, had died in 1955, had recently moved to the Howard County community east of Kokomo "after she got booted out of Somerset," according to Rose, "to be near her oldest daughter," Linda's mom, Betty. As she had in Somerset with Aunt Vernie Knee, Omie had gone to work in the school cafeteria in Greentown.

"That drive from Wabash to Greentown isn't that far, but when you are eight, it's like a road trip, and what I remember, after getting in the car, is that the weather changed, the sky darkened, it was storming, and almost black out. It had gotten very dark while we were driving," Rose said, "and I remember her pulling off the side of the road because I guess she couldn't see, that it was raining so hard. I don't know if she saw a tornado. Anyway, she pulled off into what I can only guess was somebody's driveway or farm lot or something."

Ahead, from inside the car her father, John Haines, drove, Linda saw "three funnels, one in front and one on each side," she told me. "There was no place to go. There was no place to escape. My dad had the accelerator floored, and the car was going twenty miles per hour, because the wind was so strong.

"There's a little dip in the road right before you get into Greentown from the east. We hit that dip at the same time the tornadoes went over. We were lower than what they were reaching. It was God's hand that saved us. It's a slight dip, but it was enough. Yes, we drove right into it."

Behind them, according to the account heard by Tom Snyder, Vernie Knee's grandson, the tornado flipped over Omma Sweet's car several times "like a tumbleweed."

Oblivious to all that was happening ten miles to my west, in the dim light after sunset, it looked to me like that same tornado was headed directly for us. Vern decided to get us away from there, to put Mom, Stan, and me with him into our Pontiac, rather than head for the crawl space under the new house. Linda was home from Ball State on spring break, but she had gone to the drive-in movie in Marion with her future husband, John, and we would have to leave without her. Dad hesitated, looking left and right at the end of the driveway, where he had to decide.

North or south?

"Let's get out of here."

He turned south onto State Road 13.

From out the rear window, three minutes later, I watched the monster tornado cross our road as we drove past my school, the Green Township Elementary building at Point Isabel, three miles from Normal. I wondered if it had destroyed our house, the new one Vern had built in the backyard of our old one, the one we'd now proudly lived in for a little more than a year. He turned around at State Road 26, and seven minutes after he'd pulled out with some doubt about which way to go, we discovered our new house was dark but still there. We went inside fearfully uncertain that this supernatural monster thing was done with us.

The tornado had crossed the road a mile and a half north of Normal, killing three people in their home near where we would have been had Vern decided to turn right onto State Road 13. It continued on the ground north and east, through Marion, where a veterans' hospital and a strip mall had their roofs torn away. It plowed through the Three Acres Mobile Home Park a mile from the Hi-Way Drive-In. "The sky was the strangest color," Linda told me. "We had no idea what was going on." Afterward, she said, "I saw the people walking around the trailer court, after it had been demolished."

Back in Greentown, Omma and Rose were discovered an hour after the storm had passed, in a field behind the house where they had stopped. "The wind had picked up their car and sucked them out," Thornton reported.[340] "At the hospital the doctors reported that Rose Ann has sustained numerous lacerations and a deep gash on her thigh. She would recover."[341]

"'My grandmother had wrapped her arms around my cousin,' Linda said. 'Her watch imprint stayed on my cousin's cheek for days.'"

"A thousand traces in my skin," is how Rose described that, through tears, to me. "I wouldn't be here if my grandma hadn't put her arms around me."

The woman who covered her granddaughter with her own body to protect her would not survive. Sixty-three-year-old Omma Ellen Sweet "suffered severe, untreatable internal injuries," Thornton wrote.[342]

The *Kokomo Morning Times* of June 28, 1965, reported that after surgery, Omma died in her sleep the next morning.[343]

"I don't recall when they told me that Grandma had died," Rose told me. "I just know that she made it" to the hospital. "They took her to surgery, and she died of internal injuries, I think I was told."

She added softly, "It's really part of who I am, this whole story. It's a loving story."

My sister, Linda, had given me Janis Thornton's book; Janis gave me a connection to Linda Martin, and Linda Martin quite generously put me in touch with Rose. "I'm writing a letter to my grandson about my dad" was all I ever had to say.

I had not expected Rose to be so open.

"This presence told me to get on the floor of the car. I know one hundred percent," Rose said. "This is what I tell my kids: it's a fate story, also, but I know an angel told me to get on the floor of the car. It wasn't my grandma. It was some being. I obeyed. That's the last thing that I remember.

"The next thing I knew, I wake up in a field. I get up. I somehow find my grandma and I tell her I'm gonna go get help and I like see lights or something off in the distance, and she told me to lay down and stay with her. I was in shock or hurt, but she was alive in the field, and the next thing I remember is our cousins came and found us."

Linda Haines Martin told me that after the storm had passed, "My dad and my mother wanted to go out and see if they could find my grandmother and see what happened to her car, so we dropped off my sister, her husband, their baby, and my baby brother at the house. Mother said she wanted me to go with them because Rose and I were very close, and I remember going out there. It was still raining and dark.

"There was a man walking around in a circle, saying, 'I can't find my wife, I can't find my wife.' She was laying dead in the middle of the circle he was walking around."

Linda stopped for a moment as her voice broke.

"That was traumatic," she continued. "Then we walked pretty far out into a field because my dad could see like the shape of something out there, and it turned out to be my grandmother's car.

"We were thrown not just a little ways from that car," Rose told me. "We were a field or so away from that car. It wasn't like we got pushed right out into that parking lot. We were quite a distance from where the car was, and the car was squished. You know how you see them at the junkyards when they get squished down flat? That's my impression of what the car looked like. So thank God we were thrown out."

John Haines told the *Kokomo Tribune* that when he found Rose and Omma, Rose "was clutched in Mrs. Sweet's arms."[344]

"I can only imagine what my parents were going through," Rose said. "I can just see them getting into the car. There were so many trees down between Wabash and Greentown. They had to zig and zag and zig and zag to get to where I was.

"The local undertaker got his ambulance and came back and found us, and then the next thing I remember is being in the emergency room in Kokomo. There were no lights," Rose said. "There was no power, and my mom told me that I didn't have any broken bones. I don't know if I had a concussion, who knows, but I had lots of lacerations and I was caked in mud and they sewed most of my lacerations by candlelight or flashlight, and then Mom said by the time they had gotten to my head wounds, they did have maybe some power."

The *Kokomo Tribune* reported that Kokomo's Saint Joseph Memorial Hospital "cared for at least 129 victims," forty-nine of them admitted and eighty treated and released. The Howard Community Hospital in Kokomo released the names of 160 people whom doctors there were treating in a list officials called "unofficial and incomplete."[345]

"I couldn't get enough water," Rose said. "I can thankfully remember people giving me water out of the old-style cafeteria coffee cups that are white with like a little black line, maybe two lines. I still have some at home. I'm connected to that cup because of my extreme thirst. I can remember being that thirsty."

Rose said that when it was permissible, she was transferred to the Wabash hospital to be closer to home. "They would pick sticks and grunge out of my wounds. I would get a little scab on my arm, and when it was loose, there would be like a stick or something that was hooked to that scab. I just remember dirt and stuff just coming out like no big deal. I had so much mud in my hair," Rose said. "They put a shower cap on me. Why in the hell they didn't just wash my hair, I don't know, but back in those days, they thought just keeping it dry was better. They should have just hosed me off. Any of the pictures of me at that time are me with a shower cap on because my hair was caked in mud." Rose said she was hospitalized for three weeks.

"The scars that you get when you are eight, they're part of you," Rose said. "I had big scars on my legs. I had a scar on my shoulder, my abdomen, elbows." Rose said that the experience probably kept her from ever having too much of a sense of vanity. "It is what it is," she said. "I just had a knee replaced on that side, and it was like, well, what the hell, what's another scar on my leg."

Along with several homes within the city limits, the high school in Greentown was destroyed, and a new elementary school and the Methodist church were heavily damaged. In the area where Omma had pulled over when the tornado struck, according to the *Kokomo Tribune*, "A cluster of new homes a half mile east of Greentown along U.S. 35 disappeared, leaving only the foundations to mark their locations."[346]

An eleven-year-old fifth grader named Debbie Sprague and a two-week-old baby named Tamara Lynn Harvey were among the sixteen people who were killed in the Greentown area. Another 288 were injured. There was a temporary morgue in the Mast funeral home downtown.

Rose's story represented the disaster. "I had so many cards and well wishes," she told me. She had packed her dolls for the week with Grandma. "Somehow the newspaper story got out that I lost all my Barbies, and suddenly every homemaker and grandma in a ten-county area was sending homemade Barbie clothes. I just remember I had so many Barbie clothes.

"I had a piece of Samsonite luggage that my mom had let me take," Rose said. "They never found a trace of that. That would have been a good Samsonite commercial, but they never found that. They did find a perfect check from my grandma's checkbook that landed on a porch in Ohio. A check landed on a porch in Ohio, and somehow, they reached back to find us. You hear freaky stories like that with tornadoes all the time, but no Barbies." She paused and, as if talking to herself, said, "I got a shit ton of Barbie clothes."

Rose told me that her parents were wonderful in comforting her after that awful day.

"I remember watching the sky as a kid, after this happened, and on a perfectly beautiful day, with a white cloud and a little bit of gray in it, I'd freak out. 'Is there a storm?' If there was any kind of a thunderstorm coming, I would make my parents take me over to my other grandma's house, who had a cellar. It gave me some peace.

"I didn't realize this until my mom told me not too many years ago that they got me a little transistor radio. It was almost like my security blanket, that I had my transistor radio and I could hear if there would be a storm or something. How clever of my parents. Nobody took me to a psychiatrist or anything. I was fine and normal. I turned out okay. Nowadays, they would probably take me to a counselor or something."

This story found me, Vern. Omma was Aunt Vernie's friend. She was a Somerset person. She was killed by a tornado that I watched from the front yard of the house that the man you are named for built, the man who maybe saved our lives when he turned south instead of north. Omma's granddaughter Rose has graciously shared this painful story with us only because I told her that I am writing you a letter about my dad. It's important, what she has to say:

I wouldn't be here if my grandma hadn't put her arms around me.

"We stand on the shoulders of those who went before us," Rose said. "There's fascinating studies now about how our genes do remember things. Stresses like war can be manifested generations later. There's more than we know on the surface about how our history impacts us today, not just the bread and butter of those deeds but what happened to the people. This touches a sense of magic for me. The more I learn about it, the more . . . I mean, it's not magic, but there's mystery, that we have barely scratched the surface of.

"I wouldn't be here if my grandma hadn't put her arms around me," Dr. Rose Wenrich said.

"That's what I want to tell Vern," I replied.

I feel some magic, too. I woke up at three o'clock in the morning after the day you were born with the notion that I ought to write this letter to you. Then these stories found me.

Omma Sweet lived on a farm four miles west of Somerset until the army confiscated it in the Upper Wabash Valley Flood Control Project.

Rose remembers "a kind of a quaint, beat-up farmhouse with all the charm and woodstove and smells and the kitchen where she would produce yummy baked goods and foods sitting out on the table."

While Omma worked on the cafeteria staff, Rose's grandfather Jesse "drove a Somerset school bus. I fantasized buying the land back," Rose said, "the farm where they lived. My dad said it was crappy land. From a farmer perspective, they were always sort of poor. They were the poor relatives of more prosperous farmers, but I don't think that they ever felt poor. They raised rabbits for food. I remember my grandma cutting the head off of a chicken. My grandparents had a maple syrup stand that used their tree to barter other goods. That's how they lived. It's that idyllic country life that I never experienced."

Rose paused, pondered for a moment, and said, "She was a great cook."

Rose remembers the village of Red Bridge: "a gas station, a restaurant, a little gathering place. I've been told they would put me on a table and I would sing 'I Had a Girl in Red Bridge.'" Rose said it was "a place where people would go to hang out or to have coffee, shoot the shit. Public space." The Sweets and the Shroyers were of a kind, then, it sounds like to me, Vern. More Red Bridge than Somerset. Untillable land. Chickens in the yard. With a memory of displacement that has perhaps seeped into the hearts of my generation. Foreshadowing. Dad mentioned Mrs. Sweet in his 1943 army letter home.

"I don't remember any conversation about it," the flooding of Somerset, Rose told me. "Law of eminent domain, the greater good, flooding control, suck it up, sister."

And "my grandma would never have been in that tornado had it not been for the displacement of people caused by the creation of the reservoir."

"Memory?" Rose thought aloud when we spoke. "Pulling off the highway and being compelled to get on the floor . . . by a being . . . I don't know . . . But I know . . . absolutely comfortable sharing . . . I tell it all the time . . . an angel told me to get on the floor . . . and I think my grandma probably piled on top of me and wrapped her arms around me.

"When I look back on that, anytime you have something traumatic happen to you, it does affect you. It affects the trajectory of your life, and I always point to that as, I've always known that, I have a kind of a personal . . . I had an angel that day. Certainly that experience—well, my mom was a nurse—but I think that experience made me want to help people and go into medicine. I mean I think it's definitely been a part of my story, being a physician—at one time, I did ER; most of my work has been in family medicine."

The little girl that Omma saved that day became Dr. Rose Wenrich, MD, a family medicine doctor in Wabash, who for a time specialized in emergency care. Until her retirement in 2022, she served her community that way for over forty years. She saved lives.

Omma—"Omie" they called her, like they called Verna "Vernie"—was known by most, and known to be selfless, in Somerset. Nothing unusual. That's how they lived, of a kind.

Omma Sweet was among the last three people to be buried at the Pleasant Grove Methodist Church cemetery before everyone there was disinterred in 1966 and moved to a consolidated cemetery location north of Somerset and away from the Mississinewa Reservoir water. The last time I visited my parents there, I recognized her gravestone for the first time. You gave that to me, Vern.

After their town was devastated by the Palm Sunday 1965 tornado, losing lives, homes, businesses, churches, and schools, the people of Greentown rebuilt. Since 1960, the population has nearly doubled, and its visible, if modest, prosperity stands in contrast to nearby towns like Windfall and Fairmount that have not fared as well. A continually growing, highly rated high school that opened new in 1967 is three blocks from the center of town. I graduated from that Eastern High School in 1971.

Somerset never had a chance. In 1965, the school building where Omma Sweet had worked, the last building standing in Somerset, would be closed for good and then destroyed, like the rest of that town, on purpose. Moving a few buildings up the hill to a site where Somerset did not belong only extended the tragedy. The Somerset of Omie Sweet and Vernie Knee does not exist.

The National Weather Service reported that there were forty-four tornadoes in six midwestern states April 11, 1965, killing 261 people, twenty-five killed by the storm that I saw from our front yard in Normal. It was on the ground, sometimes a mile wide, for forty-eight miles. Vernie's son, Larry Knee, worked the repair crews for Indiana Michigan Power, where he'd been employed as a lineman since he graduated from high school in 1956. The storm "dropped tower after tower" from a substation east of Greentown to the Deer Creek facility at Marion twenty miles away, Larry said. "Big old lines were wrapped around buildings. No power anywhere."

Twenty-nine people were killed by three different tornadoes in the South Bend and Elkhart area that day. Ten tornadoes killed 137 people in Indiana.

There was a man walking in a circle around his wife he could not find. There was a little girl who can never forget the loss of her fifth-grade best friend.

My sister was a mile from destruction. My dad turned south. Grandma drove Rosie. Linda Haines's dad drove hard into a dip in the road. Luck and choices, Vern. North or south.

53. JOHN HUDDLESTON

The *Kokomo Morning Times* on January 7, 1967, said in a photo feature called "Somerset: A Second Birth" that there was a "great future ahead" for residents who were given a choice, move or close down. "Many outside business concerns have invested heavily in the future of new Somerset," it said, adding that the development of the new town was being aided by state and federal funding for streets, water, and sewage.[347]

SOMERSET THRIVES IN NEW ENVIRONS was the headline for an *Indianapolis News* story on June 26, 1969, seven days after the Mississinewa Reservoir dedication. Somerset is "a hamlet that is growing and gives promise of much greater growth," the story read.[348]

"It never developed like they expected it to," Janet Weaver told me. Janet is my mom's youngest sister, and her husband, Larry, opened a body shop in the new Somerset strip mall along State Road 13. He died in 2012, but Aunt Janet told me what life was like around 1975 in the new town, nine years after the water flooded the old one. By 1975, it was clear that New Somerset wouldn't take off. "There was not a lot going on," Janet told me on the phone in 2023.

"They called it the Shopping Center, the strip mall," she said. "I think it was called Shopping Center Road for a while. It was a shopping center. It was a whole row of buildings built back when shopping centers were popular. They were storefronts. When we was there, there was a flea market that they tried. There was a restaurant that changed hands different times," Janet said. "Dave Compton had a boat business. There was big plans for that row of buildings. You know, you put a building in with a loading dock, you expect some kind of manufacturing or something." The strip mall is now vacant.

"The building in Somerset we went into was a big, huge building that belonged to Rex Snyder, who lived in town and bought [it] as an investment, but then it was empty," Janet said. "His wife had been a schoolteacher, and we knew them through the Masonic lodge." Mrs. Snyder, Mabel, was a member of Somerset's Citizens Committee and its Development Corporation, like Floyd Bowman and Fred Snyder.

"We knew about the building through Larry belonging to the Masons, and I belonged to Eastern Star," Janet said. "They had a Mason and Eastern Star chapter in new Somerset in a new building."

She and Larry made friends. Helen and Aden Adkins, she told me, were among the first people they met. Aden was a "character," she said. "He helped move the town. He was a person who, when told, 'You can't do that,' he would figure out a way to do it."

"The people there were wonderful," Janet said. "They were accepting. In our building, we basically had a stop-off point where everybody hung out. Larry would go early and make a big pot of coffee. People would go get their mail and drop by and get their coffee and chit-chat and check on each other. The women had puzzles, the jigsaw puzzles, out on the table that was out. A lot of the same people showed up all the time. A lot of them were people who lived in the old town. It just became a friendly little spot. There was a coffee can with a slit in it. People would drop a dollar in it to buy more coffee, and we had a Coke machine. They'd stop by and get a Coke. It was a gathering place in the morning.

"They grew garden plants in our front windows. There was a 'Kenny Rogers,' cool name, who lived about a mile south of the shop, and he would come in. He was a gardener, an old guy with bib overalls, what a sweetheart, and he helped them get some plants going because he always grew his own plants. There was a lady named Mary Smith. They planted the seeds in these big flats. There was good light in the windows in the front of the shop. They passed out the plants—tomato, different kinds of tomato plants, old-fashioned kind, and then the pepper plants. That's what they grew. That seems weird for a body shop, but that's the kind of people that lived there.

"There was an old guy that was interesting; his name was John Huddleston."

That's the guy, Vern, who connected an electric fence to his windmill for power in 1936, the man whose sister married Somerset Communist Milo Long in 1938, and the same guy who was guarding the old high school when it was the last building standing in the old town in 1965. John was there when Somerset fell. I wish I could have talked to him.

John Huddleston had been hired by the contractor that was to tear down the school to be the building's night watchman. Tom Snyder told me that Huddleston had been around the school because he had been hired before by the school to help remove coal waste from the furnace boiler system. "He had a place, his farm about a mile north of Somerset, where he could haul the stuff," Tom said.

What was left of the old town needed a guard because looters were taking anything they could get after the area had been decimated, Tom said. "They were ripping off everything. I lost a bicycle and tools from our farm."

Janet said she didn't know Huddleston had been the last man standing in Somerset, but like Tom, she knew that he was eccentric.

"When we knew him, he used to come in the shop and get water. He lived back a lane, outside of town to the north and to the west. He was like a hobo, almost. He was living in this house, old house, and there was part of a log cabin there.

"He initially had a driver's license that he had a habit of letting lapse, but he'd drive, anyway," Tom Snyder said. "He thought it was immoral to have to pay to get a driver's license.

"I don't think he had power back to his house." That would have been forty years after he connected the windmill to the electric fence.

"Supposedly," Janet said, "he took a chain saw and cut down a power pole because he didn't want people infringing on his property. That was the story. I don't know that that was true, but I think it could have been.

They put up a couple power poles, and he sawed them down with his chain saw."

Larry Knee remembered, "The power company set a pole too close to his drive, he thought, so he took a chain saw and cut it off and let it fall. He got in a lot of trouble there."

Huddleston's neighbor Dale, Omma Sweet's nephew, was a friend of Larry Knee and Larry's wife, Nancy. "Nancy and I would go over to Dale's to eat dinner, sit and talk," Larry said. "The Sweets had a porch with glass, and it wouldn't be nothin' to be sitting in the kitchen there to look up and John would be standing there.

"Sometimes you could hear somebody down in the basement when we were there. Dale said, 'John must be getting coal. I told him he could get coal anytime he needed it.'"

Larry said John Huddleston had "an inventor's mind" and "two daughters who were brilliant, one of them in Nancy's class."

"We became close to him in a way," Janet said. "I know he knew your folks."

He sounds like a guy who would have liked Dad.

"He liked us," Janet said, "and he didn't like very many people. He had an old tractor and that was his transportation a lot, and he had an old truck that broke down, and he would drive his tractor into town, and he'd stop at our shop and fill up his jugs with water and get a cup of coffee. He was smelly and unshaven and dirty, but we were kind to him. We took him a Thanksgiving meal, and he hardly ever let anybody back his lane, but he invited us back to his house. People . . . I wouldn't say were afraid of him, but there was a lot of rumors about him being a Communist."

A rumor that sounded absurd to me when Janet said it made sense when I later followed the trail of Ron Woodward's Commie kidnapping story. It was true, and he knew Vern.

"The fact that he let us go back there surprised all the people that was hanging out in the shop," Janet said. "It was really hard to get back there. There was ruts in the road. You had to even drive off of the road sometimes."

Snyder said that while he was never in Huddleston's house, he knew that "the ruts in the lane back were so deep you'd get hung up. You had to straddle one side or the other. You better have a four-wheel-drive pickup."

"He had a fallen-down barn with an old-fashioned thrasher in it and his little cabin thing," Janet continued. "We get back there, and he wanted to serve us coffee. 'Let me get you a cup of coffee,' he said. You know what, that place he was living in, you could see a trail through the house of leaves and dirt. It was like being outside almost. Anyway, I'm thinking, *I'm supposed to drink coffee?* He goes to this old stove he had and puts instant coffee and water in a pan, and he makes us coffee. We're looking at each other like, 'Okay?' The cup, the spoon. You know.

"Larry gave him a motor for his truck, and he, in return, had us come back to his place, and he gave Larry a desk. That was supposed to be because we gave him the motor. He wanted to give us something in return. We actually had that stripped, and we had it in our house until I moved, after Larry died. That was the relationship thing that we kind of had with him.

"We were in our forties, I guess. We'd been at the shop quite a while. That relationship developed over time."

John Huddleston died alone at his log cabin home on a windy day when the temperature hit fourteen below, January 16, 1982. There was no place there, then, for a man like him.

Janet said she's "not in much contact" with people from Somerset now. "They're gone. They're gone."

Flood

54. RALPH ROESSLER

Dear Vern,

Ralph Roessler was a self-made man, a man who made himself and then gave himself a prize for being that. Like if the first Oscar went to the man who made up the Oscars, a man named Oscar. Ralph had the prize plastered all over his office walls, the prize being a collection of a map or two or three and pictures of things and men like himself whom he collected along the way who also made it a point to have collections that hung on walls. Prize plastered.

When I went through the Indiana State Library artifacts collection that got taken down from Ralph's walls, I didn't see anybody who looked like my father, even though my father lived at a place on his map. Dad lived there with one grandparent, two parents, four brothers, and two sisters on the farm before it was made irrelevant by the water on the map, the big-one-in-the-middle-of-the-wall map, among the pictures of government men and army men and press men and businessmen and industry men.

Mostly, what Roessler wanted was to be important. I didn't see any photos in his files of people who were not important. No children. No grandparents. No family reunions at Matter Park or in Amboy. He was among important people, which makes him an important person, so why not celebrate the success of doing what he set out to do with the evidence and the creation and the prize all tied up into one big ball of something so great that it made Roessler want to leave a written account? Of course he did. Important. Even in the file folders where the diary and the pictures and three plaques went after they came off the wall before the state library attendant rolled them in on a cart for me, there's a pecking order. Too much shit to throw in your grave, so we've got a place with a lovely view here in the Indiana state mausoleum. Walk-in closets.

He did mention graves at the end, by the way, in one of his reports in his files. After a section called "General Program" came "Cost of Project," followed by "Recreational Benefits, Detailed Information, Mississinewa Reservoir, Spillway," and finally, "Graves."

No pictures, though, of Ruth Rudicel of Nineveh, Indiana, and her husband, past pastor of the First Christian Church of Clinton, Indiana, watching some strangers "respectfully" move the discolored soil beneath the grave marker of her grandfather Asa Ross, Civil War veteran and two-term sheriff of Wabash County, from the Somerset cemetery.

No pictures, though, of my grandfather, my father, and my brother, standing by to witness when those toothless strangers moved my grandma's grave from the Pleasant Grove churchyard up to the bigger, better, six-sites-consolidated, treeless cemetery on State Road 13.

Not on the wall.

Not off the wall.

Not part of the celebration.

"Father of the Mississinewa Reservoir." When the Marion Chamber of Commerce gave Ralph its Man of the Year Award in 1964, that's what they called him. There's a picture in the collection, and the plaque is in a manila envelope at the Indiana State Library that you can handle respectfully with gloves if you know enough to ask for it.

Vern

55. VERN SHROYER

Dear Vern,

To support himself and his family, Vern left the farm for factory work that served the same cash economy interests that turned the farmland into factory farms serving the same interests. People were betrayed by the leaders of their communities, the government, the army, business and industry, and the press, for the sake of a progress that defied the tradition they simultaneously claimed as their own. Rural communities have been hollowed for the greater good like Grandma and Grandpa's house on the hill by Goose Creek before it was obliterated.

I've looked for something, anything, there—the foundation, maybe, the spring—but it's all gone.

What is it? The force to tell this story to you, my grandson. The power of our father so great that we create a God in his image. And "our father who art in heaven" to rationalize our predicament when he is gone. So be it.

My fondest memories of Vern are in times we spent together when nobody else was around. That time was almost always silent. Silent prayer is the best kind.

On few occasions do I remember times not silent. I have the immediate memory of a rare conversation in the car that is, by all measures but one, insignificant. We had turned left from State Road 13 to Highway 37 south of Elwood for Wickes Lumber when I told Dad that I could identify the make and year of every car we saw. We had gone to Wickes to get something for building the new house, in the blue '61 Chevy Impala, which means I was younger than ten. Dad responded, "I can't." That is the significance of a sixty-year-old memory. I could know something that he did not.

I remember that time now as the time, also, of something known as the Cuban missile crisis, when for several days even children knew that the world might soon be destroyed. I remember at that time believing that diving into the hole-in-the-ground concrete space for a septic tank Dad had created behind the new house foundation he was building could save us.

We didn't talk any more in the times alone together on the tractor than we did in the car, but that was fine with both of us. I was proud to be with him and happy to have him all to myself for an hour. I guess he liked that I was quiet, too.

"I'm going to Wickes," he'd say, and with that as close as I'd ever get to an invitation, I'd follow him into the car. It's the story of tagging along, like the one from 1938 that his little brother, Wayne, told me, saying, "The world needs another Vern."

Vern never bought a car on time. He always paid cash. "I'll put the money away myself," he'd tell us, "ahead of time, instead of giving it to the banks, and when I've saved up enough, I'll go get a new car." Vern didn't like to owe anybody anything. Sure enough, we had a 1953, a 1957, a 1961, a 1964, and a 1967 new car, three Chevys and two Pontiacs, and he paid cash for all of them. He did borrow some money to pay for whatever he needed for the house he built, though I know it bugged him. I think it was for around $20,000, an amount that I must have overheard, or else Mom mentioned in the way she sometimes read aloud the signs that we passed on the highway when I was alone with her, trying to listen to a song I liked that had finally come on the radio.

"Gas City 7," "Burma Shave," "Impeach Earl Warren," Mom said to no one.

Sometimes I'd ride with Vern up to the Amboy State Bank on a once-a-month Saturday morning to pay the house-building loan. He didn't interrupt the songs.

I rode alone with Vern down to Wickes Lumber to get whatever he needed to build the house in the backyard. I suppose that's what made the old house bearable, the fact that there was a visible sign right there in the backyard every day, progressing slowly, but progressing before our eyes, that we would not have to live in that old, cold house forever.

Vern cleared the space: bushes and trees and stumps and buildings and the remains of buildings and places where the trash that was burned left debris. Like what was happening to Somerset. To build us a better place to live. Sacred work. He hitched the plow to the tractor and dug up the soil, and then he smashed with the disc the dirt clods that Stan and I liked to throw at each other, and then he smoothed the ground with a rake and leveled it with a rusty-brown open-sideways barrel-like device that was 240 degrees of a circle, creating a shower of dirt that I would've liked to stick my foot into up to the ankle as I ran alongside. Over and over and over again, the tractor ran over the dirt like it didn't know when the right time would be to stop. *When will the ground be level enough?* the tractor said. *And how will I know?* Vern knew, and then he made another day's worth of passes.

Vern went out into the backyard after work, before supper, with a shovel and dug a trench that was four feet deep and two feet wide in the rectangular shape of an imagined house. It took him a year to dig and form the foundation. Stan remembered, "When the guy with the cement truck came to pour the foundation, he told Dad, 'I've poured these many times, and I must say you did a really good job on this one. I've seen 'em bust wide open. A really good job.'"

The concrete was perfectly level when it dried with three-quarter-inch anchor bolts firmly rooted six feet apart all the way around the home that would someday be.

"It took him a while to build it," Stan said. "Miss Downs, the teacher at Point, when the floor was all that was in, said to me, 'Is he just building that so you can ride your bicycles on it?'

"'Who does she think she is?'" he remembers.

"It took a while for those walls to start going up. Got the foundation in, got the flooring on," Stan said. "Took a while on the walls," but there was never any doubt.

Something in Vern's head appeared on the ground because he built it. It's still there in the space behind where the old house disappeared and where my niece and her husband live now in the house Vern built, without their daughter, who has also now gone away to college. "Everything is perfect," Linda said. "Every square. Every line. Perfect. He wouldn't do it haphazard. He took such pain. He did that with everything." It took six years.

He brought home in the two-wheeled trailer he'd fashioned from an abandoned pickup truck bed a cement mixer that he'd repaired with a new belt and a new motor so he could mix the concrete that he would pour himself for the sidewalk and the driveway and the garage floor. He didn't have to call the cement truck guy back after he'd watched him that one time.

Vern dug a well, and he installed a pump. I remember the plastic sheeting that covered the ground under what would become the crawl space under the house-in-his-head, and I remember the pea gravel that covered the plastic and that everything came home in the back of that little red trailer he made that he pulled behind the 1957, 1961, and 1964 car, like the concrete mix in heavy, heavy bags, and that he did it by himself, after work and on the weekends.

Week after week, month after month, for six years.

He lifted every heavy bag. I never heard him swear. After he put the two-by-fours he brought home from Wickes in the trailer, like everything else through the foundation bolts at perfect intervals, he was next able to create a wooden base for the entire house that we could run around on, firm and strong, not sagging at all.

I remember believing that the concrete-walled hole he dug behind the new house foundation for a septic tank would suffice, just fine, for a bomb shelter around the same time that I saw a cloud in the sky in the shape of a question mark that disappeared before I could show anyone.

I remember the reddish-orange string snapping after it had spooled out from the chalk line tool, and the line it created that Dad followed through the wood exactly with his circular handsaw.

"Stay back," he said.

Stan said, "A lot of it came from those outbuildings on the property.

Recycled and put into that new house. There's probably subflooring that's still got red paint on it from those red buildings out there. He used a lot of that stuff over again."

I do not remember blueprints. I remember that Burnell helped him with the wiring, and another uncle, on Mom's side, told me once that he'd helped put on the roof, but I don't remember that, only Burnell and no one else helping Dad. Jack Zorn was that uncle's name, and I'm sure he's right, but I don't remember him being there.

My memory of when we moved into the new house is the memory of which house we were in when things were on TV. Sometimes that doesn't match what makes sense. Maybe, for a while, we lived to some degree in both, and that's the source of my confusion. I remember one Sunday Stan and I were in what had been the backyard for the old house and then became the front yard for the new house, playing catch, when Mom and Dad called us in. That would have been after church and what we called dinner at the Mangas Cafeteria in Elwood. It was early fall, when a month in, school still felt new. I can feel those days, right now, as Warm tells Cold, "Not yet." I was in fifth grade, the smartest kid in my class, and the Cuban missile crisis hadn't killed everybody after all. I wasn't a Negro and I didn't live in Birmingham, so for my ten-year-old-white-boy mind, there was no better time in American history than September of 1963.

"You have to come in," Mom said. My memory of that is connected to an historical event, and so I can look it up and pinpoint the exact date. It's Mom calling us in; she's standing on the front-Dad-poured-concrete-slab new house porch. I can see the limestone siding in the sun. "Stan Musial is taking his last at bat," she said. "You have to see this." My brother's name is no coincidence.

That was September 1963. There's a YouTube video. September 29, 1963.

I have seen the video a few times, so by this time, I don't remember if what I remember is that or the moment in which I saw it. What I really remember is Mom calling us in.

September of 1963 seems early to me for when we moved in. I thought it was 1964. I definitely remember watching the Beatles on *Ed Sullivan* in the new house, which was February of 1964, but I'm less certain about where the November 1963 Kennedy assassination unfolded on our TV. Was that old house or new house? What house did we come home to after the Country Kitchen waitress told us Oswald was dead?

That's when we moved in. The new house, Kennedy, the Beatles, Musial. This was the time of Congressman Roush helping the people at Red Bridge because it was the right thing to do.

I saw the greatest baseball players who ever lived when Vern continued the tradition Pop had started by taking his family to St. Louis: 1963, 1964, 1965, 1966, 1968. It could well have been in the car during the 1964 trip when we saw Bob Gibson pitch to Willie Mays that Dad made known his negativity toward what was becoming the Vietnam War. That Monday night game was August 10, the same day that President Lyndon Johnson of Texas authorized a war without a declaration of war in Vietnam. I looked that up, too, Vern, knowing they were both in August 1964 but not connecting the two.

Johnson signed the Gulf of Tonkin Resolution after the House of Representatives passed it by a vote of 416–0 and the Senate passed it 88–2 three days before. We were in the car for hours that week, and had the radio news mentioned it, then Dad might have reacted that day as he did later with an "I don't know about this."

From the start, Vern thought the war in Vietnam was a mistake, and he did not trust the leaders who made it happen. He said the press went along for the ride. He said it's easy to "wave the flag" to get most people to go along when they don't know enough to know what's going on.

"But they're Communists," I said around that time, confident that I was capable of knowing something Dad did not. The "domino theory" was not hard for an eleven-year-old approaching sixth grade to comprehend. Vern did not argue with me. He did not say that he knew something that I did not. He'd already said, "I don't know about that."

Because Vern was my dad, I began to thoughtfully consider the growing dissent about the war. The war opposition was never "un-American" to me. It was Dad. I heard Simon and Garfunkel's "7 O'Clock News/Silent Night" announcer quote Richard Nixon saying, "Opposition to the war in this country is the greatest single weapon working against the U.S."[349] That sentiment was pretty popular in my neck of the woods, but that sentiment would make Vern an enemy of the state. I knew that was wrong. Dad loved the country. He flew the flag.

But he never went along with things because everybody else did.

I remember a night around the campfire with junior high friends in Fairmount when someone asked us all to say which service we would be joining. Maybe I was thirteen. I was being a smart-ass, and I got a laugh when I said, "I'm going to Canada," but it immediately felt like the right thing to say. By the time "anti-war" Bobby Kennedy was assassinated while running for president in 1968, I was almost fifteen, and I was in Normal, Indiana, Green Township, Grant County, identifying with the long-hair kids in places like Berkeley who were protesting the war. I saw them on TV in the new house.

The American war in Vietnam started that summer of 1964, not long after we'd moved into the new house, when I was eleven, while we were getting ready to ride the Redbird Express from a suburban St. Louis shopping mall to the Busch Stadium that had been called Sportsman's Park. It ended, mostly without the Americans, in the spring of 1975, as your newly acquainted-to-me grandma Shroyer and I were getting ready to graduate from Indiana University in Bloomington. Formative years, transformative years, wasn't it pretty much that all our years awakening to the world had been spent in the Vietnam War? In grade school, high school, and college, in loneliness, in love, in drugs, and in rock and roll, Vietnam was there, and then your grandma Shroyer and I met as all of that fell away. I landed on the earth in 1975.

In 1975, silently waiting, Father Vern had never gone anywhere. Vern was always right there.

Writing you this letter, Grandson Vern, I've wondered some about how my life would have been different if Somerset had not been swept away. Dad wanted to farm. Might he have taken over the land that would be lost for Pop around 1957, the time when we moved from Marion to the land at Normal, where Dad could pretend to farm and think about draught horses? Might I have grown up there and lived in a place where I felt like I belonged, like I felt when I was there with my cousins playing ball in the barnyard at the bottom of the hill? Might my life away from that place be connected to the feeling in my life that I would never "belong" anywhere? Who knows? Maybe I would have run away from there, too.

I wonder sometimes, too, how different my life would have been if Vietnam had not happened. The war seemed to set a lifetime's worth of perspective for me. It was political and it was personal, but for me, it was less confusing because Vern didn't have to say a whole lot about how a person ought to act. I could see it. Dad was a rock.

When I was a kid where I was, before "sit down and shut up" had morphed sequentially into the disparagement of "political correctness" and the word *woke*, I knew the risk and the reward of being on the outside looking in. When it was, then, the culture versus the counterculture, when each side had its fashions and music and media and recreational drugs and its symbols, when the war and the civil rights movement divided the country into two camps and it felt to me like one had to pick a side, I picked the counterculture. I picked the peace symbol. "They" picked the American flag.

Dad taught me I didn't have to pick from others' choices.

At a time when war protests had already become pervasive, especially on college campuses, the United States, under the direction of then-president Richard Nixon, expanded the war with an invasion of Vietnam's neighbor, Cambodia. I was a junior in high school and probably already insufferable to my classmates when the Ohio National Guard murdered four protesting students on the campus of Kent State University, May 4, 1970. I'm still mad about that and angry that some flag-wavers said those kids "had it coming." They were shooting at me.

"That could have been me they killed," I said to Mom and Dad that day. "I would have been there." After that, my parents never again told me it was time for a haircut. They were on my side.

With my head bowed, first love a casualty, also, of all that, I got off the school bus one sunny, later-in-May day in 1970. I'm there now when I think about it. I suppose I'm always there. As I walk down our gravel driveway toward the garage, I see that Dad has put an American flag decal on the rear window of our car. Those American flag decals were a symbol of support for the war, but even more than that, they were a denunciation of people protesting the war, like the kids at Kent State. The war was a mistake, and millions were dying, and mothers and fathers and children were suffering, and I wanted to make it stop. And for that, my self-righteous sixteen-year-old self got a windshield flag thrust into my face on every drive into town that said, “Fuck you!”

“Fuck you back!” I said.

So now I’m walking toward the house built by my own anti-war dad, and I see the *Reader’s Digest* flag John Prine would later sing about on the Pontiac’s rear-window lower-right-hand corner. Maybe John wrote “Your Flag Decal Won’t Get You into Heaven Anymore” that very day. As I walked into the house, I knew that I would have to say something to Dad. The only other conversations I can remember as clearly are the one about John Brown and when I told him I knew something that he said he did not.

This time, as he stood, alone, in the doorway between the kitchen and the living room, he knew what I did not. Before I could speak, “It’s our flag, too,” he said. And that was all.

56. CLOSING

I heard him that day, Vern, and I understood what it meant, so now it feels like I got on the floor of a car in the service of an unseen entity, too, but it was Dad, no angel. He wrapped his arms around me with a four-word lesson I've never stopped learning.

I don't know . . . but I know. I'm certain that I am uncertain. It was a voice telling me to save myself, get down on the floor of the car. It's the same voice that said, "Watch number six," "John Brown was right," and "Let's get out of here."

It's the voice that's writing this letter to you. We matter, Vern. Dad's life matters. Somerset matters. It's our flag, too.

I was too young to know, but I knew. It was a voice that told me to get on the floor. Cover my head.

Save yourself. We're better than all that nonsense, he said. It's our flag, too.

"What time is it?" I said to your grandma Shroyer when we met, and when she said, "When?" and when I said "Now," all the cosmic tumblers tumbled into place, the war ended, and maybe that's God and maybe that's not, but really, what difference does it make?

It's our flag, too. We belong together. Everything else is commentary.

To attach myself to a certainty that I know is a mask that people wear, in fashion, is not something that I have to do. So when the flag is unfurled and I pledge allegiance or I pledge no allegiance, I know the truer nature of things: no capital *T* in truth, that Yossarian is right, that I'd be a damn fool to feel any different, and if that means I go to hell, well, all right, then, like Huck, I'll go to hell.

Destroying Somerset destroyed the evidence that the life there meant something. There was a truth there that transcends the illusion of progress its destruction was meant to convey. I've dug up some graves, too.

There was genuine truth in the backyard house that grew out of Vern's imagination. No one else had to know. The certainty in the self-righteous claims around me would always be a disguise that I did not need, he said by living, and I knew it to be true because I knew him and I saw the way he lived, without disguise.

"Faith" was a surrender to the idea that allegiance or not allegiance or God or no God will save us. Doubt is living free. I was young and I wanted to belong, too young to know, but I knew. "Our flag, too" was a lesson for every day, a rock, a life preserver. I was just fortunate to be his kid. Thanks, Dad.

"The world needs another Vern," said his little brother Wayne.

What is that? The power of our father so great that we create a God in his image. And "our father who art in heaven" is how we rationalize our predicament when he is gone.

"He'll be fine," I said. Vern would always be okay in my mind. My disbelief that any harm could come from the 1970 heart attack that hit him three months after a day in May I will never forget, I associate now with the shock of his death in 1986.

His death?

"My father died?"

What possibility could there be in losing something that had always been? No possibility at all.

I'd had a son.

We were gonna be friends.

It makes me sad.

But then, through your birth, and by your parents giving you his name and by my writing this letter to you, I've completed the cosmic circle. I don't know . . . but I know I was intended to deliver. I have given you each other. Now my son has a son, and his name is Vern.

I have not lost Vern at all. He is here with me. I write this letter because I would like for him to be here for you. I would like for you to be here for him. That's all. I don't need a reward.

It's our flag, too.

Imagine it, from the guy who built our house in the backyard.

That's it.

Thanks for giving me the opportunity to tell you about him.

Grandpa Shroyer

INDEX

C

D

G

H

I

J

K

P

Q

R

S

T

U

V

W

Y

Z

ENDNOTES

Chapter 1—The Beginning

1 David I. Day, "Taking a Look Around at Indiana Rural Life," *Indianapolis Star*, April 4, 1953. https://www.newspapers.com/image/105045309/?match=1&terms=%20David%20Day.

Chapter 2—Origins

2 Hosea Paul C.E., P.A. Cunningham, and R.W. Twitchell, *Illustrated Historic Atlas of Wabash County Indiana* (Philadelphia: Hosea Paul & Co., 1875). Reprinted (Mt. Vernon, Indiana: Windmill Publications, Inc., 1998), 55.

3 Hosea Paul C.E., P.A. Cunningham, and R.W. Twitchell, *Illustrated Historic Atlas of Wabash County Indiana* (Philadelphia: Hosea Paul & Co., 1875). Reprinted (Mt. Vernon, Indiana: Windmill Publications, Inc., 1998), 7.

4 "Flames Wipe Out Somerset," *Wabash Daily Times Star*, November 3, 1914.

5 Ron Woodward, "Somerset," *Family Branches: Newsletter of the Wabash County Genealogical Society*, Volume 14, Number 7, March 2009.

6 "Shoots Self Near Heart When Love Is Spurned," *Indianapolis News*, April 18, 1934. https://www.newspapers.com/image/314208607/?match=1&terms=shoots%20self.

7 Ron Woodward, "Somerset," *Family Branches: Newsletter of the Wabash County Genealogical Society*, Volume 14, Number 7, March 2009.

8 Daniel Resneck, "Animals Keep Noses Clear of Electrified Fencing," *Indianapolis Star*, August 30, 1936. https://www.newspapers.com/image/105402012/?match=1&terms=electric%20fence.

9 "News of Society, Clubs, and Churches, Hackleman," *Fairmount News*, May 1, 1936. https://www.newspapers.com/image/134010207/?match=1&terms=hackleman%20somerset.

10 "Hills of Somerset, Famous in Riley Verse, Will Be Scene of Historic Park Dedication," *Indianapolis News*, October 22, 1936. https://www.newspapers.com/image/314443169/?match=1&terms=hills%20of%20somerset.

11 Otho Winger, *The Frances Slocum Trail* (North Manchester, Indiana: The News-Journal, 1943).
12 James Whitcomb Riley, "Little Orphant Annie," *Indianapolis Journal*, as "The Elf Child," November, 1885. https://americanliterature.com/author/james-whitcomb-riley/poem/little-orphant-annie.

Chapter 3—The Idea

13 Ralph Roessler (1939–1968). Ralph Roessler papers, Rare Books and Manuscripts, Indianapolis; Indiana State Library.
14 "Millions Proposed for Flood Control," *Lafayette Courier Journal*, April 26, 1939. https://www.newspapers.com/image/1044963665/?match=1&terms=millions%20proposed.

Chapter 5—The Indiana State Library

15 Bert G. Moore, ed. *The Whetstone*, Kiwanis Club of Marion, Indiana, May 31, 1939. Ralph Roessler papers, Rare Books and Manuscripts, Indianapolis; Indiana State Library.
16 Ralph Roessler (1939–1968). Ralph Roessler papers, Rare Books and Manuscripts, Indianapolis; Indiana State Library.
17 Ralph Roessler to Forest Harness, June 3, 1939. Ralph Roessler papers, Rare Books and Manuscripts, Indianapolis; Indiana State Library.
18 Ralph Roessler (1939–1968). Ralph Roessler papers, Rare Books and Manuscripts, Indianapolis; Indiana State Library.
19 Ralph Roessler (1939–1968). Ralph Roessler papers, Rare Books and Manuscripts, Indianapolis; Indiana State Library.
20 "A Bill to Authorize a Preliminary Examination and Survey of the Mississinewa River and Its Tributaries in the State of Indiana, from Matters Park to Conners Mill in Grant County, for Flood Control, for Run-Off and Water-Flow Retardation, and for Soil-Erosion Prevention," H.R. 6713, 76th Congress, 1st Session, congressional session (1939).
21 Bert G. Moore, ed. *The Whetstone*, Kiwanis Club of Marion, Indiana, June 7, 1939. Ralph Roessler papers, Rare Books and Manuscripts, Indianapolis; Indiana State Library.

Chapter 7—Labels

22 "Communist Organizer Kidnaped in Wabash but Later Released," *Journal and Courier*, Lafayette, Indiana, January 24, 1933.
23 "Warn Communists to Avoid Wabash," *Muncie Evening Press*, January 25, 1933. https://www.newspapers.com/image/249182129/?match=1&terms=communistic.
24 "Farmer Off to Russia," *Indianapolis Star*, April 11, 1934. https://www.newspapers.com/image/105287566/?match=1&terms=milo%20long.
25 "Milo David Long," *Find a Grave*, https://www.findagrave.com/memorial/45962133/milo-david-long.

Chapter 8—Big Shots

26 "A Bill to Authorize a Preliminary Examination and Survey of the Mississinewa River and Its Tributaries in the State of Indiana, from Matters Park to Conners Mill in Grant County, for Flood Control, for Run-Off and Water-Flow Retardation, and for Soil-Erosion Prevention," H.R. 6713, 76th Congress, 1st Session (1939).

27 "Thousands Flee Flood Waters," *The Muncie Morning Star*, May 19, 1943. https://www.newspapers.com/image/251973725/?terms=the%20worst%20flood%20in%2030%20years.

28 Ralph Roessler (1939–1968). Ralph Roessler papers, Rare Books and Manuscripts, Indianapolis; Indiana State Library.

29 Ralph Roessler (1939–1968). Ralph Roessler papers, Rare Books and Manuscripts, Indianapolis; Indiana State Library.

30 Governor Henry Schricker to Ralph Roessler, November 3, 1944. Ralph Roessler papers, Rare Books and Manuscripts, Indianapolis; Indiana State Library.

31 Ralph Roessler (1939–1968). Ralph Roessler papers, Rare Books and Manuscripts, Indianapolis; Indiana State Library.

32 "Benefits of Flood Control," *Wabash Plain Dealer*, October 19, 1961. Wabash County Museum archive.

Chapter 9—Hoosiers

33 "Jackson Evens Count," *Kokomo Tribune*, January 7, 1933. https://www.newspapers.com/image/41574552/?match=1&terms=somerset.

Chapter 15—The Fix

34 Cordie Beck Johnson, July 30, 1957.

35 "Wabash Flood Bill Approved," *Indianapolis News*, July 24, 1956. https://www.newspapers.com/image/311498764/?match=1&terms=wabash%20flood%20bill.

36 "Flood Control Act of 1946," H.R. 6597, 79th Congress, 2nd Session, July 24, 1946.

37 Use of Tributaries May Cut Flood Control Cost," *Indianapolis News*, October 23, 1946. https://www.newspapers.com/image/314196692/?match=1&terms=Use%20of%20tributaries.

38 Ralph Roessler (1939–1968). Ralph Roessler papers, Rare Books and Manuscripts, Indianapolis; Indiana State Library.

39 "Urge Reservoirs to Hold Wabash," *Lafayette Journal and Courier*, March 28, 1950. https://www.newspapers.com/image/1045488430/?match=1&terms=%20Reservoirs.

40 "Urge Reservoirs to Hold Wabash," *Lafayette Journal and Courier*, March 28, 1950. https://www.newspapers.com/image/1045488430/?match=1&terms=%20Reservoirs.

41 "Benefits of Flood Control," *Wabash Plain Dealer*, October 19, 1961. Wabash County Museum archive.

Chapter 16—Necessities

42 "Funeral at Marion for Paul Stevens," *Muncie Star*, August 27, 1948. https://www.newspapers.com/image/252142483/?match=1&terms=%20Paul%20Stevens.

43 William H. Webb to Congressman John V. Beamer, May 16, 1950. Congressman John V. Beamer collection, Rare Books and Manuscripts, Indianapolis; Indiana State Library.

Chapter 17—Hard Rain

44 Robert Kellum to Congressman John V. Beamer, February 19, 1952. Congressman John V. Beamer collection, Rare Books and Manuscripts, Indianapolis; Indiana State Library.

45 Congressman John V. Beamer to Robert Kellum, February 25, 1952. Congressman John V. Beamer collection, Rare Books and Manuscripts, Indianapolis; Indiana State Library.

46 Robert Kellum to Congressman John V. Beamer, November 10, 1952. Congressman John V. Beamer collection, Rare Books and Manuscripts, Indianapolis; Indiana State Library.

47 "Act Now on Flood Crisis, Truman to Urge Congress," *The Palladium-Item and Sun-Telegram*, Richmond, Indiana. April 17, 1952. https://www.newspapers.com/image/247932957/?match=1&terms=aerial%20survey%20.

48 Johnny Burnes to Congressman John V. Beamer, December 14, 1953. Congressman John V. Beamer collection, Rare Books and Manuscripts, Indianapolis; Indiana State Library.

49 "Urge Reservoirs to Hold Wabash," *Lafayette Journal and Courier*, March 28, 1950. https://www.newspapers.com/image/1045488430/?match=1&terms=%20Reservoirs.

50 Indiana Flood Control and Water Resources Commission, Memorandum to: U.S. House Civil Functions Subcommittee, Honorable Glenn R. David, Chairman, February 1954. Congressman John V. Beamer collection, Rare Books and Manuscripts, Indianapolis; Indiana State Library.

51 E. C. Itschner, Brigadier General, USA, Assistant Chief of Engineers for Civil Works to Congressman John V. Beamer, July 6, 1954. Congressman John V. Beamer collection, Rare Books and Manuscripts, Indianapolis; Indiana State Library.

52 Ryan Albrecht, Assistant Division Counsel, Department of the Army, U.S. Army Corps of Engineers, Great Lakes and Ohio River Division to author, May 3, 2023.

53 Ralph Roessler, "Last Living Charter Member, Marion Kiwanis Club, Presents a Documentary and Autobiographical Record of a Kiwanis Dream and a Seventy Million Dollar Reality, 1939 to 1968." Ralph Roessler papers, Rare Books and Manuscripts, Indianapolis; Indiana State Library.

54 E. C. Itschner to Ralph Roessler, July 6, 1954. Ralph Roessler papers, Rare Books and Manuscripts, Indianapolis; Indiana State Library.

Chapter 18—Gonna Fall

55 "Wabash Flood Plan Outlined," *South Bend Tribune*, July 30, 1954. https://www.newspapers.com/image/515213214/?match=1&terms=Flood%20plan%20.

56 Paul Janes, "Army Engineers May Decide by October on Huge Wabash River Flood Control Project," *Indianapolis Star*, July 31, 1954. https://www.newspapers.com/image/105575430/?match=1&terms=Flood%20plan%20.

57 Congressman John V. Beamer to Robert Kellum, July 12, 1954. Congressman John V. Beamer collection, Rare Books and Manuscripts, Indianapolis; Indiana State Library.

58 Paul Janes, "Army Engineers May Decide by October on Huge Wabash River Flood Control Project," *Indianapolis Star*, July 31, 1954. https://www.newspapers.com/image/105575430/?match=1&terms=Flood%20plan%20.

59 W. D. Milne, Colonel, Corps of Engineers, District Engineer, to Congressman John V. Beamer. August 12, 1954. Congressman John V. Beamer collection, Rare Books and Manuscripts, Indianapolis; Indiana State Library.

60 W. D. Milne, Colonel, Corps of Engineers, District Engineer, to Congressman John V. Beamer. August 27, 1954. Congressman John V. Beamer collection, Rare Books and Manuscripts, Indianapolis; Indiana State Library.

61 Ralph Roessler to Congressman John V. Beamer, December 11, 1954. Congressman John V. Beamer collection, Rare Books and Manuscripts, Indianapolis; Indiana State Library.

62 Robert Kellum, Executive Secretary, Indiana Flood and Water Resource Commission to *Wabash Plain Dealer* publisher Joe Nixon, January 10, 1955. Wabash County Museum archives.

63 Robert Kellum, Executive Secretary, Indiana Flood and Water Resource Commission to Congressman John V. Beamer, December 8, 1955. Congressman John V. Beamer collection, Rare Books and Manuscripts, Indianapolis; Indiana State Library.

Chapter 20—You Could Say

64 E. C. Itschner to Ralph Roessler, July 6, 1954. Ralph Roessler papers, Rare Books and Manuscripts, Indianapolis; Indiana State Library.

65 E. C. Itschner to Ralph Roessler, July 6, 1954. Ralph Roessler papers, Rare Books and Manuscripts, Indianapolis; Indiana State Library.

66 Colonel W. D. Milne, Army Corps of Engineers, District Engineer, to Congressman John V. Beamer, August 27, 1954. Congressman John V. Beamer collection, Rare Books and Manuscripts, Indianapolis; Indiana State Library.

67 Colonel W. D. Milne, Army Corps of Engineers, District Engineer, to Congressman John V. Beamer, January 21, 1955. Congressman John V. Beamer collection, Rare Books and Manuscripts, Indianapolis; Indiana State Library.

68 Robert Kellum, Executive Secretary, Indiana Flood and Water Resource Commission to *Wabash Plain Dealer* publisher Joe Nixon, January 10, 1955. Wabash

County Museum archives.

69 P. E. Karlan, April 25, 1955. U.S. Army Corps of Engineers. Bloomington, Indiana; Archives, Herman B. Wells Library, Indiana University.

70 Colonel W. D. Milne, Army Corps of Engineers, District Engineer, to Congressman John V. Beamer, May 25, 1955. Congressman John V. Beamer collection, Rare Books and Manuscripts, Indianapolis; Indiana State Library.

71 "Army Proposes to Relocate Indiana Town of Somerset," *Muncie Evening Press*, June 1, 1955. https://www.newspapers.com/image/249676011/?match=1&terms=Army%20Proposes; and "New Dam May Force Out State Town of Somerset," *Indianapolis News*, June 1, 1955. https://www.newspapers.com/image/311321126/?match=1&terms=New%20Dam.

72 Colonel W. D. Milne, Army Corps of Engineers, District Engineer, to Congressman John V. Beamer, June 9, 1955. Congressman John V. Beamer collection, Rare Books and Manuscripts, Indianapolis; Indiana State Library.

73 Colonel J. L. Person, Corps of Engineers, Division Engineer, to Congressman John V. Beamer, August 30, 1955. Congressman John V. Beamer collection, Rare Books and Manuscripts, Indianapolis; Indiana State Library.

74 Colonel J. L. Person, Corps of Engineers, Division Engineer, to Congressman John V. Beamer, August 30, 1955. Congressman John V. Beamer collection, Rare Books and Manuscripts, Indianapolis; Indiana State Library.

75 Ben Cole, "Army to Recommend 3 Hoosier Reservoirs," *Indianapolis Star*, September 7, 1955.

76 Colonel J. L. Person, Corps of Engineers, Division Engineer, to Congressman John V. Beamer, "Notice of Interim Report on Wabash River and Tributaries, at and Above the Mouth of White River, Indiana," Office of the Division Engineer, Ohio River Division, Corps of Engineers U.S. Army, Cincinnati, Ohio, September 12, 1955. Congressman John V. Beamer collection, Rare Books and Manuscripts, Indianapolis; Indiana State Library.

77 Congressman John V. Beamer to Robert Dawes, September 30, 1954. Congressman John V. Beamer collection, Rare Books and Manuscripts, Indianapolis; Indiana State Library.

78 Colonel J. L. Person, Corps of Engineers, Division Engineer, to Congressman John V. Beamer, "Notice of Interim Report on Wabash River and Tributaries, at and Above the Mouth of White River, Indiana," Office of the Division Engineer, Ohio River Division, Corps of Engineers U.S. Army, Cincinnati, Ohio, September 12, 1955. Congressman John V. Beamer collection, Rare Books and Manuscripts, Indianapolis; Indiana State Library.

79 "Board of Engineers for Rivers and Harbors to Consider Report on November 28, 1955," Corps of Engineers, U.S. Army, November 1955. Congressman John V. Beamer collection, Rare Books and Manuscripts, Indianapolis; Indiana State Library.

80 Sam Hubley, Manager Wabash Chamber of Commerce, to Board of Engineers for Rivers and Harbors, Corps of Engineers, U.S. Army, November 25, 1955. Congressman John V. Beamer collection, Rare Books and Manuscripts,

Indianapolis; Indiana State Library.

81 Colonel H. S. Miller, Corps of Engineers, to Sam Hubley, December 1, 1955. Congressman John V. Beamer collection, Rare Books and Manuscripts, Indianapolis; Indiana State Library.

82 Ralph Roessler, "Report to Indiana Flood Control and Water Resources Commission," March 26, 1954. Ralph Roessler papers, Rare Books and Manuscripts, Indianapolis; Indiana State Library.

83 E. C. Itschner, Brigadier General, USA, Assistant Chief of Engineers for Civil Works to Congressman John V. Beamer, July 6, 1954. Congressman John V. Beamer collection, Rare Books and Manuscripts, Indianapolis; Indiana State Library.

Chapter 22—Seventy-Five Feet Above the Stream Bed

84 Rolland Bozarth to Congressman John V. Beamer, February 19, 1955. Congressman John V. Beamer collection, Rare Books and Manuscripts, Indianapolis; Indiana State Library.

85 Rolland Bozarth to Congressman John V. Beamer, March 24, 1955. Congressman John V. Beamer collection, Rare Books and Manuscripts, Indianapolis; Indiana State Library.

86 Colonel W. D. Milne, Army Corps of Engineers, District Engineer, to Congressman John V. Beamer, April 11, 1955. Congressman John V. Beamer collection, Rare Books and Manuscripts, Indianapolis; Indiana State Library.

87 Gene Smith to Congressman John V. Beamer, May 10, 1955. Congressman John V. Beamer collection, Rare Books and Manuscripts, Indianapolis; Indiana State Library.

88 Colonel W. D. Milne, Army Corps of Engineers, District Engineer, to Congressman John V. Beamer, May 25, 1955. Congressman John V. Beamer collection, Rare Books and Manuscripts, Indianapolis; Indiana State Library.

89 Congressman John V. Beamer to Colonel W. D. Milne, June 1, 1955. Congressman John V. Beamer collection, Rare Books and Manuscripts, Indianapolis; Indiana State Library.

90 "Army Proposes to Relocate Indiana Town of Somerset," *Muncie Evening Press*, June 1, 1955. https://www.newspapers.com/image/249676011/?match=1&terms=Army%20Proposes; and "New Dam May Force Out State Town of Somerset," *Indianapolis News*, June 1, 1955. https://www.newspapers.com/image/311321126/?match=1&terms=New%20Dam.

91 "Somerset May Be Moved for Flood Control," *Kokomo Tribune*, June 2, 1955. https://www.newspapers.com/image/1069073239/?match=1&terms=Somerset; and "Flood Control Project Would Move Somerset," *Bedford Daily Times-Mail*. https://www.newspapers.com/image/547228604/?match=1&terms=flood.

Chapter 23—Interested Parties

92 Florence Roby, *Spotlight on Somerset High School and the Surrounding Community*, January 1971.

93 Inez Highly to Congressman John V. Beamer, undated, approx. September 1955. Congressman John V. Beamer collection, Rare Books and Manuscripts, Indianapolis; Indiana State Library.

94 Congressman John Beamer to Inez Highly, September 7, 1955. Congressman John V. Beamer collection, Rare Books and Manuscripts, Indianapolis; Indiana State Library.

95 D. R. Dragstem to Congressman John V. Beamer, September 24, 1955. Congressman John V. Beamer collection, Rare Books and Manuscripts, Indianapolis; Indiana State Library.

96 Congressman John V. Beamer to D. R. Dragstrem, October 3, 1955. Congressman John V. Beamer collection, Rare Books and Manuscripts, Indianapolis; Indiana State Library.

97 Congressman John V. Beamer to Ralph Roessler, June 2, 1955. Congressman John V. Beamer collection, Rare Books and Manuscripts, Indianapolis; Indiana State Library.

98 Ruth Rudicel to Congressman John V. Beamer, June 2, 1955. Congressman John V. Beamer collection, Rare Books and Manuscripts, Indianapolis; Indiana State Library.

99 Congressman John V. Beamer to Ruth Rudicel, June 6, 1955. Congressman John V. Beamer collection, Rare Books and Manuscripts, Indianapolis; Indiana State Library.

100 Glenn Henderson to Congressman John V. Beamer, June 5, 1955. Congressman John V. Beamer collection, Rare Books and Manuscripts, Indianapolis; Indiana State Library.

101 Congressman John V. Beamer to Glenn Henderson, June 7, 1955. Congressman John V. Beamer collection, Rare Books and Manuscripts, Indianapolis; Indiana State Library.

102 Willard Oppy to Congressman John V. Beamer, June 28, 1955. Congressman John V. Beamer collection, Rare Books and Manuscripts, Indianapolis; Indiana State Library.

103 Fernie Trigalet to Congressman John V. Beamer, July 4, 1955. Congressman John V. Beamer collection, Rare Books and Manuscripts, Indianapolis; Indiana State Library.

104 Congressman John V. Beamer to Ira Roby, July 13, 1955. Congressman John V. Beamer collection, Rare Books and Manuscripts, Indianapolis; Indiana State Library.

105 Congressman John V. Beamer to Fernie Trigalet, July 21, 1955. Congressman John V. Beamer collection, Rare Books and Manuscripts, Indianapolis; Indiana State Library.

106 Lawrence Scheffer to Congressman John V. Beamer, July 5, 1955. Congressman John V. Beamer collection, Rare Books and Manuscripts, Indianapolis; Indiana State Library.

107 Congressman John V. Beamer to Lawrence Scheffer, July 11, 1955. Congressman John V. Beamer collection, Rare Books and Manuscripts, Indianapolis;

Indiana State Library.
108 Ralph Roessler, "Report to Indiana Flood Control and Water Resources Commission," March 26, 1954. Ralph Roessler papers, Rare Books and Manuscripts, Indianapolis; Indiana State Library.
109 "Supporters Say Flood Control Program Would Save Millions," *Marion Leader-Tribune*, June 4, 1955. https://www.newspapers.com/image/1069076676/?match=1&terms=reservoir.
110 "Moving of Somerset Seen in Flood Plan," *Wabash Plan Dealer*, June 3, 1955. Congressman John V. Beamer collection, Rare Books and Manuscripts, Indianapolis; Indiana State Library.
111 Ralph Roessler to Congressman John V. Beamer, June 5, 1955. Congressman John V. Beamer collection, Rare Books and Manuscripts, Indianapolis; Indiana State Library.
112 "Engineers Propose Reservoir System to Control Floods," *Peru Republican*, June 10, 1955. Wabash County Museum archive.
113 "Local Flood Control Plan," *Wabash Plain Dealer*, June 11, 1955. Wabash County Museum archive.

Chapter 24–The Small Dam Plan

114 "Use of Tributaries May Cut Flood Control Cost," *Indianapolis News*, October 23, 1946. https://www.newspapers.com/image/314196692/?match=1&terms=David%20Harker.
115 Wabash Circuit Court judge Byron Kennedy to Congressman John V. Beamer, June 3, 1955. Congressman John V. Beamer collection, Rare Books and Manuscripts, Indianapolis; Indiana State Library.
116 Congressman John V. Beamer to Byron Kennedy, June 4, 1955. Congressman John V. Beamer collection, Rare Books and Manuscripts, Indianapolis; Indiana State Library.
117 "Hearing on S.B. 174," Flood Control and Water Resources Commission, State House, Indianapolis, February 7, 1945. Ralph Roessler papers, Rare Books and Manuscripts, Indianapolis; Indiana State Library.
118 "Hearing on S.B. 174," Flood Control and Water Resources Commission, State House, Indianapolis, February 7, 1945. Ralph Roessler papers, Rare Books and Manuscripts, Indianapolis; Indiana State Library.
119 Congressman John V. Beamer to Donald Williams, Soil Conservation Service, Department of Agriculture, June 11, 1955. Congressman John V. Beamer collection, Rare Books and Manuscripts, Indianapolis; Indiana State Library.
120 Donald Williams, Soil Conservation Service, Department of Agriculture, to Congressman John V. Beamer, June 21, 1955. Congressman John V. Beamer collection, Rare Books and Manuscripts, Indianapolis; Indiana State Library.
121 A. G. Allen to Congressman John V. Beamer, August 31, 1955. Congressman John V. Beamer collection, Rare Books and Manuscripts, Indianapolis; Indiana State Library.

122 Colonel W. D. Milne, Army Corps of Engineers, District Engineer, to Congressman John V. Beamer, October 3, 1955. Congressman John V. Beamer collection, Rare Books and Manuscripts, Indianapolis; Indiana State Library.
123 Congressman John V. Beamer to Colonel W. D. Milne, August 29, 1955. Congressman John V. Beamer collection, Rare Books and Manuscripts, Indianapolis; Indiana State Library.
124 C. R. Leiter, "You Will Enjoy a Trip Along the Slocum Trail," *Kokomo Tribune*, October 18, 1955. https://www.newspapers.com/image/2674602/?match=1&terms=Leiter.
125 Mrs. Charles Shelley to Congressman John V. Beamer, November 7, 1955. Congressman John V. Beamer collection, Rare Books and Manuscripts, Indianapolis; Indiana State Library.
126 Congressman John V. Beamer to Robert Kellum, November 28, 1955. Congressman John V. Beamer collection, Rare Books and Manuscripts, Indianapolis; Indiana State Library.

Chapter 25–Representative

127 Cliff Funderburg to Congressman John V. Beamer, April 30, 1956. Congressman John V. Beamer collection, Rare Books and Manuscripts, Indianapolis; Indiana State Library.
128 Ivan Funderburg to Congressman John V. Beamer, November 28, 1955. Congressman John V. Beamer collection, Rare Books and Manuscripts, Indianapolis; Indiana State Library.
129 Charlotte Funderburg to Congressman John V. Beamer, November 28, 1955. Congressman John V. Beamer collection, Rare Books and Manuscripts, Indianapolis; Indiana State Library.
130 Congressman John V. Beamer to Ivan and Charlotte Funderburg, December 5, 1955. Congressman John V. Beamer collection, Rare Books and Manuscripts, Indianapolis; Indiana State Library.
131 Colonel W. D. Milne, Army Corps of Engineers, District Engineer, to Sam Hubley, Manager Wabash Chamber of Commerce, December 1, 1955. Congressman John V. Beamer collection, Rare Books and Manuscripts, Indianapolis; Indiana State Library.
132 Cliff Funderburg to Congressman John V. Beamer, February 14, 1956. Congressman John V. Beamer collection, Rare Books and Manuscripts, Indianapolis; Indiana State Library.
133 Congressman John V. Beamer to Cliff Funderburg, February 27, 1956. Congressman John V. Beamer collection, Rare Books and Manuscripts, Indianapolis; Indiana State Library.
134 Congressman John V. Beamer to Howard Houghton, publisher, *Herald-Press*, Huntington, Indiana, February 28, 1956. Congressman John V. Beamer collection, Rare Books and Manuscripts, Indianapolis; Indiana State Library.
135 Cliff Funderburg to Congressman John V. Beamer, February 29, 1956. Congressman John V. Beamer collection, Rare Books and Manuscripts, Indianapolis; Indiana State Library.

136 Congressman John V. Beamer to Cliff Funderburg, March 7, 1956. Congressman John V. Beamer collection, Rare Books and Manuscripts, Indianapolis; Indiana State Library.

Chapter 26–Minnick

137 "Empty Revolver Kills Youth," *Elwood Call-Leader*, March 13, 1956. https://www.newspapers.com/image/87714186/?match=1&terms=Empty.

Chapter 27–Opposition

138 Carlos Life, Member of the Board, Indiana Flood Control and Water Resources Commission, "Hearings Before the Subcommittee of the Committee on Appropriations," House of Representatives, 84th Congress, 2nd Session, March 20, 1956. Congressman John V. Beamer collection, Rare Books and Manuscripts, Indianapolis; Indiana State Library.

139 Congressman John V. Beamer, "Hearings Before the Subcommittee of the Committee on Appropriations," House of Representatives, 84th Congress, 2nd Session, March 20, 1956. Congressman John V. Beamer collection, Rare Books and Manuscripts, Indianapolis; Indiana State Library.

140 Robert Kellum, Executive Secretary, Indiana Flood Control and Water Resources Commission, "Hearings Before the Subcommittee of the Committee on Appropriations," House of Representatives, 84th Congress, 2nd Session, March 20, 1956. Congressman John V. Beamer collection, Rare Books and Manuscripts, Indianapolis; Indiana State Library.

141 "7 Millions Asked in Flood Control," *Indianapolis Star*, March 21, 1956. https://www.newspapers.com/image/105551862/?match=1&terms=Upper%20Wabash%20Valley.

142 Ivan Funderburg, "Letters to the Editor," *Huntington Herald-Press*, March 22, 1956. Congressman John V. Beamer collection, Rare Books and Manuscripts, Indianapolis; Indiana State Library.

143 Lucius Sheets, "Letters to the Editor," *Huntington Herald-Press*, March 22, 1956. Congressman John V. Beamer collection, Rare Books and Manuscripts, Indianapolis; Indiana State Library.

144 Lucius Sheets, "Letters to the Editor," *Huntington Herald-Press*, March 25, 1956. Congressman John V. Beamer collection, Rare Books and Manuscripts, Indianapolis; Indiana State Library.

145 Cliff Funderburg to Congressman John V. Beamer, March 25, 1956. Congressman John V. Beamer collection, Rare Books and Manuscripts, Indianapolis; Indiana State Library.

146 Mark Fisher to Congressman John V. Beamer, March 26, 1956. Congressman John V. Beamer collection, Rare Books and Manuscripts, Indianapolis; Indiana State Library.

147 Howard Houghton, publisher, *Herald-Press*, Huntington, Indiana, to Congressman John V. Beamer, March 28, 1956. Congressman John V. Beamer collection, Rare Books and Manuscripts, Indianapolis; Indiana State Library.

148 Congressman John V. Beamer to Carlos Life, March 28, 1956. Congressman John V. Beamer collection, Rare Books and Manuscripts, Indianapolis; Indiana State Library.

149 Carlos Life to Congressman John V. Beamer, April 2, 1956. Congressman John V. Beamer collection, Rare Books and Manuscripts, Indianapolis; Indiana State Library.

150 Cliff Funderburg, "Letters to the Editor," *Huntington Herald-Press*, April 4, 1956. Congressman John V. Beamer collection, Rare Books and Manuscripts, Indianapolis; Indiana State Library.

151 Congressman John V. Beamer to Mark Fisher, April 10, 1956. Congressman John V. Beamer collection, Rare Books and Manuscripts, Indianapolis; Indiana State Library.

152 Frank Dice to Congressman John V. Beamer, April 19, 1956. Congressman John V. Beamer collection, Rare Books and Manuscripts, Indianapolis; Indiana State Library.

153 Carlos Life to Congressman John V. Beamer, April 19, 1956. Congressman John V. Beamer collection, Rare Books and Manuscripts, Indianapolis; Indiana State Library.

Chapter 28–A '57 Chevy

154 Heather McGhee, *The Sum of Us: What Racism Costs Everyone and How We Can Prosper Together* (New York: One World, 2021), 23-28.

Chapter 29–Conscientious Objection

155 "Gov. Craig Endorses Plan for Control," *Marion Leader-Tribune*, January 8, 1956. https: www.newspapers.com/image/1068458390/?match=1&terms=Upper%20Wabash%20Valley.

156 Edward Keefer to Congressman John V. Beamer, January 12, 1956. Congressman John V. Beamer collection, Rare Books and Manuscripts, Indianapolis; Indiana State Library.

157 Congressman John V. Beamer to Edward Keefer, January 16, 1956. Congressman John V. Beamer collection, Rare Books and Manuscripts, Indianapolis; Indiana State Library.

158 Congressman John V. Beamer to W. R. Jones, March 12, 1956. Congressman John V. Beamer collection, Rare Books and Manuscripts, Indianapolis; Indiana State Library.

159 Congressman John V. Beamer to Howard Houghton, April 9, 1956. Congressman John V. Beamer collection, Rare Books and Manuscripts, Indianapolis; Indiana State Library.

160 Congressman John V. Beamer to Carlos Life, April 9, 1956. Congressman John V. Beamer collection, Rare Books and Manuscripts, Indianapolis; Indiana State Library.
161 Colonel W. D. Milne, Army Corps of Engineers, District Engineer, to Congressman John V. Beamer, October 3, 1955. Congressman John V. Beamer collection, Rare Books and Manuscripts, Indianapolis; Indiana State Library.
162 Cliff Funderburg to Congressman John V. Beamer, April 22, 1956. Congressman John V. Beamer collection, Rare Books and Manuscripts, Indianapolis; Indiana State Library.
163 Cliff Funderburg to Congressman John V. Beamer, April 22, 1956. Congressman John V. Beamer collection, Rare Books and Manuscripts, Indianapolis; Indiana State Library.
164 "Oliver Goldsmith," *Wikipedia Foundation*, last modified February 3, 2025. https://en.wikipedia.org/wiki/Oliver_Goldsmith.
165 Cliff Funderburg to Congressman John V. Beamer, April 30, 1956. Congressman John V. Beamer collection, Rare Books and Manuscripts, Indianapolis; Indiana State Library.
166 Cliff Funderburg to Congressman John V. Beamer, March 14, 1958. Congressman John V. Beamer collection, Rare Books and Manuscripts, Indianapolis; Indiana State Library.
167 "Californian Admits Killing Ex-Legislator," *Indianapolis Star*, August 25, 1965. https://www.newspapers.com/image/105493850/?match=1&terms=Californian%20 Admits.

Chapter 30—Big Wheels

168 William Shakespeare, *Much Ado About Nothing* (London; New York: Penguin, 2005), Act I, Scene 3.
169 Congressman John V. Beamer to Carlos Life, April 21, 1956. Congressman John V. Beamer collection, Rare Books and Manuscripts, Indianapolis; Indiana State Library.
170 Congressman John V. Beamer to Robert Kellum, April 21, 1956. Congressman John V. Beamer collection, Rare Books and Manuscripts, Indianapolis; Indiana State Library.
171 C. A. Kessler to Congressman John V. Beamer, April 24, 1956. Congressman John V. Beamer collection, Rare Books and Manuscripts, Indianapolis; Indiana State Library.
172 Congressman John V. Beamer to C. A. Kessler, April 30, 1956. Congressman John V. Beamer collection, Rare Books and Manuscripts, Indianapolis; Indiana State Library.
173 Congressman John V. Beamer to Gene Smith, May 10, 1956. Congressman John V. Beamer collection, Rare Books and Manuscripts, Indianapolis; Indiana State Library.

174 Gene Smith to Congressman John V. Beamer, April 30, 1956. Congressman John V. Beamer collection, Rare Books and Manuscripts, Indianapolis; Indiana State Library.
175 Ralph Roessler to Congressman John V. Beamer, January 28, 1956. Congressman John V. Beamer collection, Rare Books and Manuscripts, Indianapolis; Indiana State Library.
176 Carlos Life to Congressman John V. Beamer, May 22, 1956. Congressman John V. Beamer collection, Rare Books and Manuscripts, Indianapolis; Indiana State Library.
177 Congressman John V. Beamer to Carlos Life, May 22, 1956. Congressman John V. Beamer collection, Rare Books and Manuscripts, Indianapolis; Indiana State Library.
178 Congressman John V. Beamer to Robert Kellum with copies to Carlos Life and Ralph Roessler, June 23, 1956. Congressman John V. Beamer collection, Rare Books and Manuscripts, Indianapolis; Indiana State Library.
179 Ralph Roessler to Congressman John V. Beamer, May 31, 1956. Congressman John V. Beamer collection, Rare Books and Manuscripts, Indianapolis; Indiana State Library.
180 Congressman John V. Beamer to Robert Kellum, Carlos Life, and Ralph Roessler, July 24, 1956. Congressman John V. Beamer collection, Rare Books and Manuscripts, Indianapolis; Indiana State Library.
181 "House Completes Action of State Flood Control Bill," *Kokomo Tribune*, July 28, 1956. https://www.newspapers.comimage/2563177/?match=1&terms=Flood%20control%20project.
182 "Wabash Flood Plan Is Voted," *South Bend Tribune*, July 29, 1956. https://www.newspapers.com/image/514877078/?match=1&terms=Flood%20control%20project.
183 "Wabash Project Wins Ike Pledge for '57," *Indianapolis Star*, August 11, 1956. https://www.newspapers.com/image/105582258/?match=1&terms=Wabash%20project.

Chapter 31—Small Dams

184 Wabash Circuit Court judge Byron Kennedy to Congressman John V. Beamer, June 3, 1955. Congressman John V. Beamer collection, Rare Books and Manuscripts, Indianapolis; Indiana State Library.
185 Congressman John V. Beamer to Donald A. Williams of the Department of Agriculture's Soil Conservation Service, June 11, 1955. Congressman John V. Beamer collection, Rare Books and Manuscripts, Indianapolis; Indiana State Library.
186 Donald A. Williams to Congressman John V. Beamer, June 21, 1955. Congressman John V. Beamer collection, Rare Books and Manuscripts, Indianapolis; Indiana State Library.
187 Congressman John V. Beamer to Fernie Trigalet, June 23, 1955. Congressman John V. Beamer collection, Rare Books and Manuscripts, Indianapolis; Indiana State Library.

188 Congressman John V. Beamer to Col. W. D. Milne, September 27, 1955. Congressman John V. Beamer collection, Rare Books and Manuscripts, Indianapolis; Indiana State Library.
189 Gladwin Young, deputy administrator of the Soil Conservation Service of the Department of Agriculture, to Congressman John V. Beamer, June 6, 1956. Congressman John V. Beamer collection, Rare Books and Manuscripts, Indianapolis; Indiana State Library.
190 "Watershed Protection and Flood Prevention Act of 1954," Pub. L. 83-566, 83rd Congress (1954).
191 "Flood Control Act of 1936," Pub. L. 74-738, 74th Congress (1936).
192 Ralph Roessler, "Statement by Ralph Roessler, Marion, Vice-Chairman Commission. Hearing Flood Control Commission," Indiana Flood Control and Water Resources Commission report to U.S. Army Corps of Engineers, Peru, Indiana, January 23, 1945. Ralph Roessler papers, Rare Books and Manuscripts, Indianapolis; Indiana State Library.
193 "Use of Tributaries May Cut Flood Control Cost," *Indianapolis News*, October 23, 1946. https://www.newspapers.com/image/314196692/?match=1&terms=Use%20of%20tributaries.
194 David Harker, Chief Engineer, Flood Control and Water Resources Commission, "Flood Control in Indiana," *Proceedings of the Indiana Academy of Sciences*, Corydon, Indiana, May 9 and 10, 1947, 142. https://archive.org/details/proceedingsofin571947indi/page/n3/mode/2up?view=theater&q=david+harker.
195 "David H. Harker Heads Drainage Association," *Indianapolis Star*, February 27, 1949. https://www.newspapers.com/image/1045416075/?match=1&terms=Harker.

Chapter 33—In Play

1.
196 Congressman J. Harry McGregor to Ivan Funderburg, November 2, 1956. Congressman John V. Beamer collection, Rare Books and Manuscripts, Indianapolis; Indiana State Library.
197 Ivan Funderburg to Congressman John V. Beamer, November 21, 1956. Congressman John V. Beamer collection, Rare Books and Manuscripts, Indianapolis; Indiana State Library.
198 Congressman John V. Beamer to Ivan Funderburg, December 4, 1956. Congressman John V. Beamer collection, Rare Books and Manuscripts, Indianapolis; Indiana State Library.
199 Ivan Funderburg to Congressman John V. Beamer, December 4, 1956. Congressman John V. Beamer collection, Rare Books and Manuscripts, Indianapolis; Indiana State Library.
200 Ralph Roessler (1939-1968). Ralph Roessler papers, Rare Books and Manuscripts, Indianapolis; Indiana State Library.

2.

201 "$647,115,000 Sought for Civil Works Program of Army Engineers in Fiscal Year 1958," *News Release, Department of Defense, Office of Public Information*, January 16, 1957. Congressman John V. Beamer collection, Rare Books and Manuscripts, Indianapolis; Indiana State Library.

202 Congressman John V. Beamer to Congressman Charles A. Buckley, January 18, 1957. Congressman John V. Beamer collection, Rare Books and Manuscripts, Indianapolis; Indiana State Library.

203 Ivan Funderburg to Congressman John V. Beamer, January 21, 1957. Congressman John V. Beamer collection, Rare Books and Manuscripts, Indianapolis; Indiana State Library.

204 Congressman John V. Beamer to Ivan Funderburg, January 24, 1957. Congressman John V. Beamer collection, Rare Books and Manuscripts, Indianapolis; Indiana State Library.

205 Hassil Schenck, Indiana Farm Bureau, president, to Congressman John Beamer, February 8, 1957. Congressman John V. Beamer collection, Rare Books and Manuscripts, Indianapolis; Indiana State Library.

206 Ivan Funderburg to Congressman John V. Beamer, February 4, 1957. Congressman John V. Beamer collection, Rare Books and Manuscripts, Indianapolis; Indiana State Library.

207 Carlos Life to Congressman John V. Beamer, February 9, 1957. Congressman John V. Beamer collection, Rare Books and Manuscripts, Indianapolis; Indiana State Library.

208 Nancy Brown, secretary to Congressman John V. Beamer, to Carlos Life, February 12, 1957. Congressman John V. Beamer collection, Rare Books and Manuscripts, Indianapolis; Indiana State Library.

209 Congressman John V. Beamer to Robert Kellum, February 25, 1957. Congressman John V. Beamer collection, Rare Books and Manuscripts, Indianapolis; Indiana State Library.

210 Congressman John V. Beamer to Congressman Clifford Davis, March 11, 1957. Congressman John V. Beamer collection, Rare Books and Manuscripts, Indianapolis; Indiana State Library.

211 Congressman Clifford Davis to Congressman John V. Beamer, March 15, 1957. Congressman John V. Beamer collection, Rare Books and Manuscripts, Indianapolis; Indiana State Library.

212 Congressman J. Harry McGregor to Congressman Clifford Davis, March 28, 1957. Congressman John V. Beamer collection, Rare Books and Manuscripts, Indianapolis; Indiana State Library.

213 John Nixon, *Peru Tribune* manager, to Congressman John V. Beamer, March 29, 1957. Congressman John V. Beamer collection, Rare Books and Manuscripts, Indianapolis; Indiana State Library.

3.

214 "Senate Passes Wabash Flood Aid," *Logansport Press*, March 29, 1957. https://www.newspapers.com/image/3881768/?match=1&terms=reservoir.

215 Congressman John V. Beamer to Mr. and Mrs. Sam Colby, April 1, 1957. Congressman John V. Beamer collection, Rare Books and Manuscripts, Indianapolis; Indiana State Library.

216 Congressman John V. Beamer to Congressman Clifford Davis, April 2, 1957. Congressman John V. Beamer collection, Rare Books and Manuscripts, Indianapolis; Indiana State Library.

217 Robert Kellum to Congressman Clifford Davis, April 9, 1957. Congressman John V. Beamer collection, Rare Books and Manuscripts, Indianapolis; Indiana State Library.

218 Congressman Clifford Davis to Robert Kellum, April 11, 1957. Congressman John V. Beamer collection, Rare Books and Manuscripts, Indianapolis; Indiana State Library.

219 Robert Kellum to Joe Nixon, *Wabash Plain Dealer* publisher, April 22, 1957. Congressman John V. Beamer collection, Rare Books and Manuscripts, Indianapolis; Indiana State Library.

220 "Congressman Beamer Suffers Heart Attack," *Kokomo Tribune*, April 22, 1957. https://www.newspapers.com/image/2704099/?match=1&terms=congressman.

221 Robert Williams, executive secretary to Congressman John V. Beamer, to O. E. Bearse, April 23, 1957. Congressman John V. Beamer collection, Rare Books and Manuscripts, Indianapolis; Indiana State Library.

222 Robert Williams to Ivan Funderburg, May 7, 1957. Congressman John V. Beamer collection, Rare Books and Manuscripts, Indianapolis; Indiana State Library.

223 Ivan Funderburg to Congressman John V. Beamer, May 8, 1957. Congressman John V. Beamer collection, Rare Books and Manuscripts, Indianapolis; Indiana State Library.

4.

224 "Clifford David (politician)," *Wikipedia Foundation*, last modified January 20, 2025. https://en.wikipedia.org/wiki/Clifford_Davis_(politician).

225 "Hearings Before the Committee on Public Works, House of Representatives, Eighty-Fifth Congress, First Session on S. 497, a Bill Authorizing the Construction, Repair, and Preservation of Certain Public Works on Rivers and Harbors for Navigation, Flood Control, and Other Purposes," May 14, 1957. Congressman John V. Beamer collection, Rare Books and Manuscripts, Indianapolis; Indiana State Library.

226 Jerry Durnbaugh, "The Clipboard," *Wabash Plain-Dealer*, April 13, 1957. Congressman John V. Beamer collection, Rare Books and Manuscripts, Indianapolis; Indiana State Library.

227 Elisabeth Buckmam Godard, "Bearded Blue Hill Editor Determined for Change, Why I Came to Maine," *The Bangor Daily News*, December 16, 1960. https://www.newspapers.com/image/664777233/?match=1&terms=durnbaugh.

5.

228 Ivan Funderburg to Robert Williams, June 19, 1957. Congressman John V. Beamer collection, Rare Books and Manuscripts, Indianapolis; Indiana State Library.

229 "Upper Wabash Flood Control Project OK'd," *The Pharos-Tribune*, Logansport, Indiana, July 19, 1957. https://www.newspapers.com/image/28125589/?match=1&terms=Upper.

230 Ivan Funderburg to Congressman John V. Beamer, July 28, 1957. Congressman John V. Beamer collection, Rare Books and Manuscripts, Indianapolis; Indiana State Library.

231 Congressman John V. Beamer to Ivan Funderburg, July 30, 1957. Congressman John V. Beamer collection, Rare Books and Manuscripts, Indianapolis; Indiana State Library.

232 Ralph Roessler, "Statement by Ralph Roessler, Marion, Vice-Chairman Commission. Hearing Flood Control Commission," Indiana Flood Control and Water Resources Commission report to U.S. Army Corps of Engineers, Peru, Indiana, January 23, 1945. Ralph Roessler papers, Rare Books and Manuscripts, Indianapolis; Indiana State Library.

Chapter 34—Floods

233 "'Stop Fooling' Truman Urges, Wants Long-Range Flood Control Program," *South Bend Tribune*, April 17, 1952. https://www.newspapers.com/image/515078598/?match=1&terms=Truman%20flood%20control%20program.

234 Jack Ellis to Congressman John V. Beamer, February 19, 1957. Congressman John V. Beamer collection, Rare Books and Manuscripts, Indianapolis; Indiana State Library.

235 Carl Schini to Congressman John V. Beamer, February 8, 1957. Congressman John V. Beamer collection, Rare Books and Manuscripts, Indianapolis; Indiana State Library.

236 Carl Schini to Congressman John V. Beamer, February 25, 1957. Congressman John V. Beamer collection, Rare Books and Manuscripts, Indianapolis; Indiana State Library.

237 "Could This Happen Again? Not with Adequate Flood Control," *Peru Tribune*, April 1, 1957. Congressman John V. Beamer collection, Rare Books and Manuscripts, Indianapolis; Indiana State Library.

238 "Rising River Chases Residents of Wabash," *Marion Chronicle Tribune*, April 5, 1957. https://www.newspapers.comimage/1069165996/?match=1&terms=Rising%20River%20Chases%20Residents%20of%20Wabash.

239 "Rains Bring Flood Threat," *Indianapolis Star*, June 14, 1958. https://www.newspapers.com/image/105715658/?match=1&terms=%27little%20trouble%20at%20Peru%22.

240 "Flood Perils Terre Haute, Disaster Area Declared; 2,000 Face Evacuation," *Indianapolis Star*, June 16, 1958. https://www.newspapers.com/image/105708450/?match=1&terms=flood%20.
241 Mrs. Russell Keith to Congressman John V. Beamer, June 18, 1958. Congressman John V. Beamer collection, Rare Books and Manuscripts, Indianapolis; Indiana State Library.
242 Joe Nixon to Congressman John V. Beamer, June 14, 1958. Congressman John V. Beamer collection, Rare Books and Manuscripts, Indianapolis; Indiana State Library.
243 David Hicks to Congressman John V. Beamer, July 14, 1958. Congressman John V. Beamer collection, Rare Books and Manuscripts, Indianapolis; Indiana State Library.
244 Florence Sanin to Congressman John V. Beamer, July 18, 1958. Congressman John V. Beamer collection, Rare Books and Manuscripts, Indianapolis; Indiana State Library.

Chapter 35–Displaced

245 Florence Roby, *Spotlight on Somerset High School and the Surrounding Community*, January 1971.
246 Ron Woodward, "Somerset," *Family Branches: Newsletter of the Wabash County Genealogical Society*, Volume 14, Number 7, March 2009.

Chapter 36–Gratitude

247 Ralph Roessler to Congressman J. Edward Roush, March 7, 1968. Ralph Roessler papers, Rare Books and Manuscripts, Indianapolis; Indiana State Library.
248 J. Edward Roush to Robert Kellum, July 26, 1958. J. Edward Roush Congressional Papers, Indiana University Archives, Herman B Wells Library, Bloomington, Indiana.
249 Kathleen McKenzie 1969, J.Edward Roush Interview, Indiana University Oral History and Research Center, Center for the Study of History and Memory at Indiana University, Bloomington, Indiana.
250 J. Edward Roush to Ivan Funderburg, et al. August 13, 1958. J. Edward Roush Congressional Papers, Indiana University Archives, Herman B Wells Library, Bloomington, Indiana.
251 Kathleen McKenzie 1969, Joe Mettler Interview, Indiana University Oral History and Research Center, Center for the Study of History and Memory at Indiana University.
252 Bob Tillet to Joe Mettler, August 26, 1958. J. Edward Roush Congressional Papers, Indiana University Archives, Herman B Wells Library, Bloomington, Indiana.
253 J. Edward Roush to Russell Keith, September 12, 1958. J. Edward Roush Congressional Papers, Indiana University Archives, Herman B Wells Library, Bloomington, Indiana.
254 J. Edward Roush to R. D. Hall, October 28, 1958. J. Edward Roush

Congressional Papers, Indiana University Archives, Herman B Wells Library, Bloomington, Indiana.
255 Congressman John V. Beamer to *Kokomo Tribune*, August 15, 1958. Congressman John V. Beamer collection, Rare Books and Manuscripts, Indianapolis; Indiana State Library.
256 Harold Handley, "Remarks of Governor Handley on Flood Control. Marion, Indiana. Tuesday, October 7," Marion, Indiana, October 7, 1958. Congressman John V. Beamer collection, Rare Books and Manuscripts, Indianapolis; Indiana State Library.
257 Edward Ziegner, "Beamer Has Fight on His Hands in Fifth Term Bid," *Indianapolis News*, October 7, 1958. https://www.newspapers.com/image/311515983/?match=1&terms=ziegner.
258 "Beamer-Roush Head Area Political Contests," *Tipton Daily Tribune*, November 1, 1958. https://www.newspapers.com image/14875263/?match=1&terms=beamer%20roush.

Chapter 38—Money

259 "Money Sought to Halt Floods," *Indianapolis Star*, February 13, 1959. https://www.newspapers.com/image/105698756/?terms=floods%20roush.
260 "Special to Editors," *In Washington with Senator Vance Hartke,* February 16, 1959. Wabash County Museum archives.
261 Congressman J. Edward Roush to Joe Nixon, February 17, 1959. Wabash County Museum archives.
262 Ralph Roessler to Congressman J. Edward Roush, March 7, 1968. Ralph Roessler papers, Rare Books and Manuscripts, Indianapolis; Indiana State Library.
263 Congressman J. Edward Roush to Herman Elett, February 19, 1959. J. Edward Roush Congressional Papers, Indiana University Archives, Herman B Wells Library, Bloomington, Indiana.
264 Carlos Life to J. Edward Roush, February 12, 1959. J. Edward Roush Congressional Papers, Indiana University Archives, Herman B Wells Library, Bloomington, Indiana.
265 John V. Beamer to Senator Homer Capehart, February 20, 1959. Congressman John V. Beamer collection, Rare Books and Manuscripts, Indianapolis; Indiana State Library.
266 John V. Beamer, speech (March 31, 1959): "Flood Control on Upper Wabash River & Tributaries, Remarks by John V. Beamer at League of Women Voters, Wabash, Indiana." Congressman John V. Beamer collection, Rare Books and Manuscripts, Indianapolis; Indiana State Library.
267 Senator Homer Capehart to Congressman J. Edward Roush, March 11, 1959. J. Edward Roush Congressional Papers, Indiana University Archives, Herman B Wells Library, Bloomington, Indiana.
268 "Progress Report—December 1961," Indiana Flood Control and Water Resources Commission to Governor Matthew Welsh. Ralph Roessler papers, Rare Books and Manuscripts, Indianapolis; Indiana State Library.

Chapter 40–Marion

269 Charles Courtney to Congressman J. Edward Roush, February 25, 1959. J. Edward Roush Congressional Papers, Indiana University Archives, Herman B Wells Library, Bloomington, Indiana.

270 Wayne Townsend, Indiana state legislator, to Congressman J. Edward Roush, March 2, 1959. J. Edward Roush Congressional Papers, Indiana University Archives, Herman B Wells Library, Bloomington, Indiana.

271 "Engineers Ignore Recommendation on Upstream Flood Prevention," *Marion Chronicle Tribune*, March 27, 1959. https://www.newspapers.com/image/1068794667/?terms=Gas%20City%20mayor.

272 Congressman J. Edward Roush to Jim Ward, *Marion Chronicle-Tribune*, April 20, 1959. J. Edward Roush Congressional Papers, Indiana University Archives, Herman B Wells Library, Bloomington, Indiana.

273 Congressman J. Edward Roush to S. M. Bailey, chief engineer of the Louisville district Army Corps of Engineers, July 21, 1959. J. Edward Roush Congressional Papers, Indiana University Archives, Herman B Wells Library, Bloomington, Indiana.

274 Gardner Thomas, *Marion Chronicle-Tribune* publisher, to Congressman J. Edward Roush, August 11, 1960. J. Edward Roush Congressional Papers, Indiana University Archives, Herman B Wells Library, Bloomington, Indiana.

275 Jim Mitchell, executive editor, *Marion Chronicle-Tribune,* to John Nixon, publisher, *Peru Tribune,* December 1, 1961. Wabash County Museum archives.

276 John Chambers, "Dam Means move to People of the Valley, but Where to Go," *Marion Sunday Chronicle Tribune*, October 29, 1961. Wabash County Museum archives.

277 "Engineers Ignore Recommendation On Upstream Flood Prevention," *Marion Chronicle Tribune*, March 27, 1959. https://www.newspapers.com/image/1068794667/?terms=Gas%20City%20mayor.

278 "A Bill to Provide for Flood-Control Work on the Wabash River and Its Tributaries," H.R. 2957, 78th Congress, 1st Session, June 15, 1943. Ralph Roessler papers, Rare Books and Manuscripts, Indianapolis; Indiana State Library.

Chapter 41–Townsman

279 James S. Ward, "Residents of Somerset Must Move If Dam Is Built," *Marion Chronicle-Tribune,* March 12, 1959. https://www.newspapers.com/image/1068791253/?match=1&terms=Residents%20of%20Somerset.

280 "The Classified Department Is as Close as Your Phone," *Elwood Call-Leader,* December 3, 1959. https://www.newspapers.com/image/87955974/?match=1&terms=%20Somerset%20Kern%20oil%20heaters.

281 A. E. Housman, "To an Athlete Dying Young," *The Heath Introduction to Poetry* (Lexington, Massachusetts, Toronto: D. C. Heath and Company, 1984), 259-60.

Chapter 42—Grave Sights

282 Ruth Rudicel to Congressman John V. Beamer, June 2, 1955. Congressman John V. Beamer collection, Rare Books and Manuscripts, Indianapolis; Indiana State Library.

283 C. A. Kessler to Congressman John V. Beamer, April 24, 1956. Congressman John V. Beamer collection, Rare Books and Manuscripts, Indianapolis; Indiana State Library.

284 "7,000 Graves Must Be Moved in Flood Project," *Kokomo Tribune*, August 11, 1961. https://www.newspapers.com/image/2727346/?match=1&terms=graves.

Chapter 43—Witness

285 Ralph Roessler, remarks: "Three Reservoir Project, Upper Wabash River Basin," Exchange Club, Ft. Wayne, Indiana, March 10, 1964. Ralph Roessler papers, Rare Books and Manuscripts, Indianapolis; Indiana State Library.

286 *Final Report, Cemetery Relocation Plan No. 2 for Ten Cemeteries, Wabash County,* Army Corps of Engineers Louisville District, June 1968.

Chapter 44—Love Us

287 Colonel W. D. Milne to Congressman John V. Beamer, March 3, 1955. Congressman John V. Beamer collection, Rare Books and Manuscripts, Indianapolis; Indiana State Library.

288 "Moving of Somerset Seen in Flood Plan, Call Press Conference at Peru to Explain Details of Upper Wabash Project," *Wabash Plain Dealer*, February 11, 2022. Congressman John V. Beamer collection, Rare Books and Manuscripts, Indianapolis; Indiana State Library.

289 Ralph Roessler to Congressman John V. Beamer, June 5, 1955. Congressman John V. Beamer collection, Rare Books and Manuscripts, Indianapolis; Indiana State Library.

290 Congressman John V. Beamer to Lawrence Scheffer, July 11, 1955. Congressman John V. Beamer collection, Rare Books and Manuscripts, Indianapolis; Indiana State Library.

291 Congressman John V. Beamer to Cliff Funderburg, February 27, 1956. Congressman John V. Beamer collection, Rare Books and Manuscripts, Indianapolis; Indiana State Library.

292 Congressman John V. Beamer to Hueston Schaaf, December 4, 1956. Congressman John V. Beamer collection, Rare Books and Manuscripts, Indianapolis; Indiana State Library.

293 "Flood Control in This Area," *Peru Tribune*, April 10, 1957. Congressman John V. Beamer collection, Rare Books and Manuscripts, Indianapolis; Indiana State Library.

294 John V. Beamer, speech (March 31, 1959): "Flood Control on Upper Wabash River & Tributaries, Remarks by John V. Beamer at League of Women Voters, Wabash, Indiana." Congressman John V. Beamer collection, Rare Books and

Manuscripts, Indianapolis; Indiana State Library.

Chapter 45—Windfall

295 "Grit (newspaper)," *Wikipedia Foundation*, last modified September 9, 2024. https://en.wikipedia.org/wiki/Grit_(newspaper).

Chapter 46—Resettlement

296 Congressman J. Edward Roush to Robert Dawes, March 7, 1960. J. Edward Roush Congressional Papers, Indiana University Archives, Herman B Wells Library, Bloomington, Indiana.

297 Congressman J. Edward Roush to Reverend LeRoy J. DeLong, December 20, 1961. J. Edward Roush Congressional Papers, Indiana University Archives, Herman B Wells Library, Bloomington, Indiana.

298 Robert Kellum, Indiana Flood Control and Water Resources Commission, memo: "Meeting January 4, 1962, in Somerset High School Gymnasium on Corps of Engineers Plans for Purchase of Lands and Easements for Mississinewa Reservoir," January 5, 1962. J. Edward Roush Congressional Papers, Indiana University Archives, Herman B Wells Library, Bloomington, Indiana.

299 Robert McCallen to Congressman J. Edward Roush, July 10, 1962. J. Edward Roush Congressional Papers, Indiana University Archives, Herman B Wells Library, Bloomington, Indiana.

300 Congressman J. Edward Roush to Congressman Clarence Cannon, July 11, 1962. J. Edward Roush Congressional Papers, Indiana University Archives, Herman B Wells Library, Bloomington, Indiana.

301 "Help Sought for Utilities at Somerset," *Wabash Plain Dealer*, October 27, 1962. Wabash County Museum archives.

302 "Moving of Somerset Seen in Flood Plan, Call Press Conference at Peru to Explain Details of Upper Wabash Project," *Wabash Plain Dealer*, February 11, 2022. Congressman John V. Beamer collection, Rare Books and Manuscripts, Indianapolis; Indiana State Library.

303 Ralph Roessler to Congressman John V. Beamer, June 5, 1955. Congressman John V. Beamer collection, Rare Books and Manuscripts, Indianapolis; Indiana State Library.

304 "Buy White Farm," *Wabash Plain Dealer*, January 8, 1963. Wabash County Museum archives.

Chapter 47—Roush

305 Frank Campbell to Congressman J. Edward Roush, September 12, 1963. J. Edward Roush Congressional Papers, Indiana University Archives, Herman B Wells Library, Bloomington, Indiana.

306 L. Ferol Bussert to Congressman J. Edward Roush, November 26, 1963. J. Edward Roush Congressional Papers, Indiana University Archives, Herman B Wells Library, Bloomington, Indiana.

307 L. Ferol Bussert, minutes: Red Bridge Group, November 7, 1963. J. Edward Roush Congressional Papers, Indiana University Archives, Herman B Wells Library, Bloomington, Indiana.

308 Colonel W. Roper to Congressman J. Edward Roush, November 15, 1963. J. Edward Roush Congressional Papers, Indiana University Archives, Herman B Wells Library, Bloomington, Indiana.

309 Congressman J. Edward Roush to L. Ferol Bussert, November 20, 1963. J. Edward Roush Congressional Papers, Indiana University Archives, Herman B Wells Library, Bloomington, Indiana.

310 Kathleen McKenzie 1969, J. Edward Roush Interview, Indiana University Oral History and Research Center, Center for the Study of History and Memory at Indiana University, Bloomington, Indiana.

Chapter 48—Real Estate

311 Kathleen McKenzie 1969, J. Edward Roush Interview, Indiana University Oral History and Research Center, Center for the Study of History and Memory at Indiana University, Bloomington, Indiana.

312 "Somerset, Ind," *Chronicle Tribune Magazine*, December 4, 1977. https://www.newspapers.com/image/1071862320/?match=1&terms=Somerset.

313 "Somerset, Ind," *Chronicle Tribune Magazine*, December 4, 1977. https://www.newspapers.com/image/1071862320/?match=1&terms=Somerset.

Chapter 49—Packing

314 "Starting a New Era," *Indianapolis Star*, October 2, 1961. https://www.newspapers.com/image/105694200/?match=1&terms=Salamonie.

315 "Ralph Roessler, 'The Father of the Mississinewa Reservoir,'" *Wabash Plain Dealer*, June 24, 1965. Ralph Roessler collection, Rare Books and Manuscripts, Indianapolis; Indiana State Library.

316 Paul M. Doherty, "Reservoir Job Started with Bang," *Indianapolis Star*, April 28, 1962. https://www.newspapers.com/image/106396726/.

317 Dale Burgess, "Somerset, Old Indiana Town, to Disappear," *Anderson Herald*, April 22, 1962. https://www.newspapers.com/image/975192482/?match=1&terms=Somerset.

318 Dale Burgess, "Mississinewa Reservoir to Kill Town of Somerset," *Terre Haute Tribune*, April 22, 1962. https://www.newspapers.com/image/80247586/?match=1&terms=Somerset.

319 "Mississinewa to Flood Town, Dam Project to Start," *Indianapolis Star*, April 22, 1962. https://www.newspapers.com/image/106387506/?match=1&terms=Somerset.

320 "Somerset, Ind," *Chronicle Tribune Magazine*, December 4, 1977. https://www.newspapers.com/image/1071862320/?match=1&terms=Somerset.

321 "New Dam Gives Hoosier Town Chance to Rebuild," *The Call-Leader*, Elwood, Indiana, April 27, 1962. https://www.newspapers.com/image/87903227/?match=1&terms=Somerset.

Chapter 51—Gotta Wear Shades

322 Congressman J. Edward Roush, radio address: "Recreation Industry Boom," July 5, 1963. J. Edward Roush Congressional Papers, Indiana University Archives, Herman B Wells Library, Bloomington, Indiana.

323 Ken Atwell, "Reservoirs on Wabash Expected to Boost 5 Counties' Economy," *Kokomo Tribune*, October 9, 1963. https://www.newspapers.com/image/44694134/?match=1&terms=Atwell.

324 "Somerset - The Old and the New," *Columbia City Commercial Mail*, November 1, 1963. https://www.newspapers.com/image/132772255/?terms=somerset.

325 Ron Woodward, "Somerset," *Family Branches: Newsletter of the Wabash County Genealogical Society*, Volume 14, Number 7, March 2009.

326 "Says Reservoirs Will Improve Area Income by $13.5 Million," *Wabash Plain Dealer*, November 18, 1964. Wabash County Museum archive.

327 "Fort Wayne Firm Buys New Somerset Location," *Kokomo Morning Times*, July 21, 1965. https://www.newspapers.com/image/32413967/?match=1&terms=fort.

328 "Expect Local Reservoirs to Attract 2,000,000 Annually," *Wabash Plain Dealer*, February 3, 1966. Wabash County Museum archive.

329 Congressman J. Edward Roush, "Past Studies Indicate. . . . ," File folder: *Roush, Legislative, Working, Reservoirs*, 1968. J. Edward Roush Congressional Papers, Indiana University Archives, Herman B Wells Library, Bloomington, Indiana.

330 US Army Corps of Engineers, Institute for Water Resources, www.iwr.usace.army.mil/Missions/Value-to-the-Nation.

331 Philip F. Clifford, "Old Town of Somerset Soon Will Be No More, By Next Spring Under Water," *Indianapolis Star*, June 19, 1966. https://www.newspapers.com/image/105526214/?match=1&terms=toschlog.

332 Don Timmons, "Village and Indian Chief Moved to Tame Wabash," *Daily News*, Dayton, Ohio, September 27, 1966.

333 Congressman J. Edward Roush, "Past Studies Indicate. . . . ," File folder: *Roush, Legislative, Working, Reservoirs*, 1968. J. Edward Roush Congressional Papers, Indiana University Archives, Herman B Wells Library, Bloomington, Indiana.

334 C. Gerber, "Study: 4,100 More Peru Properties Flood Risk." *Kokomo Tribune*, August 28, 2020.

335 US Army Corps of Engineers, www.ird.usace.army.mil.

336 Indiana Flood Control and Water Resources Commission "Comments on Preliminary Report on Three Mid-Wabash Valley Reservoir Sites, as Presented by U.S. Army Corps of Engineers at Public Hearing Attended by More than 1,000 Persons in Lob Playhouse, Memorial Center, Purdue University, West Lafayette, Indiana, February 15, 1963. Col. James L. Lewis, District Engineer, Had Charge of the Hearing," February 22, 1963. J. Edward Roush Congressional Papers, Indiana University Archives, Herman B Wells Library, Bloomington, Indiana.

337 C. Gerber. "Mississinewa Lake Sees Record-Setting Crowds," *Kokomo Tribune*, July 22, 2012. https://www.kokomotribune.com/news/mississinewa-lake-sees-record-setting-crowds/article_eadac15c-e8b9-11eb-8347-7748f46095a4.html.

Chapter 52—Ripple

338 Wendell Berry, "Horse-Drawn Tools and the Doctrine of Labor Saving," in *The World-Ending Fire: The Essential Wendell Berry*, ed. Paul Kingsnorth (Berkeley, California: Counterpoint, 2018), 151–158.

339 Janis Thornton, *The 1965 Palm Sunday Tornadoes in Indiana* (Charleston, South Carolina: The History Press, 2022), 108.

340 Janis Thornton, *The 1965 Palm Sunday Tornadoes in Indiana* (Charleston, South Carolina: The History Press, 2022), 108.

341 Janis Thornton, *The 1965 Palm Sunday Tornadoes in Indiana* (Charleston, South Carolina: The History Press, 2022), 109.

342 Janis Thornton, *The 1965 Palm Sunday Tornadoes in Indiana* (Charleston, South Carolina: The History Press, 2022), 109.

343 Boyd Gill and Don Wallis, Jr. "Most Springs Are Marvelous . . . but This Wasn't," *Kokomo Morning Times*, June 28, 1965. https://www.newspapers.com/image/32411891/?match=1&terms=gill.

344 Mark Mast, "Tornado Smashes Kokomo Area, Eastern School, Housing Additions Destroyed," *Kokomo Tribune*, April 12, 1965. https://www.newspapers.com/image/44711991/?match=1&terms=John%20Haines.

345 "List of Treated," *Kokomo Tribune*, April 12, 1965, https://www.newspapers.com/image/44712142/?match=1&terms=129%20victims.

346 Mark Mast, "Tornado Smashes Kokomo Area, Eastern School, Housing Additions Destroyed," *Kokomo Tribune*, April 12, 1965. https://www.newspapers.com/image/44711991/?match=1&terms=John%20Haines.

Chapter 53—John Huddleston

347 Bill Nangle, "New Somerset: A Second Birth," *Kokomo Morning Times*, January 7, 1967. https://www.newspapers.comimage/32506709/?match=1&terms=Somerset%3A%20A%20Second%20Birth.

348 Wayne Guthrie, "Somerset Thrives in New Environs," *Indianapolis News*, June 26, 1969. https://www.newspapers.com/image/312628425/?match=1&terms=Guthrie.

Chapter 55—Vern Shroyer

349 Josef Mohr and Franz Gruber, "7 O'Clock News / Silent Night," *Parsley, Sage, Rosemary, and Thyme*, Simon and Garfunkel, October 10, 1966, Columbia Records, Bob Johnston, producer.

DISCUSSION QUESTIONS

Elements for Consideration

Transformation of history taught as the story of "them" to the story of "us"

The present is also the story of us

Providing for your own identity

Overcoming the separation of the observer from the observed

How a personal story evolves into universality

The impact of status on access to avenues of communication

The destruction of rural American culture in the post–World War II dominance of "progress" and profitability

The destruction of Indigenous culture

The Indigenous lifestyle as a model for behavior

“Leadership is rooted not in power and authority, but in service and wisdom” (Kimmerer)

The diminishment of the concept of value from that with a basis in morality to only money

The transformation of environmental destruction from nuisance to threat

What the destruction of community means to succeeding generations

Eliminating a problem is not the same as solving a problem

STUDY GUIDE

I. The Power of the Press

Brothers Joe Nixon and John Nixon are publishers, editors, reporters, and writers for the *Wabash Plain-Dealer* and the *Peru Tribune*, respectively. They are also the stepsons of Wabash industrialist Mark Honeywell.

Agree or disagree: Their editorial decisions clearly limit public input into the policy decisions that affected the people most immediately affected by the Upper Wabash Valley Flood Control Project. Support your position with evidence.

Agree or disagree: The impact the Nixon brothers had on the Upper Wabash Valley Flood Control Project is as likely to occur today. Support your position with evidence.

II. Historical Perspective

How do the descriptions of grave relocations by Stan Shroyer and Tom Snyder differ from those of Greg Hoback and Bonnie Truss? Which do you find most likely accurate? How is that connected to their closeness to the event? How might the way the procedure was described by Indiana Flood Control and Water Resources vice-chairman Ralph Roessler and

Indiana Third District congressman J. Edward Roush affect how moving graves was perceived at the time and how it is perceived today? How might that be significant as an example in the telling of history?

Three sources in the book–Wabash County historian Ron Woodward, retired Somerset and Southwood elementary teacher Frances Roby, and the Wabash County Museum–report separately that Somerset residents found out about the impending destruction of Somerset in 1958. They are easily interpreted as "official accounts," presented as historical fact. And yet, state and area newspapers published accounts of its demise in June 1955 that were revealed by the US Army Corps of Engineers to Congressman John Beamer in late May of 1955. Draw on evidence from the book to suggest meaning behind the difference.

Author Robin Wall Kimmerer notes in her book *Braiding Sweetgrass* that "science is rigorous in separating the observer from the observed." "History" has traditionally done the same.

In what manner and with at least one developed example can you assert that in *When Once Destroyed* the author sought to counter that traditional approach?

Why might "history" be better taught in a literature class? Why better in a history class? Why better as a combination of both?

Provide examples of accounts of historical events that are told in a way that does not separate the observer from the observed. Do not limit yourself to your social studies book. It could be a song.

The author's second cousin Tom Snyder, retired chief of operations at the Salamonie element of the Upper Wabash Valley Flood Control Project and Somerset historian, said that the project wouldn't happen today. With what evidence would you agree that memory and mistrust of the government would make the Mississinewa Reservoir that covered Somerset impossible?

III. Identity

Congressman John Beamer often appeared conflicted in the story. Compare and contrast his conflicts with project supporter and Indiana Flood Control and Water Resources Commission member Carlos Life and project opponent and former state lawmaker Cliff Funderburg.

Why does "It's our flag, too," make a lifelong impact on the author? Why is it significant for the manner in which he tells the story? How might you describe it as a theme of the story, what the story is about?

On October 6, 1846, just more than three hundred Miami people from near what became Somerset were herded onto canal boats at gunpoint and taken down the Mississinewa River to Peru, where they began a month-long journey to their new "home" south of Kansas City, Kansas. Elaborate on the similarities between their forced migration and that of around three hundred Somerset people almost 110 years later. Consider the causes, consider the methodologies, and consider the effects of the removals.

How do the values of "country folk" differ from those of "city folk" in *When Once Destroyed*? If those value systems were in conflict in the story, which side won? What makes you say so? How does that result impact you?

ACKNOWLEDGMENTS

I must begin with my team at Wise Ink Media, Minneapolis, and especially my project manager Lindsay Bohls. Thank you, Lindsay, most of all for your patience. Wise Ink vice president Hanna Kjeldbjerg, marketing manager Crown Shepherd, editors Imani Josey and Sara Robb, designer Emily Mahon, and proofreader Caitlin Fultz have been active creators, meticulous and kind. Of course, none of it would happen without the vision of Wise Ink cofounders Dara Beevas and Amy Quale. They believed in my story.

Thank you to Matt and Shannon Shroyer for giving their child my father's name; a story that was always in me would not have seen the light of day without that.

My partner Judy Shroyer never questioned the obligation that I created for her with this project. Judy was with me in our research at the Indiana State Library, the Indiana University Herman B Wells Library, and the Wabash County Museum; she led me in the planning of the book launch, she directed me to newspapers.com, and she took the photo that's on the cover. Judy and I had the thoughtful guidance of Kathleen Cruikshank in the Archives, Indiana University Herman B Wells Library, Bloomington; Laura Eliason, Rare Books and Manuscripts assistant, Indiana State Library, Indianapolis; and T. J. Honeycutt, director of archives and outreach, Wabash County Museum.

Thank you to the people who made a financial commitment to the creation of this book: Mara Boettcher, Mel Brown, Janice Firestein, Rose

Firestein, Frank Hobart, April Lidinsky, Sandy Murray, Judy Shroyer, Lily Shroyer, Stan Shroyer, and Phil Webster.

Thank you to Ari Krause for sharing his insight and encouragement throughout this endeavor, to Mel Brown for telling me "You need to talk to people down there [at Somerset]," and to Peter Firestein for telling me my voice should be heard. This book would not exist without my acceptance into the WVPE-FM 88.1 Michiana Chronicles radio essay group by its director Ken Smith and the warm encouragement of April Lidinsky.

This book would not exist without my experience as a Holocaust educator, which provided a basis for my practical understanding of the significance of marginalized perspectives. Thank you to New Prairie High School and the New Prairie United School Corporation Board for providing me with the opportunity to teach semester-long English Department courses on the literature of the Holocaust and the literature of the Vietnam War.

Thank you to everyone I interviewed in preparing this work:

Linda Shroyer, Stan Shroyer, Lucinda Holderman, Larry Stouffer, Greg Bowman, Dave Compton, Kay Peas, Janet Schenkel, Helen Adkins, Tom Snyder, Wayne Shroyer, Bonnie Truss, Duane Truss, Greg Hoback, Janet Weaver, Janis Thornton, Linda Martin, Dr. Rose Wenrich, Larry Knee, Ronald Woodward, and Carson Gerber. Especially Tom Snyder.

All I ever had to say was, "I want to tell my grandson about my dad."

Acknowledgement of Land

There is no adequate acknowledgement for the loss for the Indigenous men and women who lived harmoniously for many generations on the land that invaders called Indiana, as a reserved space that gradually dissolved in the face of expediency and progress. The loss is great, also, for those Europeans who ignored an opportunity to learn. The world carries that burden today.

When Once Destroyed occurs on the land of the Miami. The European American settlers who built Somerset emulated the wisdom of the Miami Nations people that they displaced by constructing their community among natural springs on the small flood-proof cliffs above the Mississinewa River. Downriver, however, other European American settlers ignored the obvious hazard and created communities on commerce-friendly floodplains. Their descendants sacrificed Somerset to protect their flood-prone communities.

The land seizures and genocide committed by the United States were projects of spiritual and cultural destruction that denied the Miami free and unhindered access to the land that fundamentally shaped their identity. We must acknowledge that that trauma has occurred, that harm continues to occur today, and that it is incumbent upon all of us residing on this land to work toward an equitable future where everyone has the opportunity to thrive. I encourage you to learn and consider the history of the land on which you reside, as well as the resilient peoples and complex legacies that have made it what it is today.

What developed in the telling of *When Once Destroyed* is not the result of an intention. The intention is the result of the telling.

I see now that in using a direct address tradition in addressing my grandson to reveal from the inside out the history of our ancestral family home and its destruction, I do not, to paraphrase *Braiding Sweetgrass* author Robin Wall Kimmerer, separate the observer from the observed.

I follow academic standards for research and documenting sources in order to substantiate the veracity in the details of my account, but I do not adhere to a traditional academic perspective. With my grandson at my figurative knee, I tell the story of "us," not the story of "them."

What I hope to have gained through this approach is an acknowledgment of the people whose perspectives are rarely considered in community histories, both large and small, the people on the ground when the bombs fall from the sky.

I believe it is the absence of this perspective that makes the bombs permissible.

Thank you.
Sid Shroyer
South Bend, Indiana
February 17, 2025